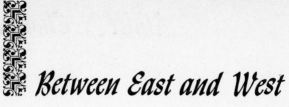

Between East and West

André N. Chouraqui

Between East and West

A history of the Jews of North Africa

translated from the French by Michael M. Bernet

The Jewish Publication Society of America
Philadelphia   5728 · 1968

389

This book is dedicated to
the memory of my father
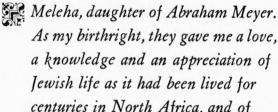 *Isaac, son of Saadia Chouraqui*
who erected a synagogue
at Aïn-Témouchent
which now stands deserted;
and to my mother
Meleha, daughter of Abraham Meyer.
As my birthright, they gave me a love,
a knowledge and an appreciation of
Jewish life as it had been lived for
centuries in North Africa, and of
which these pages record the history. . . .

 *Preface*

This book is the result of a series of studies on various aspects of North African Judaism which I have made over a period of years. My sincere thanks are due to Dr. Solomon Grayzel for the valuable advice he extended to me during the preparation of the English edition. I would also like to express my appreciation for the fine work done by Mrs. Yael Guiladi in the revision of the manuscript and its arrangement in the present form.

A.N.C.
Jerusalem, Spring, 1968

Contents

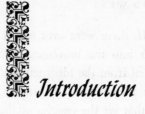

Introduction

North Africa has been in the forefront of world events since World War II, when its strategic importance to the Allied campaign thrust it into prominence. As Theodor Herzl had foreseen, the twentieth century, particularly the second half, became the era of emancipation for Africa and Asia. In the course of their struggles for national freedom, Morocco, Tunisia and Algeria have emerged from the shadows and stand today in the fierce glare of history. The international importance of the "Maghreb," a name traditionally given by Arab writers to the Moslem countries west of Egypt, has become obvious. By its nature, its history and its geography, the Maghreb forms an immense crossroads between Europe to the north, Black Africa to the south and the lands of Islam to the east. From Europe it assimilated much during the period of French colonization. From Africa, Negro influences have left their mark on the people and folklore. But of transcending significance has been Islam, the religion common to the inhabitants of the Maghreb and to the vast numbers of Moslem peoples in the area. Two other factors add to the importance of North Africa today: the quality of its cultural élite which, numerically and in the extent of its education, leads all other countries of Africa and Asia; and the natural resources of the region, primarily the petroleum and natural gas in the Sahara.

At the end of World War II, there were over half a million Jews in North Africa. Drawn into the movement that swept their countries, they too emerged from the hibernation to which they had been relegated since the seventeenth century. By an irony of fate, the very events that set the peoples of the region once more upon their feet and led to the independence of Tunisia, Morocco and Algeria brought about the mass exodus of the Jews from North Africa and the resettlement of the majority in Israel. Communities that had been rooted in their countries for two thousand years were destined to disappear in less than a decade. Their sudden dissolution was the more astounding because Jewish life had been the one unchangeable constant in all the changing history of the Maghreb. Indeed one might say that the best way to understand the past and present of the Maghreb is to regard it through the prism of the history of its Jews. Among all the races of the Maghreb today, only the Jews, while retaining their own identity, have known the long series of empires that governed this territory from the Phoenicians to the French. They arrived with the victory of the first conquerors and left twenty-five centuries later, after the defeat of the last, to return to their starting point, the Holy Land.

The Jews first appeared in the Maghreb when, as a result of Phoenician influence, the area was emerging from its dim prehistory. They were in a favorable position, for they were familiar with the ways of the land's conquerors, whose neighbors they had been in the Holy Land. Before the Phoenician conquest, the inhabitants and language of the region had been of Indo-European origin. Till the fall of Carthage in 146 B.C.E., the Jews, in partnership with the Phoenicians, molded North Africa with Semitic influences and won over many of its inhabitants to the Jewish religion.

With the defeat of Carthage, the Jews came under Roman

domination. Their number increased two centuries later when, after the destruction of Jerusalem by the Emperor Titus in 70 C.E., many of the survivors chose North Africa as their refuge. Before long, however, the communities were once more engulfed, this time under the tide of Christianity. When Emperor Constantine made Christianity the state religion, North Africa became one of the first regions of the Empire to accept the faith. The Romans were succeeded by the Vandals, the Vandals by the Byzantines, and the Byzantines by the Arabs and the Turks. The Jews firmly withstood the ebb and flow of each successive tide until the State of Israel was reborn.

Their coexistence with the Arab conquerors lasted more than a thousand years, alternating between periods of splendor and periods of obscurity. Decay set in after the sixteenth century, when the Jews and the Moors were driven from, and soon thereafter lost contact with, the Spanish mainland. The decline was further aggravated by a number of geo-economic factors: the discovery of America, which caused a shift in the center of civilization from the countries bordering on the Mediterranean basin to those fronting the Atlantic Ocean; the industrialization of northern Europe, which brought about changing patterns in world commerce; and finally, the discovery of the sea route to the Indies which bypassed the Maghreb, formerly one of the main land routes to the East. North Africa, now practically isolated from the rest of the world, was brought close to economic and cultural ruin, a condition that was shared by the entire Middle East and by the Sephardi and Oriental Jews who had till then held a prominent place in Jewish life.

The Jews had watched with trepidation the attempts of Spaniards and Turks to obtain a foothold in North Africa and welcomed the French as saviors when they took possession of Algeria in 1830, of Tunisia in 1881, and of Morocco in 1912.

Their presence meant the end of spiritual decadence and economic stagnation, the beginning of a new era in which North
Africa, torn from its isolation, would be introduced once more
into the great currents of modern life and would reassume its
traditional position as an international crossroads. The French
conquest was of even greater importance for the status of the
Jews themselves. With its gospel of liberty, equality and fraternity, France was to raise them from the condition of inferiority
that had been their lot under the domination of Islam. The Jews
of North Africa were the first among those in all Moslem countries to benefit from the privilege of emancipation. The new
status applied to the entire Jewish population of Algeria, to the
majority of those in Tunisia and to an important section of the
Jewish urban population in Morocco.

With a speed that has always amazed sociologists, the emancipated Jews passed, in the space of one, two or at the most
three generations, from the medieval life of their Moslem neighbors into the world of twentieth century science and civilization.
The Jews of Europe who were emancipated after the French
Revolution experienced the Industrial Revolution, living through
it at the pace of their Christian compatriots. The process of their emancipation had not yet been completed when the
Nazis put a brutal end to it. But for the Jews of the Maghreb,
the Western world appeared with an apocalyptic suddenness
that demanded instant adaptation. They started from a level
that was incredibly lower than that of the European communities. The worst miseries of the European ghetto are not comparable to the moral and material degradation that existed in the
mellahs of the foothills of the Atlas or of the remote Sahara
until they were emptied with the migration of their inhabitants
to Israel. Those Jews who settled in France or who still linger in
Morocco or Tunisia have often in a single generation leaped

from their former abject condition into a new world in which they are gradually coming to assume their just role.

The French conquest introduced progress to the Maghreb, but it also brought about the drama in which the three protagonists—the Moslem, the Frenchman and the Jew—together controlled the dynamic internal force and the social, economic and political evolution which was a result of their coexistence. However, in their religious, political and economic life the three groups formed entirely separate entities. The way of thinking, the social structure and the ethnic characteristics of each were clearly defined; they were centered on axes whose poles were as far apart as Paris is from Mecca, Jerusalem from Rome. The separate groups were superimposed. They never attempted to create conditions that might lead to their fusion. When the hour of reckoning came, they faced each other in a merciless struggle between the Arabs and the French in which the Arabs were victorious. The equilibrium in which the three entities had been poised was upset and the weakest, the Jews, were forced to leave.

This departure had not been intended by either the French or the Moslems, and certainly not by the Jews themselves. It became an unavoidable necessity that only the existence of the State of Israel prevented from becoming a disaster. The exodus that circumstances had made inevitable at least now had goal and direction. France had assumed that in any event the Jewish communities would stay where they were, as the demographic constant that was necessary to maintain the balance in the great socio-political complex that was envisaged for the future. The French administration in Algeria used all the means at its disposal to dissuade the minority groups from a hasty departure; but at the last minute a panic-stricken population was in full flight, the Jews in the lead.

The Moslem nationalists had not wanted this to happen. Neither the King of Morocco nor the Istiqlal leaders nor Bourguiba and the leaders of the Néo-Destour, nor the leaders of the Algerian National Liberation Front (F.L.N.) had even imagined the possibility of the departure of the Jews, who were for them all the more valuable as their contribution to the work of national reconstruction was considered irreplaceable. No nationalist leader had ever uttered anything but idyllic promises regarding the future of the Jews of the Maghreb once their countries had secured their independence.

The Jews themselves believed to the last minute in the permanence of their presence in an area of which their ancestors had been the earliest inhabitants. They frequently took up arms alongside the nationalists in Tunisia and Morocco, and even in Algeria, in the belief that they were serving a just cause. Suddenly, however, impelled by an irresistible force, they were torn from the land in which they had been born, from their homes and their share in the country, to be carried away on the wave that swept the French settlers out of North Africa. The departure of the French put an end to the longest succession of colonial rulers in history, beginning with the foundation of Carthage in 813 B.C.E., and continuing unbroken to the middle of the twentieth century.

The extraordinary length and richness of the history of North Africa's Jewry has no parallel in the history of the Diaspora. Rooted in the biblical past, the Jews of the Maghreb retained through the centuries the influence they had acquired from Rome's contemporaries, the Carthaginians; they faced the Vandals and the Byzantines, assimilated Arabic culture and Berber traditions inherited from the Jewish communities expelled from Spain in 1492. They were skilled in the use of the Hebrew language, and, as if in preparation for its rebirth, brought into

existence the earliest Hebrew grammars and lexicons. Inclining
to the philosophical, they prepared the groundwork for neo-Pla-
tonic studies. They regarded themselves as the trustees of the
cabalistic tradition they had inherited. After three centuries of
somnolence, North African Jewry was suddenly integrated into
the mainstream of nineteenth and twentieth century French culture which formed the character of the community until its final
redemption from the Maghrebian exile.

A historian can scarcely undertake to recount the history of
the Jews of North Africa without a certain trepidation. The
history of twenty-five centuries that saw the successive over-
throws of mighty empires remains to this day virgin territory in
the world of scientific research and is a *terra incognito* even to
Jewish scholars. The immensity of the task is made the more
difficult by the lack of the necessary groundwork of previous
publications and scholarship on which the researcher may draw,
as a quick glance at the bibliography at the end of this book will
show. Furthermore, the characteristic diversity of the Jewish
population of North Africa—diversity between eras, and between the social strata within each era—does not facilitate the
historian's work. Each wave of conquerors exerted its own influence, but in a manner that changed from region to region and
that varied according to distance from the coast, isolation in the
Sahara desert or in the Atlas mountains.

The same variation persisted under French rule. Algeria was
a colony, Morocco and Tunisia were protectorates; in each
there were profound differences in the structure and organization of the Jewish community. There were even greater regional
divergencies within each country, and the racial and cultural
environment could be Berber or Arab, Spanish or French.

That the great wealth of history and diversity that is North

Africa has so seldom drawn the attention of historians and sociologists is indeed surprising. Every Jewish community in North Africa formed a microcosm in which it was possible not only to observe at first hand an ancient heritage that had been faithfully preserved but also the rapid transition from a civilization based on the Arab Middle Ages to one that is part of twentieth-century France or Israel. All the steps of the transformation are still visible—from the illiterate peddler who hawks his wares through the inaccessible hamlets of the Atlas foothills, to the industrialist blazing a trail in Europe; from the Cabalist, a stranger to all that is new in the modern world, to the university professor in Paris, opening up new fields of learning. Thus, the history of mankind may often be summed up in the changes that have overtaken one community, one family or one man.

Despite the difficulties inherent in the preparation of a comprehensive history of the Jews of North Africa, I was eager to assume this task in order to make up what I feel to be a lack in the literature available on the subject. In my journeys throughout the length and breadth of my native North Africa, and later in France, America and Israel, where the Jews whose ancient homes I had known have rebuilt their lives and communities, I was able to collect documents and first-hand information which completed my earlier experiences. Around these I have constructed this book.

Part 1 From Antiquity to the Byzantine Period

1

The Carthaginian Era: 813–146 B.C.E.

The Origins of the Jewish and Berber Populations

The origin of the Jews of North Africa stretches back to the earliest history of that region. While it is probable that members of the Israelite tribes were among the earliest Phoenician traders who colonized the African coast and founded Carthage, this must remain speculation in the absence of more conclusive historical proof.

Of some significance to the later history of the North African Jewish and Berber populations are the conclusions which can be drawn from the frequently recurring legend that ascribes a Palestinian origin to the indigenous Berbers. The Byzantine historian Procopius, for instance, stated that the Phoenicians, fleeing before Joshua, left their Palestinian homeland and migrated across Egypt, spreading out as far as the Pillars of Hercules. In support of this view, Procopius pointed out that in his days the natives of North Africa spoke Punic, a language closely akin to Hebrew. He also mentioned a Punic inscription on two stone columns at Tigisis, which, he claimed, read: "It is we who have taken flight before that bandit, Joshua son of Nun."[1] It is generally agreed that the extraordinary persistence of this legend derives from the profoundly Semitic character of North Africa during the nearly seven centuries of Carthaginian domination.

In the first century C.E., Christian and Jewish polemicists added to the existing legend the idea that the Berbers were of Canaanite origin, a theory which was taken up by Moslem writers with equal enthusiasm. Ibn Khaldun, the ingenious Moslem historian, wrote[2]: "The Berbers are the descendants of Canaan, son of Ham, son of Noah. . . . They received their Judaism from their powerful neighbors, the Israelites of Syria."[3] It would thus seem that the legend of the Berbers' Canaanite origin was already widespread at the time of the compilation of the *Book of Jubilees*,[4] probably in the first century B.C.E. The *Book of Jubilees* spoke of Ham as dividing Africa among his descendants. Josephus, however, went further, ascribing to the Berbers a Semitic origin and tracing their descent from Midian, son of Abraham by his second wife Keturah.[5]

Rabbinic literature frequently repeated the legend, further reinforcing the connection between the Berbers and the biblical Israelites.[6] A talmudic text, which a Tosefta of the second century C.E. considered "old," spoke of the migration to Africa of the Girgashites, one of the seven nations dwelling in Canaan at the time of Joshua. "The Girgashites departed (voluntarily from Palestine at the request of Joshua) and for this reason they were given a fine land for their patrimony: Africa."[7] In the Middle Ages the legend, preserved in Jewish writings, was further enriched and descendants of Esau were added to the Canaanite begetters of North Africans. According to Yosippon (I.2), a descendant of Esau in flight from Egypt founded a people in Carthage.[8]

Among early Christian writings, a text by Saint Augustine is particularly revealing: "If you ask our countrymen what they are, they will reply 'Chenani.' It is their corrupt patois, one letter has been changed. It is to be understood as Canaani."[9]

This ancient tradition in its various forms is highly important, for it makes the Berbers cousins of the Jews by race and language and, as will be shown later, by religion. It has been repeated by both Jewish, Christian and Moslem writers and cannot be lightly dismissed. Only a few of the many texts on the subject that have been collected and analyzed by Marcel Simon[10] have been presented here, but the core of undisputed truth is that as from the eighth century B.C.E., the beginning of Phoenician colonization, North Africa was subjected to Semitic influences.

A converse of the legend of the Berbers' Canaanite origin related that the Jews had originated in North Africa and had migrated from there to Palestine. Tacitus[11] repeated another version according to which the Jews had originated in Crete and migrated to Libya, while a third century Christian account of unknown authorship[12] extended this to include the inhabitants of the Balearic islands. North African folklore gives considerable importance to legends concerning Joshua, as R. Basset's monograph *Nedromah et les Traras* shows.[13] Many Moslems are convinced to this day that Joshua warred in the Maghreb, thus adding further substance to the legend which derives from the inscription reported by Procopius—except that the Berbers would now seem to have been allies of Joshua who helped to put his enemies to flight. Joshua is supposed to have died at Nedromah, near Tlemcen, where his tomb is widely venerated to this day by Jews and Moslems.[14] The extent of the veneration accorded to him is an indication of the extent to which such tradition is rooted in the Maghreb. The tendency to identify local history with the biblical past can be ascribed to the Punic and Hebrew influences on the region which will be discussed in the following pages.

The Rule of Carthage

The recorded history of North Africa begins with the founding of Carthage in 813 B.C.E. For 667 years, till its fall in 146 B.C.E., Carthage molded North Africa into its own Semitic image. Not even the efforts of the Roman conquerors, in ploughing up the site of Carthage and sowing it with salt, were able to uproot the Oriental civilization left by the oldest and most tenacious colonizers of the Mediterranean. For over six centuries, a circle of towns dependent on Carthage exerted on the indigenous inhabitants the steady influence of one language, Punic, and one culture, the Semitic, both of Palestinian origin. To quote Gsell,[15] by the end of this period, the natives of North Africa "by their language and by their customs, had become Phoenicians"—in other words, Semites, closely related to the Hebrews of Palestine.

The widespread use and the long survival of the Punic language were undoubtedly at the root of the popular legend of the Berbers' Semitic origin. The oldest extant Punic manuscripts date from the fourth to the second centuries B.C.E.[16] and are all that have survived from a presumably extensive literature of which a number of texts are believed to have survived into the Middle Ages.[17]

Nothing remains today of Punic writings on philosophy, history, literature or poetry. Our knowledge of Carthage is limited almost entirely to what has been recorded by its Roman enemies, thus leaving a regrettable gap in the knowledge of Jewish life in the Punic settlements in North Africa.[18] A precise knowledge of the areas of Punic penetration and its rate of progress might have allowed certain conjectures on the development of the Jewish communities, but historians have been satisfied with generalities concerning this era. In the eighth and seventh centuries B.C.E., the Semitic language was localized in the coastal colonies; during the sixth century it began to penetrate to the interior. All the documents available concur on the surprising spread of the language in the subsequent period among all sections of the population, the aristocracy as well as the peasants and laboring classes. The Roman historian Sparticus recorded that Septimius Severus, the Roman Emperor of Semitic descent who was born in Leptis Magna, retained his Punic accent throughout his life. His sister, arriving at the court of Leptis Magna, knew almost no Latin.

The major source on the spread of the Punic language in North Africa is Saint Augustine.[19] His writings confirm that the peasants were speaking Punic almost exclusively several centuries after the fall of Carthage, thus leaving no doubt that the Latin culture never succeeded in supplanting the deeply-rooted Phoenician civilization.[20] Valerius, a predecessor of Augustine, is mentioned by him as having questioned some peasants on the meaning of the Punic word "salus" which he had overheard them use. When they explained that it meant "three" in Punic (as also, with a variant pronunciation in Hebrew), he was overjoyed to find an additional connection between the Trinity and salvation.[21] In his sermons, Saint Augustine freely fell back on Punic to explain Hebrew or Aramaic words from the Scriptures, Punic naturally being familiar to his audiences. Moreover, he was accompanied by an interpreter on his preaching tours in the countryside to make sure that he would be understood by the Punic-speaking peasants.

Saint Augustine pointed out that the Circumcellians referred to their bludgeons, with which they forcibly converted the masses to Christianity, as "Israel"; thus the dreaded sectarians dubbed their weapons of persuasion by a name which in He-

brew means "God fights." Marcel Simon deduced from this that
presumably "the Circumcellians, and very likely large masses of
the rural population, read and understood the Bible in its original language."[22] One assumption may be safely made: the
similarity of Hebrew and Punic was bound to bring about, right
from the start, a deep interpenetration of Jews and Berbers in
the Maghreb. Saint Jerome,[23] whose authority on this subject is
undisputed, and whose views were echoed by Priscian,[24] commented on the similarity of the two sister languages. Modern
research has indeed confirmed the ancient traditions by showing
that Hebrew and Punic shared a common ancestry.[25] These
similarities explain the extraordinary extent of the spread of
Jewish beliefs in North Africa that prepared the ground for the
acceptance of Christianity and eventually of Islam.[26]

The Jewish Communities

It would be futile to try to fix a precise date for the establishment of the first Jewish settlements in North Africa, but it is
generally accepted that the first communities of any importance
date from about the time of the destruction of the Temple in
Jerusalem by Nebuchadnezzar in 586 B.C.E. The second exile
to Babylon was also accompanied by a westward migration.
Certain communities, among them Djerba, maintain an oral
tradition that they were founded at that time, a view accepted
by Marcel Simon, although he disputed Nahum Slousch's conclusion that this was proof of a large-scale colonization.[27] The
existence of Hebrew-speaking Jewish communities in North Africa substantiates the theory[28] that they left Palestine before
their original language, Hebrew, had been supplanted by
Aramaic. The first Jewish settlers retained in their new environment the use of their own language which their Punic neigh-

bors understood. The similarity in background made it easy for them to adapt to their new home and find an atmosphere that was similar to the one they had been forced to abandon.[29]

The Jews of the Maghreb maintained close ties with the Holy Land at all times. The Talmud relates[30] the journeys of Rabbi Akiba to the Maghreb, in which he doubtlessly helped to stir up the revolt against Rome. Several rabbis were born in Carthage.[31] Hillel, in a rather curious passage, explains the prevalence of flat feet among inhabitants of the Maghreb by the number of swamps in that region.

The knowledge, and presumably the use, of Hebrew among the Jews of North Africa continued till the beginning of the fifth century C.E. We know of a dispute between Saint Jerome and Saint Augustine on the correct translation of the Hebrew word *Kikayon,* the biblical name of the shrub under which Jonah slept; Saint Augustine asked the Jews of Oea (ancient Tripoli) to resolve the dispute.[32] The early Christian writer Tertullian[33] added further convincing evidence of the tenacious persistence of Hebrew in North Africa, a phenomenon which is hardly surprising in what was undoubtedly the most intensely Semitic of all countries of the Diaspora. Indeed, Carthaginian domination so thoroughly permeated North Africa with Semitic culture that it may be considered to have been a Semitic region in every respect many centuries before the Arab conquest made it so in name.

The bonds between Jews and Punics, based on their long coexistence and the similarity of language and culture, were further tightened in the face of the Roman invasion after the fall of Carthage. From this a Judeo-Punic syncretism came into being which, as will be shown in the following chapter, paved the way for Christianity and later Islam, both developments of the biblical revelation.

The initial military successes of the Jews indicate an effective organization and an intensive penetration of the Jews among the Berber masses, but the revolt, like the last insurrection of the Jews in Palestine against the Roman world, was foredoomed. Trajan, preoccupied by the war in the East against the Parthians, appointed Marcius Turbo to quell the uprising in North Africa, and there do not seem to have been any military repercussions in Tunisia or the Caesarean province. The brutal repression of 118 C.E.[8] marked the end of the development of Judaism in Cyrenaica. The survivors fled westward into the Caesarean province and southward, crossing the Sahara from oasis to oasis, eventually perhaps reaching as far as the Niger River.[9]

Sites of the Jewish Colonies

The twelve boatloads of Jewish captives that Titus had deported from Palestine to North Africa about the year 71 C.E. reinforced the existing Jewish colonies.[10] According to Saint Jerome, Jewish communities formed an unbroken chain from India to the limits of Africa and scholarly research has made it possible to fix the precise sites of those in North Africa.

Besides Carthage, which was the most important, there was Hammam-Lif, the city of Naro, where a synagogue of the Roman era, with important inscriptions referring to the synagogue and the *archesynagogus,* the religious head, has been uncovered.[11] Inscriptions, and the writings of Saint Augustine, refer to Jewish communities at Utica, Simittra in Proconsular Numidia, and at Thusurus (Tozeur). In the Byzacena province, the main Jewish centers were Henchir-Djuana, to the west of Kairouan, where an inscription reveals the existence of semi-proselytes; Yudia; and above all the great maritime city Hadrumetum (Sousse), where inscriptions referring to the God of the Hebrews[12] have been discovered. In Numidia there were communities at Hippo Regius (Bône),[13] Cirta (Constantine),[14] Henchir-Fuara on the route from Souk-Ahras to Theveste (Tebessa)[15] and Ksour El Ghennaia between Lambaesis (Lambessa) and Diana. At Henchir-Fuara a limestone column decorated with a seven-branched candelabrum was found. It bears the inscription: "Deus Abr)aham, Deus Isac."[16] The existence of Jewish semi-proselytes at Ksour el Ghennaia is shown in an inscription referring to a *metuens*. In Mauritania there were communities at Sitifis (Sétif), Auzia (Aumale), Tipasa, where the Jews built a synagogue toward the middle of the fourth century,[17] Cherchel and Volubilis, the site of the oldest Jewish inscription so far discovered in North Africa. According to Philippe Berger this inscription, engraved in Hebrew characters on a stone about eight inches high, reads "Matrona, daughter of Rabbi Yehuda, Rest [in Peace]."[18] Ibn Khaldun[19] wrote that when the Arabs reached North Africa, "a number of the Berbers professed Judaism. Among the Jewish Berbers there were the Jerawa,[20] a tribe which inhabited the Aurès region and to which belonged Kahena, a woman who was killed by the Arabs at the time of the first invasions. The other Jewish tribes were the Nefusa, Berbers from Ifrikya, the Fendelawa, the Medyuna, the Behlula, the Ghratha and the Fazaz, all Berbers of the Maghreb-el-Aksa" (extreme west).

In Tripolitania, there was a lively Jewish community at Oea (Tripoli). From the writings of Saint Augustine[21] it is evident that this community counted biblical scholars among its members. (In a letter to Jerome, whom he accused of an imperfect knowledge of Hebrew and of straying from the Septuagint text, Augustine recorded the reaction of the Bishop of Oea's community to the reading of Chapter IV, verse 6 of the new Latin version of the Book of Jonah. The bishop, faced with the irritation of his listeners who accused Jerome of falsifying the Scriptures, promised to bring the matter before the Jewish scholars of Oea. These condemned the new translation.) The importance and antiquity of the Christian community at Leptis Magna (Labdah in Libya), whose baptistry is the oldest in Africa, would lead one to hope that archeological evidence of a flourishing Jewish community there may yet be discovered. As an indication, there is a point on the seashore not far from Leptis Magna still known as "Ras el Yihudi," the Cape of the Jew. Mention may also be made of Iscina,[22] still known as El Yehudiya (the Jewess),[23] among the Jewish communities that lined the route from Volubilis to Cyrenaica and, even further, to Alexandria.[24] The existence of a widely distributed Jewish community in North Africa that extended far inland is thus proved by much direct evidence, though its relative importance has tended to be somewhat exaggerated by certain writers.[25]

Jewish Life

Life in the Jewish communities of North Africa during the Roman era was highly developed, well organized, rich and vital. The repeated struggles between Jews and Romans in the first and second centuries C.E. hampered the cultural and economic development of the Jews, but once peace had been restored and they were integrated under the *Pax Romana,* Judaism entered a new phase of development. The Romans allowed the Jewish faith to organize under a *Nasi,* a Patriarch resident in Palestine, who was both spiritual and temporal leader. His hierarchy reached into every community, through the primates who headed each province and through the local heads of the communities, thus foreshadowing to some extent the later development of the Christian hierarchy.

The many inscriptions which have been discovered in North Africa serve to reinforce the information that historians have been able to glean from Greek, Latin and talmudic texts in giving a picture of the evolution of the specific, in some measure Oriental, way of life that had been developing there since the days of Carthage. Among the most important finds have been the inscriptions in the richly decorated synagogue of Naro on the shore of Hammam-Lif,[26] the largely unknown necropolis of Gamart near the entrance to Tunis,[27] and a Greek inscription engraved on a marble column at Berenice around the year 14 B.C.E. which was discovered in Tripoli.[28] The column was erected by the Jewish assembly of the town in honor of the Prefect Marcus Titius who had been outstanding in his benevolence to the Jews. The precision of the inscription has made possible a practically authentic reconstitution of Jewish community organization in the Pentapolis.

Each community was headed by a religious assembly in which full Jews, proselytes and semi-proselytes shared equally, and an administrative council, usually of nine members, which was elected by the community. Inscriptions show that occasionally women were members of the councils. The Council of Elders administered the community. It directed the finances, supervised the religious organization of the town, represented the interests of the community before the courts and the authorities. It distributed relief, decided on the construction of synagogues, schools and libraries. The assembly, which was presided over by the *Gerousiarch,* named the administrative council members, the archons. The secretary (*grammateus*) was responsible for keeping minutes of the sessions and for the preservation of the archives. The *archesynagogus* was largely independent of the Council and was responsible for the religious ritual, preaching, and teaching the law. In this he was aided by readers, translators and *shammashim* or sacristans. The synagogue was the center of all Jewish activity, of prayer, preaching, study and justice. The Jewish communities were granted a large measure of judicial autonomy, of which they were temporarily deprived only during the worst of their struggles against the Roman rulers.

The active religious life, which was characteristic of all the Mediterranean communities, was the result of the close relationship between the communities themselves, and between them and the Palestinian center. This contact continued even after the destruction of Jewish autonomy in Jerusalem, and the religious activity it produced enabled the Jews to influence the pagans around them and so lay the foundations for the spread of Christianity. The peace was temporarily disturbed by the Jewish rebellion in Emperor Trajan's time, and by the efforts of the Emperor Hadrian to destroy Judaism. Hadrian realized that Israel's power stemmed from its religion and its religious organization and, like Antiochus Epiphanes, he tried to destroy this inner source by forbidding circumcision, the observance of the Sabbath, the teaching of the Bible and the ordination of rabbis. It was in the course of his struggle against Hadrian that Rabbi Akiba had to yield his life.[29] Emperor Antonius Pius (138–165) restored the former situation, repealed the intolerant decrees[30] and reestablished the Patriarchate as the religious and judicial authority under which the Jews of the Roman Empire,[31] without exception, were united.[32] Like all the provinces, the head of each North African province was considered a representative of the Patriarch. These primates possessed certain judiciary powers, the extent of which is unknown, and appointed the officials of the larger communities.

The Jews, along with the residents of North Africa who were of foreign origin, were rapidly accorded the rights of citizens and, as such, were eligible for the highest offices.[33] Liberal legislation excused them from participation in pagan rites associated with civic activities, since such rites were incompatible with the Jewish faith. A clear distinction between the spiritual and the temporal made it possible for a person to be a full Roman citizen while remaining spiritually part of the "Jewish Nation." Jews were thus excused from obeisance to the guardian deities of their respective cities and, in the rites connected with the person of the Emperor, they were allowed to omit all references to his divine attributes. On imperial and national feast-days, the Jews were not compelled to attend the pagan temples, but instead gathered in their synagogues to ask for God's blessings on Caesar.

Exempted from any law that would have clashed with their religion, the Jews were free from conscription, as this would have forced them to violate the Sabbath. On the Sabbath a Jew could not be compelled to appear before a court of law or to perform statutory labor duties. The Romans went so far as to change from Saturday the day on which free distributions were made, so that the Jews might also benefit. When foods forbidden by Jewish law were distributed, the Jews received their value in silver. As Roman citizens, the Jews were subject to the Roman penal code and its punishments, but were exempt from local tortures. (Thus, the apostle Paul, Jew and Roman citizen, was decapitated, whereas those of his coreligionists who did not possess the rights of citizens were generally crucified.) Augustus waived the last restrictions connected with the exercise of the *jus honorum.* Jews who had been elected to the magistracy, the equestrian class or the Senate were to be found even among the prefects and were eligible to be proconsuls. (Agrippa the First was named proconsul by Claudius.) Under the *jus com-*

mercii they could conclude contracts and litigate, and under the rights of *connubium* they could contract marriages, limited only by talmudic restrictions.[34]

The administrative structure which the Romans had allowed the Jews to maintain throughout the Empire enabled them to survive through the trials of the first century C.E., and in North Africa, where the indigenous Jews were reinforced by those fleeing from Palestine, it enabled them to spread the influence of Judaism among the Berber masses, ignoring the limits of national or racial origin. That Judaism had a marked success among the Berbers can be inferred from the measures against the Jews that the Christians took during the fourth century, measures that were a direct reflection of the concern felt by the Church over the spread of Jewish beliefs.

The Spread of Judaism among the Berbers

Having adopted the Punic faith, the pagans of North Africa already possessed the two essential principles of the later monotheistic religions: the belief in the transcendent divinity, and the submission of mortal man to the will of his Master.[35] Moreover, the fundamental similarities between the Punic language and Hebrew, the result of their common semitic origin, enabled Judaism to spread and flourish in Africa, to attract the Berber masses as proselytes or semi-proselytes to a degree which made it indisputably influential, though it is not known precisely to what degree.

Marcel Simon attributed the spread of Judaism to political factors, as well as to affinities of language or religion. As a result of the wars against Rome and the massacres in Cyrenaica, the Jews turned away from the Roman world and, with their subsequent dispersion across the African continent, drew closer to the Berbers. This era, the second and third centuries, marks the first break between the Judaism of Africa and the Hellenistic elements of the Judaism of the Diaspora. Marcel Simon held that the philo-Semitism of the Severus dynasty, "African by origin, Semitic by culture and by relationship," was also a contributing factor. Under the Severi, Jewish influences became more marked throughout the Empire. The benevolence of the dynasty and the Jewish particularism born of the events in Cyrenaica served to strengthen the Judeo-Berber solidarity.

Account must also be taken of the never-ending struggle between the nomadic and sedentary populations of Ifrikya. The Romans, as also the Severi, had pushed the nomad Berbers into the desert and confiscated the lands over which they had wandered[36] for the benefit of the colonizers. Ibn Khaldun wrote of two main branches of the Berbers, the nomadic Botr and the sedentary Beranese.[37] Jewish proselytization had its greatest success with the Botr, among the Jewish Berbers being the Jerawa in the Aurès mountains and the Behlula, the Ghratha and the Fazaz in the extreme western Maghreb.[38] Two of the principal Botr tribes who traditionally wandered between the confines of Tunisia and those of Tripolitania are thus seen to have been permeated by Jewish influences.

Again according to Ibn Khaldun, there were Jews in the Berber surroundings of Tamina (Chaouia), and Tadla (on the Oum-er-Rebia River). At Gurara, in the Touat region in the extreme north between Tamentit and Gerara, Arab historians record the existence of a small Jewish kingdom in a region where the race and the language of the Berber Zenatas has been preserved to this day. Gravestones engraved with Hebrew characters have been found there. This kingdom managed to survive the triumphs of Islam, but succumbed during a general massacre in 1492 that was fired by the recrudescence of Moslem religious fervor following the expulsion of the Jews from

Spain.[39] The existence of nomadic Jews would explain the diffusion of Judaism beyond the confines of Carthaginian influences, such as among the Judaized tribes of the Maghreb-el-Aksa[40] and perhaps even as far as Black Africa where there is evidence of the influence of immigrant Jews from North Africa on the development of the Fulani civilization.[41]

Having rediscovered the patriarchal life of the Bedouin, the Jews of North Africa came also to exert a deep influence on other sedentary elements of the population who were practicing a Judeo-Punic syncretism.[42] The Abelonians and Coelicolians, mentioned by Saint Augustine and in the Theodosian Code, were sects composed of Jews who had abandoned the rigid orthodoxy of Palestine, and of semi-Judaized pagans who had been drawn principally from Semitic peoples, particularly from the Phoenicians.[43] These Judeo-Punics were familiar with the Bible and practiced circumcision and were, to quote Marcel Simon, "on the indistinct borderline between Judaism, Christianity and Semitic Paganism."[44] However, the Christians and the Romans regarded them as Jews, a name they themselves used somewhat indiscriminately.[45] This tendency to a religious syncretism was always a feature of Jewish life in North Africa and was due in part to the varied sources of its components. It poses an interesting question on the role played by the *ger,* the proselyte, within the Jewish community.

Historical evidence, meager for earlier centuries, is abundantly available for the third and fourth centuries C.E. The spread of the Jewish faith among the Berbers appears the more remarkable since the Jews lacked the support and prestige of an empire and of the temporal power which backed the Christians and later the Moslems. "Judaism, on the other hand, had no other means but the immaterial weapons of the preacher."[46]

The weapons were the concepts of monotheism, a moral code

and a liturgy inspired by the Bible.[47] The Berbers, semitically inclined through centuries of Carthaginian influence, were only too ready to abandon their idols and swell the ranks of the Jewish faithful, or at least of their sympathizers—those who frequented the synagogues and picked up ideas which they integrated in some form or another into their pagan beliefs.[48] Tertullian, in the third century, reported that the Berbers observed the Sabbath, the Jewish festivals and fasts, and the dietary laws.[49] The poet Commodianus, also in the third century, contended with pagans who were neither exactly Christians nor Jews but who, above all, remained outside the Church.[50] An inscription on a leaden tablet dating from the Roman period which was discovered in the necropolis of Hadrumetum contained an invocation to "the God of Abraham, Isaac and Jacob" to bring two separate beings together. Though it may be regarded as an example of exorcism, in keeping with the Berbers' taste for magical practices, it clearly reveals the place that Jewish teaching had assumed in the life of the country. Similar proofs are frequently found in Punic antiquities.[51] From the end of the second century, in North Africa as in the rest of the Roman Empire, Jews and Christians frequently clashed in their attempts to convert the gentiles.[52] In the beginning the two faiths were often confused by the pagan legislators. Septimius Severus, for example, outlawed both proselytization by the Jews and missionary activity by the Christians.[53]

The Beginning of Suppression

Constantine the Great, who would have liked to force all the Jews of the Empire to submit to the cross, began, however, by issuing his Edict of Toleration in Nicomedia (Izmit) in 313,

which gave all Roman subjects, Jews included, the right to practice the religion of their choice. But at the Council of Nicaea in
325 the first steps were taken toward the establishment of
Christianity as the state religion. From then on the Jews were
gradually excluded from civic rights and relegated to a position
which permitted them to survive, but not to expand.

They were deprived by the Christian emperors of their right
to accept proselytes or to convert pagans; they were excluded
from certain types of contracts that involved non-Jewish slaves,
Christian ceremonial objects and transactions involving
Church property such as churches, cemeteries, etc.; they
were forbidden to hold Christian slaves; their rights to bequeath
and to inherit were limited; finally their juridical autonomy,
which had been permitted under the rights of arbitration, was
suppressed.[54] These discriminatory measures were accompanied by virulent anti-Jewish polemics conducted by Tertullian, Saint Cyprian, Saint Ambrose, Saint Augustine, Saint John
Chrysostom, and others. The inflammatory exaggerations of
their oratory are evidence at least of the vitality of Judaism
which was able to hold its own in North Africa till the advent of
Islam, despite the success of Christian missionary activities
among the Berbers.[55]

Carthage, the capital of Christian North Africa, was a tragic
arena in which the two sister faiths had become enemies. The
Jews, considered hostile both to the Empire and to the Christian
faith, were regarded by the authorities of the African provinces
as "a foreign body, hostile and unable to be assimilated." Oppression became progressively heavier and more relentless, the
Jews were excluded from all public offices, the taxes that had
earlier been paid by the Jews to their primate now went to
enrich the finances of the Empire. A law was passed forbidding
the construction or repair of synagogues and frequently syna-

gogues were forcibly converted into churches. Thus at Tipasa the synagogue was turned into the Church of Saint Salsa at the beginning of the fourth century.[56] Over the centuries the status of the Jews was lowered to an ever more precarious position that foreshadowed their future under Moslem rule. Intensive Christian missionary activity was often accompanied by force, the earliest known case of forced conversion being at Borion.[57]

These excesses only served to strengthen the spiritual resistance of the Jews against the appeal of Christianity. Meanwhile Jewish propaganda was carried out in those regions farthest from the centers of Christian influence, unwittingly preparing the path for the future spread of Islam among the population of the interior of the Maghreb. From this intimate and prolonged contact with the pagan Berber way of life, Judaism in North Africa absorbed many influences of which some were retained till the advent of the modern era.

3

Vandals and Byzantines: 430–642 C.E.

The Effects of the Vandal Conquest

The Vandals, who had been established in the Spanish peninsula from the year 406, set out to conquer Africa in May 429. Under their king Gaiseric, they embarked at Tarifa in Spain and landed on the coast of the Riff in northern Morocco, whence they moved eastward through Oran to the rich lands of Numidia. The fall of Carthage in October 430 marked the beginning of a century of increasing Vandal domination over the whole Maghreb which lasted till 533.[1] The death of Saint Augustine in the siege of Hippo in 431 forces us to rely on Procopius for the history of the period of Vandal domination. His account, however, is mainly a paean of praise to the victories of Belisarius, of whom he was a faithful companion. The only sources of information on this period are the observations of the enemies of the Vandals; a few coins discovered at Carthage; and the Thermae of Gibbamond, a unique monument near the mosque of Ezzituna which was brought to light by Rabbi Arditti and is attributed to the Vandal period.

Nevertheless two facts about the Vandals throw some light on the history of the Jews under their domination. Firstly, the Vandals, unlike the Romans, were destroyers and despoilers. According to Procopius, Gaiseric was once asked toward which new country he would turn next. The reply was: "Toward the one that God wishes to punish in His anger." The Vandals ravaged the cities and began destroying the immense projects undertaken by the Romans.[2] The havoc they wrought gave a new impetus to nomadism, always an important element in North African history. The Botr nomadic tribes had acquired new power and mobility after the introduction and general acceptance of the camel in Roman North Africa in the third century C.E. (In battle, they would arrange their camels in a fan-shaped formation and fight under cover of the animals' bodies. The horses, terrified by the camels, would run away.)[3] The anarchy spread by the Vandal conquest further spurred the development of nomadism. At one point the nomads allied themselves with Belisarius in the final struggle against the Vandals; later they rose up against the Byzantines after Belisarius abandoned Carthage; and finally they faced up to the Arab invaders, stemming the tide of their invasion for seventy years. Many of the Botr tribes were Jewish or Judaized. Their chiefs, such as Gabaon, who fought against the Vandals, frequently bore Hebrew-sounding names.[4] Their resistance was undoubtedly bolstered by the Catholic Christians who viewed the Vandals as the champions of the Arian heresy. The growth and spread of nomadism in North Africa is directly traceable to the effects of the century of Vandal domination.

The second factor that influenced the lives of the Jews during this period is that the Vandals supported the Arian heresy, denying the co-eternity, consubstantiality and, therefore, the true divinity of Jesus. This heresy had been formally condemned at the Council of Nicaea, but it continued to undermine Christianity everywhere, particularly in North Africa from the time of the Vandal invasion. The religious conviction of the Vandals may in part have been based on their hatred of the

Roman Empire which culminated in the sack of Rome by
Gaiseric in 455.[5] In Africa, their main preoccupation seems
to have been in fighting Roman Catholicism, hounding priests
and bishops relentlessly and destroying their churches. A
Church council met in Carthage in 535, two years after the
defeat of the Vandals, to recall the sufferings of the Church
during the century of Vandal oppression.[6]

During this period the oppression of Jews by the Christians
was halted. As they had done in Spain, the Vandals looked for
all the available support in their main struggle, which was that
against Rome. They found it in the Jews, whom they freed from
oppressive laws and to whom they gave complete freedom to
practice their religion. This freedom, however, was only a
respite, and with the advent of the Byzantines the earlier persecution was intensified.

Renewed Repression under Byzantium

In 533, the Byzantine Emperor Justinian overruled his hostile
chief of staff Belisarius and ordered war against the Vandals.
With his victory, his initiative came to be regarded as an act of
divine inspiration. The first measure of the conqueror, therefore, was to restore to the Catholic Church in North Africa all
the powers of legal and moral jurisdiction of which it had been
deprived by the Vandals, and to take possession of the buildings, ceremonial objects and property that had been confiscated.
Then came the condemnation of heresy in all its forms. In 534,
Solomon, Belisarius' successor, was ordered to expropriate all
Jewish, pagan, Arian and Donatist[7] places of worship and con-
secrate them to the Roman Catholic faith.

The jurisdiction of the rabbinical courts in civil matters between Jews had already been suppressed in 398 when all Jews had become subject to the civil courts of the Empire—courts in which Jews were denied the right of serving as magistrates. In 533, Justinian published Regulation 146, which gave a new juridical basis to the suppression. For the first time the law began to intervene in the internal life of the Jews who were being more closely confined into areas which eventually became ghettos. The Empire now decided which translation of the Bible should be permitted for use in the synagogue. It limited still further the jurisdiction of the rabbinical courts, substituting it with Imperial authority. Marriages between Jews and Christians became subject to the death penalty,[8] and Christian laws of consanguinity replaced Jewish ones, outlawing in this way the biblically prescribed practice of levirate marriage, as well as the practice of polygamy.[9]

Thus the legislative apparatus which had been prepared against the Jews in the fourth and fifth centuries was expanded during the sixth and became the instrument of the campaign against all manifestations of Jewish life and beliefs which were carried out in all the territory effectively controlled by Byzantium.

But the Byzantine domination of North Africa was far from complete. The Berbers harassed the frontiers of Byzantine rule, themselves well inside the old Roman defense lines. The greater part of Sitifian Mauretania, all of Caesarean Mauretania, all of Tingitania, the hinterlands of Tripolitania and the region of the great Chotts (saline lakes) of Tunisia remained unconquerable bastions of the nomadic Berbers. Whether converts to Judaism or to one of the Christian heretic sects, or, more frequently, Jewish or Christian in name but practicing a Judeo-pagan syncretism, these nomads waged relentless battle against the sedentary pro-Byzantine population.

With Palestine's Jewry destroyed, with the established Church of the Empire waging open battle against Judaism and denying the Jews the possibility of life in the cities which had been dedicated to Christ, the Jews sought to escape the jurisdiction of the Empire. It may be assumed that large numbers headed for the territories under the control of the nomads who in part had already been converted to Judaism, reinforcing the tribesmen with their own religious passion of resistance to the inroads of Christianity. A revolt by the Jews of Borion was brutally repressed and was followed by the forced conversion of the rebels and the kindling of the first pyres of the Jews who refused conversion. At Ifren a burial grotto houses the remains of fifty Jewish martyrs slain, according to tradition, under Christian persecution at an unknown date.

The end of the sixth century saw an abatement of the religious persecution. The Emperor Maurice forbade the forced conversion of Jews and ordered their synagogues restored to them. The arrival in 613 and 622 of two groups of Jewish refugees fleeing from the Visigoths in Spain brought a renewed flowering to Judaism in North Africa. Thus, at the time of the Arab invasion, Bizerte was inhabited mainly by Jews and semi-proselytes and governed by a Jewish magistrate. After the fall of the city, as an act of revenge on the alleged insolence of its Jews during the period of prosperity, the peasants of the surrounding area chose Saturday as their market day so that the Jews would be unable to buy provisions without desecrating their Sabbath.[10]

Although the Byzantines attempted to continue the task of Romanizing North Africa during the century which followed the Vandal occupation, they were able to do little more than stave off the inevitable, and buoyed themselves with the myth of an undivided Empire and with the more tangible reality of a Catholic Church.[11] While the historians[12] may have exaggerated by claiming that Justinian exploited North Africa solely for the purpose of draining its wealth, engaging in pillage and massacre to achieve his ends, it is clear that the net result of Byzantine rule was a failure. The influence of Byzantium failed to penetrate to any appreciable extent and the Berbers, hostile to the Roman Empire and to its religion, were continuously hovering around the borders of Byzantine territory which were only a short distance inland from the coast. The enfeeblement of Byzantium, and the seeming incompatibility between the spirit of the Berbers and that of decadent Rome, created a void in the area which was filled by the approach of a new conqueror.

Part
2

The Rule of Islam

4

The Moslem Conquest of the Maghreb: 642–ca. 900

Berber and Jewish Resistance to the Arabs

The conquering wave of the followers of Mohammed poured out from Medina and began to engulf North Africa in 642. In that year the Arab governor of Egypt, Amr ibn Al-As, seized Cyrenaica and Tripolitania. Caliph Omar feared to provoke the Berbers[1] who were viewed as unconquerable warriors, seasoned as they were by a century of combat against Byzantium, but Amr's successor, Abdallah ibn Saad, overcame his apprehension. An army of twenty thousand Arab tribesmen was put into the field under Saad's command and easily overcame the Byzantine forces. The patrician Gregory, who had proclaimed himself basileus (king), fell in the final battle at Sbeitla in Tripolitania in 647, and thus the last European rulers were expelled from North Africa, not to return for over a thousand years.

Though the Byzantines were defeated, the real resistance of the Maghreb to the Arabs had not yet begun. In 670, Carthage having been reduced to ruins, the Arabs established their main base and capital at Kairouan ("Stronghold" in Arabic). It nevertheless required another half century for the entire Maghreb to be captured and for the Arabs to be in a position to consider launching their assault on Spain. Despite the conquest of Africa and even the almost complete conversion of its inhabitants to Islam, the Berber resistance had not been broken. The Botr and the Beranese had made good use of the camel since its introduction by the Romans into North Africa, and over the centuries, in their struggles against Romans, Vandals and Byzantines, they had become the undisputed masters of the Maghreb. The wars between them and the Arabs lasted into the ninth century, ending only when the Berbers, now Moslems, had driven the last of the Arabs from North Africa. They seized Tripolitania and Egypt, continued into Mesopotamia, overthrew the Caliphate and established the new Fatimid dynasty.

Kahena

For the purposes of this history it is unnecessary to recount the details of the long wars between the Berbers and the Arabs, but the episode involving the warrior-priestess Kahena (or Kahiya),[2] heroine of the Berber resistance and famous for her supernatural powers, is worth recalling. Kahena was the chief of the Jerawa tribe which inhabited the eastern Aurès mountains. The tribe was one of many which Arab historians mention as professing Judaism in the seventh century. Later historians, though unanimous in regarding them as Jews, differ as to their origins.[3] However, it seems reasonable to suppose that, at the time of their struggle with the Arabs, the Jerawa were sedentary, the progressive settlement of nomads being a phenomenon common to the borders of steppe and desert areas. Leadership of the resistance fell to the Botr tribes led by the Jerawa under Kahena's command in 687. In that year Kusaila, the Christian chief of the Beranese Aureba tribe, who had established his mastery over the entire Maghreb after his victory over the Arab leader Okba al Tahuda in 682, was defeated and fell in battle near Kairouan.

Hassan ibn al Nu'man el Ghassani, the Arab governor of Egypt, led the Arab forces at that period. "Hassan, having destroyed Carthage, demanded to know which was the most powerful chieftain in Ifrikya. He was told of a woman who ruled the Berbers and who was commonly known by the name of Kahena. She dwelt, so he was told, in the Aurès mountains. This Jewish woman could foretell the future and all that she predicted came to pass without fail. If she were killed, Hassan was told, he would meet no further resistance or rivalry. Hassan marched against her."[4]

According to Ibn Khaldun, Hassan took up a position to the north of the Aurès, on the banks of the El Meskyana River. This was in the year 69 of the Hegira (688 C.E.). Kahena threw her Berber forces, her powerful army of camelry and the remnants of the Byzantine forces against the Arabs, routing them, and expelling the Arab tribes from the Aurès and the Gabès regions so that they were forced to take refuge in Tripolitania.[5] This victory made Kahena queen of the Maghreb; but her kingdom lasted only five years. Ibn Khaldun recorded that eventually "The Berbers deserted Kahena to make their submission to Hassan. The general took advantage of this fortunate occurrence and, having succeeded in sowing dissension among the supporters of Kahena, he marched against those Berbers who still obeyed this woman and put them to full flight. . . . (On the eve of the battle) when night fell, Kahena told her two sons that she considered herself already dead;[6] that she had seen her severed head offered to the great Arab prince to whom Hassan owed allegiance. In vain Khaled[7] suggested that she abandon the country to the invader. She objected that this would be a disgrace for her people.[8] El Bayan wrote that

"Kahena herself was killed in the Aurès mountains at a place that is today still called Bir-el-Kahena (Kahena's Well)."[9] There is no agreement among Arab historians on the exact year of her death. Ibn al-Athir has it variously as 74 and 79 of the Hegira (693 or 698); it was in 82 (701) according to El Bayan, in 84 (703) according to El Kairouani.[10] The name of the battle in which she was killed has not come down to us.

From the victory of Kusaila in 682 to the death of Kahena the Maghreb was under unified rule, a feat that had eluded the Romans, the Vandals, the Byzantines and the Arabs. Neither were the Turks and the Spaniards eventually able to accomplish this, and it was not achieved to some extent till the twentieth century under the French. The cause of the collapse of the Berbers under Kahena may have been due to the unquestionable cruelty of her reign, as the Arab historians maintain and as the following ballad, collected from the folklore of the Constantine Jews, seems to indicate:

> O! Sons of Yeshurun!
> Do not forget your persecutors
> The Chaldeans, Caesar, Hadrian and Kahiya—
> That accursed woman, more cruel than all the others together.
> She gave our virgins to her warriors,
> She washed her feet in the blood of our children.
> God created her to make us atone for our sins,
> But God hates those who make his people suffer.
> Give me back my children
> So that they can mourn me.
> I left them
> In the hands of Kahiya.[11]

But the defeat of the Berbers may also have been the result of the inherent inability of the Maghreb to set itself up as a single independent entity.

The dying Kahena ordered her sons to surrender to Hassan,

and her defeat and death were a signal for surrender by the other Berber tribes. The Arab conquerors had the wisdom to grant them full honor and to incorporate them in their forces. According to Ibn Khaldun, the sons of Kahena were given command of the Jerawa and control of the Aurès mountains. Twelve thousand Berber horsemen were conscripted, according to El Bayan, under the command of the sons of Kahena, and used to conquer the rest of the land and convert its inhabitants to Islam.

The Nefusa, another tribe that had adopted Judaism, were treated in a similar manner. In 695, the Arab armies on their way from Kairouan to Tripoli requested from the Nefusa the right of transit along the seashore, a narrow path "the width of a turban."[12] When they refused, a battle developed in which many of the Berbers were slain and the others were converted to Islam. A short time later the surviving tribesmen requested their Arab overlords to designate a successor to their slain chieftain.[13] Surrender was henceforward accompanied by conversion to Islam and thus, toward the end of the seventh century, Islam began to make headway among the indigenous tribes.

This pattern was, in the view of Gauthier, a natural reflex on the part of the Berbers—the expression of their desire to survive even if it meant joining their conquerors. They submitted in order to attain an eventual triumph. But the Arabs, unlike earlier conquerors, demanded not only physical submission but also, in the name of *Jihad*, the holy war, the soul of the Berbers for Islam. This mass conversion was made possible only by the centuries of persuasion to a monotheistic faith to which the Berbers had been subjected by the earlier spread of Judaism and of Christianity. But, while the last Christian communities of the Berbers survived only to the twelfth century,[14] Judaism in North Africa retained the loyalty of its proselytes down to our own days. In the middle of the twentieth century, an estimated one half of the Jews of North Africa were descendants of Berber converts.

The Early Years of Moslem Rule

In the early years of the conquest of North Africa, the imposition of Islam seems to have been accompanied by a large measure of tolerance. When Sidi Okba ibn Nafi founded Kairouan in 670, he is said to have settled there a thousand families of Copts and Jews to assure the cultural future of the city. Indeed, Kairouan soon won fame for the excellence of its talmudical schools, as will be seen in Chapter Six. While there were cases of forced conversion, these were generally the result, in the early centuries, of wars between Berber Jews or Christians who continued to fight the Arabs even after the defeat of Kahena.[15] Roud el Kartas tells of the assault launched by Idris against the Jews and the Christians of the Maghreb in 789 C.E. "Though they were heavily entrenched and fortified in the mountains and inaccessible fortresses, they were eventually defeated by the Imam and forcibly converted to Islam. He seized their lands and their fortresses; he had put to death the majority of those who would not submit to Islam and he pried the others from their families and despoiled them of their property. He ravaged the Maghreb and destroyed the fortresses of the Beni Luwata, of the Medyuna and of the Behlula and the citadels of Rhiata and of Fez."[16] That even the Idrises did not always have their way with the indigenous population is illustrated by a story related by Ibn Khaldun concerning Yahya ben Yahya ben Mohammed, the last emir of the elder branch of the Idrises. Yahya had taken a fancy to a young Jewess of Fez and attempted to carry her off while she was in her bath. The townspeople revolted and Yahya was forced to seek refuge in the Andalusian quarter where he succumbed during the night. This episode shows that the townspeople of Fez were concerned for the welfare of their Jews and of their women, and may be accounted for by the strong Berber influence that remained in the town.

At the end of the eighth century the situation in the Maghreb was still confused. While tribes of Berbers, among them those who had adopted Judaism or Christianity, were showing desperate resistance to the Arab conquerors, others were more or less meekly accepting the new faith and, while massacre and battle were the rule throughout the region, numerous communities were able to ride out the storm by withdrawing into their own territory. By the ninth century there were well-organized Jewish communities in Kairouan, Constantine, Tlemcen and Fez.[17] The Arab conquest of Spain opened up new avenues and allowed the Jews of Africa to have contact once more with Europe by way of the Jewish Communities of Toledo and Andalusia. The unity of the Moslem Empire, though frequently disrupted by pockets of anarchy, replaced in a way the old *Pax Romana.*

The Dark Ages

The defeat and surrender of the last Jewish warriors in North Africa marked the beginning of a wretched period in Jewish history. To be sure, the Jews in Europe were denied civil rights in the cities they inhabited and thus were increasingly segregated from the general community. Under Islam, however, the stubborn Jews who clung to their ancestral faith were subjected to such repression, restriction and humiliation as to exceed anything in Europe.

To detail the history of the Jews in Moslem North Africa is

impossible. From the seventh century on, the region was divided and split up into ever-changing, ephemeral dominions whose boundaries were never clear. The present-day division of the Maghreb into Tunisia, Algeria and Morocco bears no relationship to the geographical realities of the past.[18] Dynasties clashed with overlapping dynasties to smash the Maghreb into ever-hostile states. European powers, too, tried repeatedly to return to the continent from which they had been driven in the seventh century and only added to the chaos and confusion resulting from the long succession of crumbling kingdoms and provinces that were related to no intrinsic development of the region, its people or its ideals. Islam itself was not enough to co-ordinate the sundry elements of the Berber spirit into one entity, as should logically have been the case.

The life of the Jews under such circumstances was full of contradictions and paradoxes. It is impossible to speak of the history of the Jews of North Africa as a unit, but at best only of countless histories of disparate communities, each subject, in a separate place or at a different era, to a particular ruler. What may have been true at any date for the Jews living in the kingdom of Tlemcen, for instance, would not hold for those of Tunis, of Kairouan or of Marrakesh. At a time when Jews in one region were being massacred, those in another may have been living through one of their most prosperous periods. It was a succession of days, or more accurately of moods, in no apparent logical sequence, that varied only with the pleasure or lust of the Moslem overlords.

The thread of Jewish history is further complicated by the extent to which it has been ignored by contemporary Arab historians.[19] Jews featured in their chronicles only as chance accessories to throw light on the doings of some important Arab personage. History for the Arab writers was concerned with events that befell the followers of Islam; and Jews, in this context, were accorded little attention above that which was given to inanimate objects. The best sources are therefore to be found in the unpublished manuscripts and records of the ancient Jewish communities. Those who suffered the blows remembered them better than those who gave them, and what might have seemed quite unimportant to the Moslems was frequently of supreme importance to the Jewish communities and received appropriate mention in their chronicles. So far, little work has been done on the collection and research of these records.[20] The libraries of rabbis and the *genizot* where unused books and old manuscripts were stored remain to be searched, and the many unpublished manuscripts that have been acquired by collectors in America and elsewhere have yet to be studied. These may be supplemented with the first-hand descriptions that have been recorded in the various Western countries which had direct contact with North Africa.[21] To attempt a comprehensive history of Jewish life in North Africa during that disorganized era before all original sources have been brought to light might only obscure the true facts. Neither can the oral traditions among the Jewish communities of North Africa be regarded as reliable. Too often, when historians try to learn oral tradition and folklore from members of the Jewish communities, they receive instead a pale reflection of what their informant has read or heard discussed in an insufficiently critical volume of their history which has acquired an aura of authority.[22]

A precise detailing of the fortunes and sorrows of individual Jewish communities in North Africa is not, however, necessary for the purpose of this book. From the little that is available from Arab historians and extant Jewish texts, together with the available nineteenth century records, an overall picture emerges of Jewish life in the Dark Ages under Islam and of Moslem attitudes that shaped Jewish life in those days.

5

The Status of the Jews under Islam

The Attitude of Islam toward the Jews

The attitude of Islam toward the Jews was based in large measure on a zealous devotion to what they considered the true will of their God. It developed out of the first relationships between Mohammed and the Jews of Arabia, the early opposition of the merchants of Medina, the first battles and triumphs of the followers of the new faith over the resistance of Jews and Christians, and finally the establishment of a vast empire governed by the progressive revelations of the Koran. It is possible to follow through the Surahs of the Koran the gradual crystallization of the Prophet's attitude to Jews and Christians, hesitant at first but gradually becoming more and more rigid.

Originally he was favorably disposed toward them for his inspiration had its sources in the stories of Abraham and in the later Hebrew revelations. But, as his difficulties deepened in Medina, so his resentment increased toward both Jews and Christians who would not recognize him as the Prophet of Allah. The disappointment of the Prophet in being rejected by the very people he hoped most to attract was further aggravated by the mockery and provocations that were his lot, requiring him to expend vast efforts to establish his faith in Medina and to spread it by religious and political conquests.

When he had lost hope of seeing the Jews support his religion en masse, Mohammed attacked them openly, accusing them of the worst vices and threatening them with infernal chastisement. His many hostile remarks in the Koran still have the force of revealed truth in Islam and still color the attitude of many Moslems today. The Jews are "hostile to the Moslems" (V.85); they are "mutually hateful toward each other" (V.69); "they are more attached to the possessions of this world than are other men" (II.90); "they have defiled the most sacred objects and slandered the Virgin Mary" (IV.155); "they are so avaricious that they would not offer to give the sliver from the hollow of a date-pit" (IV.56). "They have falsified the Scriptures and, through this, even worse, have rejected the belief in the Prophet and the Koran" (II.98; IV.48); "some of them believe in the Prophet while the others have kept away: the fires of Hell will be their punishment; a painful punishment awaits them for having falsified the Scriptures" (IV.184–185). The Koran forbids any intimate dealings with the Jews for they will use every advantage to corrupt the Moslem whose downfall they seek (III.183). Another verse says of the Jews: "Their hate pierces through their words but that which their heart harbors is even worse" (III.114–115). The second Surah contains a list of the kind acts of God toward the Jews and of the ingratitude they have shown in return: "You will find them more avid for pleasures than other men, than even idolators. . . . Whenever they enter into an undertaking, will there be found even one among them who will respect it? Yes, the majority among them do not believe in anything."

The implication of these words should not, perhaps, be exaggerated. The words of prophets, including those of the Bible, are notoriously full of invective. Because of the structure of Islam, however, where dogma and law are one, and where no distinction between spiritual authority and temporal power is admitted, the verses of the Koran indirectly assume juridic force. Thus, these particular verses determined the conditions under which the Jews lived under Islam.

The Dhimmi and the Charter of Omar

According to Mohammed, the Koran and its numerous commentators, it was the refusal of the Jews to accept the enlightenment of the faith that exluded them from the privileges and responsibilities conferred by the new religious fraternity. "If they (the Jews and the Christians) accept your belief they are on the right path; if they turn away from it, they create a split between us: God will satisfy you, He understands and knows all" (Koran, II.131).

This split introduced into the political ideology of Islam the fundamental principle of discrimination between true believers and those who did not accept the teachings of the Prophet. The Koran makes a clear distinction between Believers and Infidels. Infidels had to be completely expunged from Islamic society in order not to contaminate it. They were reduced to slavery, converted or exterminated. But between the Believers and the Infidels Mohammed allowed for a third group—*Ahl el Kitab,* the People of the Book, which included both Jews and Christians— those who had received a revealed Scripture that had been accepted by Islam. "We believe in God and in those whom He has sent us from above," the Prophet proclaimed. ". . . in Abraham and in Ishmael, in Isaac and in Jacob and in the Twelve Tribes as well as in the books revealed by God to the Prophets. We make no distinction between them and us; we entrust ourselves to God . . ." (II.130).

Based on these principles, the canon law of Islam[1] elaborated the special laws for the "dhimmis," the protégés of Moslem society, among whom the Jews and the Christians were included. The drawing up of this law is attributed to Caliph Omar, Mohammed's successor, who ruled from 634 onward, but it was probably enacted only two centuries later. The Charter of Omar, as the law was called, while recognizing the right of the dhimmi to live and declaring his person and property inviolable (as was not always the position for the Jews of Mediaeval Europe under Canon Law), also laid down the limitations and the conditions of inferiority to which the Jew was to be subjected, for it was inconceivable that the dhimmi could aspire to equality with, or share the same duties and privileges as, the Faithful. The law was finally codified in the eleventh century by Al Mawardi. Since the dhimmi was entitled to his life solely by virtue of this contract, any breach of it entailed the forfeiture of his life.

There were altogether twelve laws which limited the conditions under which the dhimmi was allowed to dwell within the community of the Believers, the first six of which were considered of binding and absolute importance. The Jews, like all non-Moslems, were forbidden to touch the Koran lest they mock it or falsify its text; they were forbidden to speak of the Prophet in false or contemptuous terms; they were forbidden to speak of the faith of Islam with irreverence; they were forbidden to touch Moslem women, marriage between a dhimmi and a Moslem woman also being forbidden (but not the converse); they were forbidden to do anything that would turn a Moslem against his faith and were ordered to respect the life and property of the Moslem; they were forbidden to do anything that would aid the enemies of Islam or their spies.

The other six laws were considered by Al Mawardi to be of

secondary importance and their infringement was not considered automatically to entail a breach of the dhimmi contract. They compelled the dhimmis to wear a distinctive habit with a sash (*zunnar*) and a piece of cloth (*ghiyar*) in yellow for the Jews and in blue for the Christians; the dhimmis were not allowed to build their houses, their synagogues or their churches higher than the Moslems' tallest buildings; they were not allowed to perform their religious ritual in public, or to let their bells, trumpets, prayers or chants be heard in the Moslem city; they were not to drink wine in public or, for the Christians, to display their crucifixes or their pigs; they had to bury their dead discreetly without letting their prayers or their lamentations be heard abroad; they were forbidden to own horses (which were considered noble animals) but were to satisfy themselves with donkeys or, in a pinch, mules.[2] These restrictions weighed heavily on the lives of the dhimmi, for the normal method of proof in Moslem law was by oath and the oath of a Moslem automatically nullified the oath of a dhimmi. Moreover, any personal dispute might be turned into an accusation by the Moslem that the dhimmi had blasphemed Islam or its Prophet, against which the dhimmi could have no defense. This accusation is an ever-present threat to all Jews still living where traditional Islamic legislation remains in full force.

In return for being spared his life and property, the dhimmi was obliged to recognize the supremacy of Islam by the payment of a special head tax, the *djezya*,[3] and a property tax, the *kharaj*. The basis for this was the Koran (IX.29): "Fight all those who believe not in Allah or in the last day, who do not regard as forbidden that which Allah and His Prophet have forbidden, and those among the People of the Book who do not profess the True Religion. Make war against them until they pay tribute with their own hands and till they are humiliated."[4] The severity of the laws against the dhimmis depended on the degree and manner in which they were enforced. When the Moslem ruler was liberal-minded and understanding, the laws were bearable; when the ruler was tyrannical and cruel, the condition of the dhimmi was that of a virtual slave.[5] The head tax could be crushing and the property tax could amount to expropriation. To this the ruler could always add supplementary taxes for the support of his army, not to speak of "good-will" gifts that the weaker paid to those in power. If the dhimmis accepted conversion, the special taxes were no longer levied. The Unbeliever was forbidden to bear arms. His life, except under the Hanafi rite, was not protected against the Moslem, and the "blood price" of the dhimmi was always less than that of a Moslem.

The Charter of Omar aimed to convince every Moslem that the Jew was part of some unimportant sub-species that it was necessary to accept and respect to a certain degree in order to remain faithful to the teachings of the Prophet. Its principles, which inspired all Moslem legislation in the Maghreb down to modern times, caused the departure of virtually all Christian communities from North Africa, and subjected the Jews to the harshest conditions of inferiority even under the most benevolent rulers. At times, the more enlightened rulers or lawmakers passed certain hadiths to ameliorate the dhimmis' condition without, however, ever approaching the concept of equality among men. The boldest of these laws never went further than assuring the rights and equalities of the ruler's subjects within the limitations of the privileges extended to each group.[6] The nature of Islamic law concerning the dhimmi explains the place that the Jews occupied in Islamic society during the past twelve centuries, and, further, explains to some degree the urgency of their flight from the countries where Islamic law held sway as soon as the establishment of the State of Israel made this possible.

The Dhimmi in the Maghreb

From the tenth century on, restrictions against the dhimmi were applied more rigorously against the Jews of North Africa, more especially as the Christian communities rapidly disappeared, either because they left the Maghreb or because they were converted to Islam. By the twelfth century, the Jews remained the only distinct group. Almost from the beginning of the Arab conquest they had been compelled to live in special quarters in every town. By the end of the twelve centuries of Moslem rule, the mellahs of Morocco, the haras of Tunisia and the Jewish quarters in Algeria—the ghettos of North Africa —had reached a state of indescribable misery and squalor, as will be shown in Chapter Eight. In the twelfth century, the Almohad Sultan Yakub el Mansur ordered the Jews to wear distinctive clothes—black cloaks with wide sleeves and black caps that covered the ears. Later, his successor permitted yellow robes and turbans to be worn.[7]

The conditions under which a dhimmi was allowed to hold public office were laid down by Al Mawardi in the eleventh century.[8] They stipulated that a Jew or Christian could become vizier for execution but never a vizier of delegation: he could carry out orders but he could hold no position of responsibility. Thus, he had no judicial powers, could not appoint officials, give orders to troops or administer the treasury directly. While in theory there were many responsible positions left for a dhimmi to fill, records show that in the entire Maghreb only one Jew ever rose to real power. When Ibn Yakub Yusof ascended to the throne in 1286, he named his favorite, the Jew Khalifa ben Ragasa, as superintendent of the palace, and may even have appointed him to the post of chamberlain (*hajib*). This so offended the Moslem nobility that the Sultan was eventually obliged, in 1302, to massacre ben Ragasa and his entire family.[9]

Certain Jews managed to surmount the obstacles with which they were beset and to amass fortunes—not always with favorable results. Thus, the rich Jew of the Dar ben Meshal family was stripped and killed by Mulay Rashid in the seventeenth century. This act of lawlessness took on a legendary character and came to be associated with the famous Tolbas student celebrations at Fez. The legend has it that Ibn Meshal had become the King of Taza who demanded that each year a young girl of Fez be brought to his harem. To rid the country of this scourge, Mulay Rashid, disguised as a woman, took the place of the girl to be delivered to the King. Forty students hid in the chests which were to contain the gifts.[10] But not all the rich or influential Jews met the same fate as Ibn Meshal. Some gained the favor of princes, sultans, pashas and caids who accorded special protection to those who were in a position to advise them.

Eventually North Africa, and its Jewish communities, was split into two opposing kingdoms: Tunisia and Algeria under Turkish suzerainty,[11] and Morocco which, under the reigning Alaouite dynasty, found itself quite isolated. The Jewish élite in Morocco, who had always been numerous and of a high intellectual caliber, were able to find outlets for their ability in intellectual and commercial activities as well as in public affairs. A Jewish family named Pallache played an important role as advisors and diplomats to the sultans of Morocco. In 1609, Mulay Zidan appointed Samuel Pallache ambassador to the court of the Prince of Orange. His sons, David, Moses and Isaac Pallache, were also given diplomatic assignments. David was received by Louis XIII and Cardinal Richelieu in 1631.

While the rights of the dhimmis under the Charter of Omar were often curtailed at the whim and caprice of the rulers, the reverse was also true and at times the burdens on the Jews were lightened. The Jew was not usually regarded as a stranger and an adversary, but as a protégé who could compensate for the contempt which was his due by fulfilling certain indispensable functions in the Moslem social structure, notably as trader or petty artisan. As traders and merchants at all levels, the Jews formed a necessary link between Europe and the Maghreb on the one hand and between town and country on the other. They kept the towns provisioned and supplied the most distant oases with their requirements. An indication of the size of this trade is that, in 1553, 640,000 pounds of linen and 900,000 pounds of paper and hardware were exported from France to Morocco.[12] From his peddler's bundle the Jew drew forth both the necessities of life and fascinating novelties. No wonder that in the eyes of his customers he acquired the status of a magician. At the price, at times, of his personal dignity, the Jew was thus able to purchase the confidence of his Moslem compatriots who generally could not do without his services.

The humiliations that accompanied the status of dhimmi were accepted by the Jew as inescapable realities of life—the slap in the face with which he was rewarded when he paid his annual *djezya* to the caid, the customary degradations, the blows administered in passing, the deliberate jostling, the swallowed insult. The important thing was to work obstinately to try and surmount the misfortunes of life in order to survive.

Outbreaks against the Jews

Virtual outcasts of inferior status, the Jews became the victims of every crisis. As Omayyads, Idrisids, Almoravids, Almohads, Marinids, Saadi and Alaouites succeeded each other, the Jews were easy prey for a population constantly embroiled in inter-tribal and inter-dynastic warfare. Usually unarmed, they were at the mercy of the mob eager for rape and pillage. Every change of regime, every famine or epidemic, every incident, however small, was likely to mark an outburst of gory uprisings against the Jews. Such tragedies were so frequent that it is impossible to list them, but the details varied little. The chronicles of the Jewish communities of North Africa repeat the same phrases again and again: "They plundered all the Jews. . . . They dishonored many young women. . . . They carried off many Jews. . . . They slaughtered so many women, so many children, so many Jews. . . . They burned this number of synagogues and ripped up that number of Torah scrolls. . . . Who can know our unhappiness. . . . Epidemics followed the famine. . . . Those that survived the mob were mowed down by death. . . . We fasted to implore the help of the Lord. . . . In our unhappiness we put on sack-cloth and ashes." The Jewish poet, Abraham ibn Ezra, writing in Spain in the twelfth century, summed up the sufferings of the Jews of North Africa in the following plaint:

> I rend my clothes for Fraa, the first victim
> On the Sabbath day; son and daughter poured out their
>   blood like water . . .
> I call for mourning and for grief, for the people of Sijilmasa,
> City of glory and of scholars, whose light has been covered
>   by darkness;
> Island of beauty—people of Tlemcen—its splendor destroyed;
> O royal city that is lost—sumptuous Marrakesh!
> Your precious forces have been transfixed under the insatiable
>   eye of the Enemy.[13]

The events referred to took place during the struggles between the Almoravid dynasty and the supplanting Almohads between 1132 and 1145, when the towns of Fraa, Sijilmasa,

Tlemcen, Marrakesh, Fez, Ceuta and Meknès were pillaged and
their Jews struck down. Between 1146 and 1150 the tide of
terror rolled eastward as far as Tunisia and Tripolitania.

Though violent, these crises were of a passing nature. Fez
was again considered to be so safe a town that, within a few
years, Maimonides' family chose to find refuge there after they
had been forced to leave Cordova. Tradition even has it that
Maimonides stayed in a house in the Moslem medina and that
he taught in the Mosque of the Kairouanis. He left Fez in 1165
for Palestine and later for Egypt.

The Almohad outbreaks and the atrocities committed by the
soldiers of Abd al-Mu'min left bitter memories. At the instigation of ibn Tumart—a mystic disciple of al-Ghazali, who proclaimed himself *Mahdi* (divinely inspired)—the Jews who escaped the massacres were given the choice of emigration or
conversion to Islam. Many of those who chose to stay behind
accepted Islam outwardly, but secretly remained true to Judaism. Some, like Judah ha-Cohen ibn Shoshan of Fez, chose a
martyr's death. Occasionally, the Jews defended themselves,
sword in hand, against their attackers[14] but the inescapable realities of a life in exile had taught them that it was not always
advisable or possible to defend themselves against the pogroms,
and that it was often better to bend with the storm and hope
that the worst would blow over quickly. Once the local population had been aroused, the Jews could only retreat to their
quarter where they cringed in fear till the crisis abated, either
due to the intervention of a local ruler or through some outside
factor.

In Morocco, the condition of the Jews deteriorated further
when, in the sixteenth century, that country was cut off from the
rest of the Maghreb.[15] The fate of the Algerian communities was
not much different. Indeed, there were few communities in

Morocco and Algeria which escaped pillage and even massacre, and the advent of Mulay Yazid in 1790 was accompanied by especially wanton attacks. In Tunisia, on the other hand, the Jews were on the whole better off, as they had been at most periods of their history.[16]

The underlying causes for the situation in which the Jews found themselves are to be found not only in the theological attitudes toward the dhimmis and the political realities of rival rulers and dynasties, but also in the abject misery in which feudalism had plunged the entire population of the region, Moslems as well as Jews. When warfare was the rule, it was hardly possible for the Jews to escape the general lot which was superimposed on the misfortunes which overtook them as Jews. In normal times, the life of the Jews was closely interwoven with that of their Moslem neighbors. The outrages committed against them were not usually coldly prepared long in advance, and their aim was usually pillage rather than massacre. The Jews purchased their protection, limited as it was, in certain ways: all, except for the rabbis who were exempt, paid the *djezya* tax to the sultan;[17] they were subjected to compulsory labor duties; they paid duties and taxes on all their commercial transactions. In addition, they gave generous gifts to the sultans, pashas, caids and lesser notables to assure themselves of their good graces. In wartime they paid special tribute to support their overlords' armies, and they paid for the guards who provided limited protection for the mellah.

Under such conditions, pogroms were the means by which a miserable and unhappy populace manifested its ascendancy over the even more unfortunate Jews, engaging at the same time in pillage so that it might gain some material profit from the general misfortune.[18] Lust and envy, rather than outbursts of hate, were at the bottom of the most popular outbreaks. There was never at any time in the Moslem Maghreb a philosophy and tradition of anti-Semitism such as existed in Europe from the Middle Ages down to modern times. Accounts of such innate traditions among the Moslems of North Africa that have been published by European writers reflect on the whole the anti-Semitic prejudices of the writers, and show a lack of understanding of the realities of North African attitudes. During most periods of history, the Jews of North Africa were happier than those in most parts of Europe, where they were the objects of unrelenting hate; such extreme sentiments did not exist in the Maghreb. The scorn that the adherents of the different faiths expressed for each other could not obliterate the strong bonds of a common source of inspiration and a way of life intimately shared. Even the haughtiest Moslem noble would not have hesitated to recognize that he was the brother of the humblest Jewish peddler, and, what is more, he would have expressed the great truth that Jews and Moslems in the Maghreb were both grafts on the original Berber trunk.

Two separate but similar events in Algerian history illustrate to what extent the welfare of their Moslem overlords was of positive concern to the Jews of North Africa. On October 23, 1541, Charles V of Spain attempted to conquer Algiers;[19] on July 8, 1775, the Spaniards were led in a similar attack by Count O'Reilly. In both battles the Jews fought side by side with the Moslems to repulse and defeat the Spaniards, who for a long time evoked bitter memories among the Jews. The Jews of Algiers celebrated the Moslem victory as their own with songs of praise, with a day of fasting and a day of joy. They still commemorate these events by celebrating a *Purim Katan* (Minor Purim) on both the fourth of *Heshvan* and the eleventh of *Tammuz*.

To paint an idyllic picture of the relations between the Jews and the Arabs would be false, but leaving aside the contempt that was based on tradition and ritual rather than on passions, and taking into consideration the animosity of rival tribes whose victims were the entire population, Jewish and Arab alike, one may safely say that the lot of the Jews in North Africa was no worse than that of the lowest classes in the Moslem society who were exploited with equal harshness by the dominating feudal system.

6

Judaism in the Maghreb:
The Oriental Components

The Nature of Maghrebian Judaism

That the Jewish communities of North Africa were able to survive and retain their identity throughout the centuries of degradation to which they were subjected says much for the power of
Maghrebian Judaism to which they clung so tenaciously. We
must now interrupt the thread of our historical narrative to
examine in detail the components, the character and the development of that Judaism—a subject so far only very superficially
documented by both Jewish and non-Jewish writers.

The essence of Maghrebian Judaism lay in its diversity. It
was composed of heterogeneous elements which were themselves the natural products of the historical events which took
place or had repercussions in North Africa. The basic biblical-
Phoenician ingredient was interwoven with Berber tradition,
this synthesis being later modified by Arab culture into predominantly Oriental characteristics. This was overlaid with the powerful influence of the Spanish and Italian refugees who reached
the shores of North Africa during the fourteenth and fifteenth
centuries, and finally there were the effects of the modern Western civilization introduced by the French.

This sedimentation of history and cultures, which occurred
nowhere but in North Africa, went beyond national borders to

follow geographical features. The Jewish communities that lived on the edge of the Sahara, from the palm groves south of Marrakesh, past the red rock fastness of Ghardaia to the shores of Tunisia at Gabès and Djerba, were alike in showing the predominant cultural influences of the biblical and Oriental past. Tetuan, Meknès, and Fez in Morocco; Tlemcen, Oran and Algiers in Algeria; and Tunis, Sfax and Kairouan in Tunisia all showed strong Spanish or Italian influences. Nevertheless, the fact that Berber and Arab traditions considerably modified these "European" cultures is an indication of the degree of secular contact which existed between the Jews and the Moslem majority. The mystic tendencies and cabalistic practices, whose transcendentalist philosophies and austere outlook deeply affected many aspects of Jewish life, contrasted sharply with the other, more colorful, influences. Finally, the impact of the French presence was most deeply felt in northern Algeria and in the main cities of Tunisia and Morocco.

The isolated communities in the small towns of the Grand Atlas of southern Morocco, in the villages of the Algerian desert, in southern Tunisia and in particular on the island of Djerba, which was cut off by the sea from any adulterating influences, provide us with the best source of information regarding Jewish life in North Africa before the arrival of the Spanish refugees. Here, where neither Spanish nor French influences penetrated to any appreciable extent, Jewish life as it had been lived for centuries was retained in an almost pure state of preservation into the middle of the twentieth century. The towns themselves breathed the atmosphere of the Orient, with their narrow alleys, low houses and crude bazaars that had changed little since biblical times.

If, together with the way of life preserved in these remote communities, one observes those aspects of Judaism which in other parts of the Maghreb remained substantially unchanged, particularly among the older generation, down to modern times, one can trace with a fair degree of accuracy the Hebrew, Berber, Oriental and Arab influences which shaped the character of Maghrebian Judaism. It would be misleading to attempt to ascribe a particular time or place to this or that religious, or quasi-religious phenomenon. Some trends were stronger in some regions than others; certain were adopted or abandoned at different periods. Nevertheless, from the most widespread characteristics, a reasonably clear picture emerges.

The Synagogue

The synagogue was the pivot of the Jewish community. Here life was lived in all its reality and intensity, rich and poor commingling with surprising intimacy. Worshippers brought with them more than just their formal presence, for this was not only a religious, but also a sociological manifestation of a group that existed by virtue of its religious traditions. It was the sociological function which the Jewish community fulfilled that conferred on this Judaism its essentially popular character. It was not a religion reserved for an élite, but involved in the rhythm of its being the masses of the people who participated in it.

At dawn, the men would congregate for the hour-long morning prayers. A smaller number would attend the afternoon service, merchants and traders preferring to assemble in someone's shop to repeat *Minchah* and recite a few readings from the holy books. At sunset, the whole community, except of course the women whose place was in the home, would gather once more in the synagogue for the *Arvit* (evening) prayer that lasted half an hour. On the Sabbath and festivals services were longer, and on *Yom Kippur* the entire congregation spent the whole day praying, fasting and repenting.

On feast and holy days, the men, enveloped in sumptuous white burnouses, gave a deep impression of Oriental splendor. The Hebrew prayers were pronounced with strongly articulated gutturals[1] but the chants closely resembled those of Gregorian form used in the tenth century. The setting was plain, resembling a mosque. An air of devoted prayer was combined with a surprisingly relaxed attitude of familiarity in the presence of the Divine. Altogether, the atmosphere was thoroughly Eastern in spirit, seeming but little removed from the era that stretched from Abraham to the sages of the Talmud.

The Bible and the Talmud

For the Jews of North Africa, down to practically modern times, the sources of their religion, their literature and their culture were ever close. Palestine had always remained a tangible neighbor known to all through the precise accounts of scholars, pilgrims and travellers who, en route to and from Babylon and Spain, passed through the Maghreb. The Talmud had penetrated to North Africa at a very early date. It had been accepted and studied, as it could not have been in Europe, as a living reality under conditions close to those of the times and regions in which it had originated. There was not in the Maghreb the attitude of stiffness and reverence in relation to the Talmud that was found elsewhere, where the Bible and its commentaries lacked immediacy and reality in relation to the local scene. A child in North Africa could picture Abraham riding to Mount Moriah on donkey-back; Hillel and Rabbi Gamliel teaching their disciples were compared with the rabbi of the village; the oppression by the Eyptian taskmasters was compared with the exactions of the Moslem overlords—and in this light life in the Maghreb could be accepted as being relatively easy. For North African Jewry, there was no sharp break between the ancient Jewish heritage and the Jewish tradition of the time.

The famous teachers of the rabbinical schools and academies of the Maghreb permeated the Jews of the region with a rabbinical tradition, and a thorough understanding and deep love of the Talmud and all its subsequent elaborations and commentaries. Throughout the Maghreb, even in the most distant oases of the south, there were rabbis and scholars to whom the Talmud and all its ramifications was an open book with which they were completely familiar. Many rabbis, especially in Morocco, were considered authorities and consultants in Jewish law, and their opinions were solicited from the entire district that came under their influence. Indeed, some of them were renowned far beyond the confines of the Maghreb, and even down to recent times there were those who received inquiries for rulings and opinions from as far as Israel, Europe and even America.[2]

Talmudic study in the Maghreb was not an academic pastime or an erudite exercise. It was a vital function, a part of traditional Jewish society which, like Islam, had not yet made the distinction between spiritual and temporal obligations. The Word of God, as interpreted through His Law, determined down to the smallest detail every part of the daily life of the individual and of the group, and there was therefore a continuous need to refer to the Torah in order to be able to obey the commandments and requirements correctly. The Talmud was an encyclopedic collection of all religious precepts to which the rabbi would apply his knowledge and learning to clarify any doubtful point, whether it was a matter of ritual or civil litigation.

But even where talmudic learning was most deeply ingrained, there was never in North Africa a type of Judaism which might be singled out as orthodox. The very concept of Orthodox Judaism, in which every daily act had to be performed in accordance with rigid religious precepts, did not exist in North Africa to the extent that it did in Europe. In fact, the Jews of North Africa did not even have a word to describe this phenomenon. Public opinion would quickly have cut down to size anyone who would have dared to censure the acts of others, for everyone knew in general what religious practices required of him. Further initiation was left to the natural development of each person's private life.

The Judaism of the most conservative of the Maghreb's Jews was marked by a flexibility, a hospitality, a tolerance, that was far removed from the unbending and aggressive orthodoxy that sprung up among European Jewry in opposition to, and defense against, the movement toward reform that resulted from the emancipation of the Jews of Europe at the end of the eighteenth century. Not only were historical circumstances different, but so were the nature of life and outlook. The Jews of North Africa, with their ignorance of sectarian disputes and their innate distaste of regimentation, had a touching generosity of spirit and a profound respect for meditation.

The Rabbi and the Rabbinical Court

Traditionally, each Jewish community in North Africa was headed by a chief rabbi whose purely spiritual authority was exercised in the form of preaching, and in teaching Judaism,

Talmud and theology in the *yeshiva* or rabbinical school where he trained his disciples. The rabbi was distinguished by his learning and his saintliness. He took part in the major cere-monies of religious life where he embodied the prayers of all present, he shared the sorrows and joys of his congregants at births and marriages, at sickness and in death. Judaism has lacked a specific priesthood from the time of the destruction of the Temple of Jerusalem, and the rabbis were teachers rather than priests. The word rabbi, meaning "master," was more an honorific title than a definition of a specific function. In the Maghreb as elsewhere, it was applied equally to those who were called upon to accept a religious honor in the synagogue. In-deed, it was not uncommon for rabbis in the Maghreb to earn their living by some trade or craft, as the sages of the Talmud had done.

Around the rabbi of the community there were, at least theoretically, other functionaries whose duties were indispensa-ble for the orderly performance of the ritual and for the well-being of the community. There was the cantor, known as *shaliach tsibur* (the delegate of the public) who lead the con-gregation in prayer; the *shammash* (sexton) who was charged with minor duties in the administration and exercise of the ritual; the teachers of Hebrew and religious subjects who in-structed the children; the *shochetim* (ritual slaughterers) who slaughtered the animals in accordance with traditional Jewish precepts; *bodekim* (examiners) who examined the cattle after the slaughter to make sure the animal's state of health had been in conformity with the requirements; the *mohalim* who circum-cised male infants on their eighth day.

In practice, anyone who fulfilled any of these duties might call himself a rabbi and, in the majority of cases, the rabbi was teacher, preacher, cantor, scribe and slaughterer at the same time. The instruction he received at the *yeshivot* of the Maghreb prepared him for all or any of these functions. The versatile rabbi of the smaller communities was no less loved for the fact that he fulfilled such a variety of duties. On the contrary, he was born of the common people, and the nature of his tasks made it impossible for him to withdraw from everyday contact with his community. At the same time, his authority and prestige undoubtedly suffered (particularly, as will be seen later, in the nineteenth and twentieth centuries) when he was called upon to give counsel on any matter which lay outside the realm of the Torah and the Talmud. In general, he was sadly untutored in secular subjects of general interest.

Lacking as they may have been in certain qualities, the rabbis of the Maghreb did possess a vital ingredient of religiosity—the profundity of the sense of prayer. Jewish liturgy, with the magnificent sobriety of its psalms, with its hymns and its prayers that swept the exiled soul toward Redemption, conducted the entire being of those who abandoned themselves to its gifts to new heights of illumination. In the remotest of isolated villages, where the foot of a visitor seldom trod, could be found old and venerable rabbis who, together with their profound knowledge of the Bible, which they knew by heart, and the Talmud, which they studied and taught, and even of the Cabala on whose mysteries they meditated, possessed a spiritual purity, a simplicity of life and of manner, and an indefinable heritage of saintliness which gave them a moving nobility, a grandeur that, in their humility, was consecrated entirely to the service of the Lord. Faith, rather than intellect, was the fashioner of their thought.

Each Jewish community in the Maghreb had a rabbinical court which was responsible for the legal matters that fell within its competence. The internal autonomy of the Jews had been a feature of the first communities ever established in North Africa, and the advent of Islam did not change the rights or autonomy of the Jewish courts. The koranic principle (I.51) that "The People of the Book will be judged according to the Book" was rigidly adhered to, and the Jewish courts thus regulated all matters of personal status, marriage, divorce, inheritance, civil disputes, business transactions, debts and conveyancing.[3] The administraton of the theocratic Moslem state was facilitated by this provision of special juridical institutions for the non-Moslems.

Of the structural organization of the Jewish communities of the Maghreb before the arrival of the Spanish Jews little is known.

Language

The Aramaic that the Jews of twenty centuries earlier had spoken was largely replaced in the Maghreb by a language equally semitic in form, the Judeo-Arabic vernacular.[4] However, in certain sections of Morocco the Jews usually spoke Berber, the language of the Grand Atlas. (It has been estimated that in the twentieth century 15 per cent of Morocco Jews still spoke Berber, 29 per cent spoke Arabic and 59 per cent spoke both languages.) But elsewhere, centuries of living and daily contact with an Arabic-speaking population had caused the Jews to adopt and adapt the prevailing language, but with that peculiar distinction that was to be found wherever Jews adapted a local language to their own dialect—the adapted language was preserved in its archaic form. Thus in the Maghreb, the old pre-Islamic Arabic was more carefully preserved in the mellah than in the most conservative of medinas. The language spoken by the Jews evolved from this

Arabic with many borrowings from biblical Hebrew, especially for terms connected with religion or with intellectual life. The proportion of words of Hebrew origin so used increased as one ascended the social scale. The women and the lower classes who had absorbed less of the Hebrew culture tended to speak a dialect that was closer to the Arabic of the time.

According to a survey made by the late Chief Rabbi Maurice Eisenbeth in 1936,[5] almost half the surnames of Jews in the Maghreb were of Arabic or Berber origin. First names too were still most often in Arabic, despite the rapid inroads of French in this field. There were Yahya, Ayush, Makluf, Yehish, Khalifa, Khalfon, Mes'od, Sa'dun, Sa'id, Sa'adia, Mimun, La'ziz, Lahbib, Sellem, Huitu for men, and for women Nedjami, Kemmra, Meleha, Aziza, Mess'uda, Aysha. Some of these names were endowed with magical significance which was supposed to extend protection to their bearers: thus, Khmiss meaning five which stood for the protecting hand; Huitu meaning fish; Ussayef meaning blackamoor; Yakota, precious stone; and Allilesh, lamb.

Dress

The manner of dress retained down to modern times by the Jews of southern Morocco and southern Tunisia who had remained largely free of Spanish and French influences, is indicative of their Oriental heritage, and gives some idea of what must have been current usage until the fifteenth century. The men wore a *jellaba,* similar to that worn by Moslem town dwellers, usually in black for older persons or those of importance, but in white for the others, once the old laws restricting Jews to wearing black were no longer in force. Those rabbis who did not wear a *jellaba* wore a long grown called *zoha,* a one-piece woollen garment that fell majestically from the shoulders to the ankle without lapels or collar, with sleeves open from elbow to wrist. Men also wore the *zabador* and the *tesmir* similar to the *jellaba,* and the *behdia*—a vest richly embroidered with forty buttons—the *sarawal*—breeches of satin or of grey or black wool, narrow or wide according to fashion and gathered at the waist and ankle. Headgear was the classic black skullcap of the mellahs of Morocco in varying forms, the tarboosh and the *sheshia* which disappeared under a large black turban. The children were dressed in a *blusa* under which, in many areas especially in Gabès and Djerba, they wore a small mauve vest to protect them from the cold. For shoes they wore the slippers of the Moslems or the *belgha,* a slipper of goatskin which was held in the hand when walking along dusty roads.

The clothes of the women were even more colorful. An important garment was a blouse with bouffant sleeves and a square-cut neckline, decorated with a profusion of flounces, Valencian lace or broderie anglaise. This was worn above the *sarawal,* ample breeches of cambric, drawn together at the waist and gathered at the ankle. After a certain age, young girls would give up wearing the blouse and wore instead a brightly colored knitted jumper in red, green or bronze. Underwear was not usually worn, especially in the south, except for an underbodice made of multi-colored straps. In the streets the young women arrayed themselves in a *futa,* a length of brightly striped silk or cotton which both hid and emphasized the roundness of their hips. A scarf of cotton or of silk embroidered with gold encased the face and completely covered the hair. Uncovered hair was considered akin to nudity. For formal occasions, the head was covered with a sumptuous *coffia* (headdress) embroidered with gold, embellished with pearls, gold and silver, like a royal diadem. Fine slippers with high heels or heavy *ḳab-ḳab* (wooden) shoes gave a biblical majesty to the gait. The women never went out without being wrapped in an immense silken or cashmere *haiḳ*.[6]

The *Kessua Kbira* was the bride's wedding outfit.[7] It consisted of white embroidered linen decorated with ribbons; a wimple; the *ḳtef* (bodice) of gold-embroidered velours; the *ghembaz,* a corselet of velours with gold braid and a low neckline; the *ḳmam-tsmira,* wide sleeves of embroidered silk voile, fastened at their lower ends mid-way down the arms, the other end covering the shoulders and part of the back; with this was worn the *zaltila,* a wide skirt of gold-braided velours; the *mdamma,* a waistband of velours with gold embroidery and pearls; and lastly the *ḳhmar,* a mitred diadem encrusted with gold, silver, emeralds, pearls and rubies. The women tended to be plump if not obese for, in the tradition of the Orient, a plump woman was considered more comely than a slender one; from puberty onward the young girls were often given over to the most intemperate habits of over-eating.

Popular Customs, Superstitions and Occult Practices

The Jews of the Maghreb, dwelling in close proximity to their Moslem neighbors and sharing the same hardships, lived and traded in an intimacy that permitted a complete interchange of folkways, customs and manners. The temptations for the Jews to stray from the strict letter of their faith were thus many. Simultaneous and successive polygamy was practiced among the Jews as it was among the Moslems.[8] The Jewish woman, though queen on her wedding day, suffered from severe discrimination that at times reduced her to near servitude. Her legal status, an interaction of talmudic legislation and the influence of the Moslem environment, continued to remain an anomaly until the mid-twentieth century, a phenomenon that will be discussed in more detail in Chapter Fourteen.

Like their Moslem neighbors, the Jews were given to the practices of witchcraft and superstition that belonged neither to the Law of Moses nor to that of Mohammed. The rabbis were powerless to control these manifestations of ideas that had grown out of the centuries-long interaction of Berber, Jewish and Arab credulity and superstition. These were so intermixed that it was impossible to draw a dividing line between those of the Jews and those of the Moslems. Likewise the origin of the practices could seldom be determined. It might almost be said that all superstitions were shared equally by both races. All believed alike in the evil eye (*ayin ha'ra* in Hebrew), in the *djnun* (demons), in the *ubeyta* who were born of the mixture of the blood of a brother and a sister who had died a violent death,[9] in the efficacy of talismans and in all the protective devices against the occult powers such as ritual phrases that included the mention of God's name, of fishes, of the protective hand and the figure five and all its multiples that signified the same.

Special ornaments were worn to repel the *djnun*. Thus, a necklet of cloves, because of its shape, its color and especially its smell, was considered to possess the power of protection. The designs on tapestry, the color of scarves, protective pom-poms, perfumes, incense, flowers, water—each object had a special language that could speak to, and protect against, the *djnun,* and at times even turn their evil powers against an enemy. A Moslem witchdoctor, often of Moroccan origin, was frequently called upon to dispense love potions and invocations, spells and counter-spells, to tell fortunes and make sacrifices and offerings to the *djnun*. Seldom could a house be built until the blood of a sheep or fowl had been sprinkled on the foundations—a custom that was an obvious carryover from Punic antiquity. All these magic symbols, rites and talismans, and the devout prayers which accompanied their use, symbolized the magic and mysticism which lurked in the dark soul of the Maghreb and held the Jews of the mellah in the grip of the "forces of the netherworld." All aspects of life were caught up in the frightening maze of menaces which bore down with the full weight of the occult powers.

Superstition was but little removed from magic and witchcraft. One of the magic ceremonies that was prevalent in certain areas among Jews of the Maghreb was the rite of *Tahdid,* of which a ceremony in the mellah of Casbalanca was described by J. Matthieu.[10]

"If, by good fortune, a male child is born, the house takes on a festive air. Friends and neighbors are invited for some light refreshments, a chapter from the Book is read together in Hebrew, over the childbed is hung a sachet containing *khezama* (lavender blossoms), *zaater* (thyme), *jaui* (benzoin), *fasukh* (galbanum) and *kebrit* (sulphur). The evening is passed in chanting, charades and *muhajiia* (riddles). At midnight, when all the doors are closed, the strange practice of *Tahdid* takes place; this lasts a week till the *Milah,* the circumcision.

"The father takes an old sword especially reserved for this purpose or, lacking that, any kind of sharp iron implement. (We have seen especially a large butcher's hatchet used for this.) While those present pronounce exorcisms against the *djnun,* the father makes wide slashes with the sword along the walls of the room to destroy or chase away the evil spirits. After this performance is over the sword or a knife or any iron implement, previously sprinkled with salt, is placed under the pillow or the

mattress of the mother to protect her. We have seen the knife
replaced by a horseshoe which was slid under the bed where the
infant rested. . . . At the same time as the rite of the sword is
being enacted, the women throw *harmel* (incense) in the four
corners of the house; they fumigate with *harmel,* thyme and
mugwort."

A Berber-Negroid magic rite was practiced by Jews in Tunis
who believed that when a woman was stricken by a inexplica-
ble disease (consumption, nervous or mental trouble) it was
because an evil spirit had entered into her and corrupted her.
The spirit could only be exorcised in the course of a magic
dance, the *Rabaybiya.*

Some Arab or Negro musicians would form an orchestra of
bagpipes, a Basque tambourine, and sometimes a flageolet.
When the music was of Negro inspiration (the ceremony was
then called *Stambali*), castanettes of black leather, an enormous
drum whose single stick was a small bludgeon, and a tambourine were used. The musicians would squat in the yard, their
backs to the wall; sometimes they would sit on small benches.
Care was taken to invite friends and relatives. Younger girls
would be present at the ceremony but could not take part;
men were excluded altogether. The spectators would press
around the musicians, leaving enough space for the performance
of the rite.

The stricken woman would advance into the center of the
circle, her face to the musicians, and would start to dance. The
music, starting slowly and in monotone, would gradually speed
up, become precipitate, then jerky and panting, not allowing
itself to subside before the dancer's ecstatic exhaustion. With
her hands behind her back, her hair flying, the woman would
throw her head backward and forward spasmodically. At times
a scarlet scarf was thrown to her which she would then wave in

her hand. When she became overtaken with fatigue, a companion would join her to give her support. Occasionally a harsh-voiced musician tried out fragments of a frantic chant. When the atmosphere was heated, two women would enter the circle and stimulate each other with mutual frenzy. From the silent audience would rise at times the yu-yu of an ululation—an augury, no doubt, that the cure was near.

The dance would continue obstinately, overpowering and triumphant. The bosom was shaken, the body bent, straightened, and, shivering and exhausted in a frantic whirling, it would fall down, lifeless. The soul was then freed. The bystanders, solemn and attentive, would freeze for a moment around this scene where obscure occult powers met face to face. In a *kanun* (brazier) aromatic herbs would be sprinkled; an acrid, penetrating smoke would envelop the crowd and free them from the concepts of time, isolating them in a universe where the hurly-burly of reality could not reach them. At this point, a *Cera'a* might enter into a delirium and begin to prophesy.[11]

Usually superstition was kept within decent limits. Birth, the putting on of the phylacteries by the *Bar Mitzvah,* marriage and death were surrounded by numerous practices. Unfortunately no proper study has yet been made either of the Judeo-Berber or other specific influences which gave rise to the special practices and beliefs peculiar to the Jews of the Maghreb.

The Veneration of Saints

The ardor of the faith of Maghrebian Jews found expession in the veneration of saints, a peculiarly North African characteristic virtually unknown among Jews elsewhere. While it is true that the Hassidim of Eastern Europe held their *tsadik* in veneration, gathered around his grave and placed written supplications on the earth that covered it, the practice was never as widespread there as it was in North Africa, and it met with strong opposition on the part of the Mitnagdim. Judaism in general repudiated the veneration of saints and sacred images as contrary to the Second Commandment, but nevertheless it was an integral, and vastly important element of Judaism in North Africa. It was obviously inspired by Moslem examples—among the Arabic-Berber population of North Africa the veneration of the *marabout* (monk or hermit) held a most important place in the faith. There were few villages and sites in the Maghreb that did not have the characteristic *kubba* of some local saintling to which the piety of the crowds was directed. The Jews adopted this Moslem custom. Moslem influence on their devotion was so strong that frequently there were no sharp lines between the saints venerated by the Moslems and those venerated by the Jews. The same *tsadik* or the same *marabout* would be the recipient of pious offerings by Jews and Moslems alike.[12] A special case is the tomb of Sidi Sifiane, the "Sid with the Two Swords," a scholarly rabbi of the Grana of Tunis, who was converted to Islam. His tomb, more easily understandable than in the case of many others, is the object of Moslem veneration. However, in the nineteenth century, Rabbi Uziel Alsheikh went there to pray for the salvation of his soul.[13]

A study of venerated tombs made by L. Voinot in 1948 in Morocco[14] revealed the existence of thirty-one saints who were claimed at the same time by both Jews and Moslems, fourteen Moslem saints revered by the Jews and fifty Jewish saints revered by the Moslems. An example of the depth of this interfaith phenomenon is the cult of Sol Ha-Tsadika whose tomb stands in the picturesque Jewish cemetery of Fez. Solisa was a seventeen-year-old Jewess who was martyred in 1834 for refusing to accept Islam and be inducted into the Imperial harem.

Her defiant death, which symbolized in a way the Jewish resistance to the pressures of Islam, quickly led to popular veneration and to the growth of a cult around her tomb. What is particularly remarkable about the cult of Sol Ha-Tsadika is that the Moslems too venerated this tomb—and this despite the fact that the veneration of women was so rare among the Moslems. This was the only tomb so honored in Morocco.[15] The cult of Sol Ha-Tsadika persisted for a long time but recently Moslems openly denied that this tomb is a center for their veneration. The cult nevertheless persists among them, if not as strongly as before.

Saints in Morocco may be divided into three groups: those who were known and venerated throughout the country, usually rabbis from the Holy Land who died in Morocco; saints whose fame was confined to a particular region; and lesser saints venerated only on a strictly local basis. The most famous of the Jewish saints of Morocco was Rabbi Amran ben Divan who was born in Hebron, Palestine, in the eighteenth century. On a journey to North Africa to collect funds for the Holy Land he was staying in Fez when his son fell gravely ill. The father offered his life if the life of his son would be spared and, indeed, a short time later, Rabbi Amran died in Ouezzane and was buried in the cemetery of Asjen in 1782. His tomb became the object of veneration of a magnitude that is commensurate with that of many Christian holy sites. The sainted rabbi is reputed to have worked endless miracles, healing the blind, the lame and the insane.[16] His intercession was sought especially for barren women; a certain family in Ouezzane possessed a relic of the saint, a belt, which women in childbirth put on to have an easy labor and those who were sterile in order to conceive. Moslem women and even Christians would come to seek the help of the saint.

The tomb of Rabbi Raphael Alnaqua at Salé near Rabat was

the scene of pilgrimages from all over North Africa. Rabbi Alnaqua, whose saintliness was recognized during his lifetime, died in 1935, and thereafter thousands of pilgrims visited his grave annually. Many miracles were attributed to his intercession.

The most famous Jewish holy site in Algeria was in Tlemcen where, on the road to Brea, stood the tomb of Rabbi Ephraim ben Israel Alnaqua, known as Rab, who arrived from Spain in the fifteenth century. Around the tomb of the saint, on an elevated strip of ground dominating a wide plain, are situated the graves of members of Rabbi Alnaqua's family and of some of his disciples. Jews from all over Algeria used to flock to this tomb and when, some years ago, the Consistoire in Tlemcen made an appeal for funds for the maintenance and improvement of the site to accommodate the crowds of pilgrims, sizable contributions were received from all over Algeria. The tomb of Er-Rkyese, a rabbi of the fifteenth century, which is not far from the tomb of Rab, is also greatly venerated.[17]

In Algiers, the Jews venerated the tombs of the illustrious rabbis of the city, and the same applied in Tunis; in Testour it was the tomb of Rabbi Fragi Shuar; at El Hamma, Rabbi Joseph Alfassi. In Djerba the main synagogue, the Ghriba, was also venerated, its foundations, according to legend, dating back to the Exile of the Jews following the destruction of the First Temple in Jerusalem.[18]

Of the many Moslem and even Christian holy sites to which Jews in the Maghreb flocked to offer up their prayers and gifts, the most famous was that of the Marabout of Nedromah. Many Jews came in search of blessings and healing, and went away carrying the precious amulet received during their pilgrimage, guarding it carefully to preserve its curative powers. Saints who were not buried in North Africa and had not even visited it were also greatly venerated. Of these the most important were the "fathers" of the Cabala, Rabbi Simon bar Yochai and Rabbi Meir, both Palestinians of the second century.

The Jews of the Maghreb, especially those most deeply steeped in the ways of the natives of the region, commended their persons to the care of their favorite saints at every important event or crisis in their lives. Even disappointment at the nonfulfillment of their hoped-for assistance did not dim the faith of the devotees. When an infant fell, when a wish was formulated, when a foot slipped, when a minor accident was survived or when someone was startled, an invocation was automatically made to the saint of one's choice. "O! Rabbi Simon!" or "O! Rabbi Meir!" the person would call out in his fear or in his hope, much as a Moslem might invoke the name of Allah or a Catholic the name of Jesus or Mary.

Offerings to the saints were made in the form of candles or oil lamps which were lit in front of the tomb or, if there was no tomb, in the synagogue or some other holy place. In Marrakesh, the main occasion for these votive offerings was on Saturday evening after the close of Sabbath. When the synagogue service was over the worshippers would gather in the immense cemetery adjoining the mellah, around the tombs of those who were especially venerated. Along the roadway that led to where the crowd was gathering, a row of beggars would be squatting begging for *tsedaka* (charity). Their misery was indescribable as they crouched on the stony earth where neither tree nor greenery could be seen, only stones roughly engraved to mark the graves. At the end of the cemetery the crowd gathered under carbide lamps. It was made up chiefly of old men, women and children. They congregated around a small structure among the tombs where toothless old men were auctioning the right to light the oil lamp at each of the saintly tombs, some dozens in number.

Each saint had his devotee who would give expression to his ardor by the amount he offered at the auction. Each year the communities would confirm the right to conduct the ceremony from which it drew revenues for the benefit of its charitable works.

There were definite rites connected with pilgrimages to the tomb of a venerated saint. Important events in the family, such as marriage, sickness, healing, a wish that was fulfilled, a death, a birth would, under normal circumstances, give rise to a pilgrimage by the individual or the entire family. At times, the pilgrimage was undertaken to counteract the evil forces released through an act of witchcraft. The pilgrims often came from a great distance; before they approached the tombs, they would undergo ritual purification (*tevila*) by immersion. A rabbi, or some other man renowned for his piety, would accompany the pilgrims to the tomb itself. There they would conduct themselves with the utmost piety: they would take off their shoes, light tapers, extend their hands toward the tomb in adoration, bring their fingertips to their eyes and then to their lips. They would kiss the tomb and place a cube of sugar on the stone, pour water on it, then kneel down and eat the diluted sugar off the stone as a sign of communion with the saint. Psalms would be recited before the tomb and a prayer said for the repose of the saint's soul. Naturally a prayer would be said also for that which the pilgrimage was intended to accomplish and the intercession of the saint would be invoked. Sometimes a meal would be eaten near the tomb itself so as to permeate the food with the sanctity of the place and with the beneficial powers of the saint.

Most characteristic of all was the collective pilgrimage known as the *Hilula*. This ceremony took place on the anniversary of the death of the saint. The Aramaic name, meaning "wedding," referred to the union of the saint's soul with God. The most popular and fervently celebrated was that of the Cabalist, Rabbi Simon bar Yochai on the eighteenth of *Iyyar,* which fell on the thirty-third day of the *Omer* (usually in May). A week before this date, preparations were made in all those communities that possessed the tomb of some saint (Rabbi Simon's tomb is in Meron, in Israel) to receive the visiting crowds from out of town. The greatest activity was around the tombs of those saints who were venerated all over the country, such as at Tlemcen or at Ouezzane where there were special and quite elaborate installations for the reception of the thousands of pilgrims. A thriving and lively bazaar operated there during the *Hilula.* Each evening the members of the pious fraternities, the *Chevrot,* would gather to chant psalms, read the Cabala and other sacred works. With the approach of the great day the crowds would get thicker and thicker, entire families arriving from afar on foot, on mule-back, by horse cart, by motorcar and by omnibus. Rich and poor mingled in their thousands in the same fervor; each had come to fulfill an earlier vow by participating in the sanctity of the occasion.

On the evening of the *Hilula,* the crowd drew near to the holy site. The exaltations of the previous days rose toward midnight to the peak of frenzy. By the light of oil lamps and tapers that had been kindled in honor of the saint, groups of people stood or squatted reciting psalms or loudly chanting hymns. The eerie light that bathed the cemetery highlighted the emotions that overcame the features and the spirits of the crowd. There was a feeling that mysterious forces were being generated by the powers of the chanted prayers. From this mass of humanity that was tensed toward the same exaltations arose cries in growing numbers, piercing through the veil of reality to give voice to the event that all desired. "The saint is here!" the shout went up from the throats of those most carried away. "Ha Huwa Ja"—

"There! He's there!" Soon the whole crowd, carried away by its ecstatic excitement, would shout. Braziers were kindled and fed with entire cartons of candles; flames shot high into the night; pilgrims, endowed with some unknown strength, would leap over the flames while around them the chanting, shouting and dancing would continue ecstatically. Those who had been dumb would start to speak, the lame to walk, the blind to see. The miraculous cures would gain in magnitude as they were repeated from ear to ear. Some of the pilgrims would claim to have received personal directives from the saint; others that they had seen a miraculous spring gushing from the venerated tomb.

At midnight the soul of the saint would visit the crowd and gratify the long wait of the pilgrims. For the rest of the night the rabbis would occupy themselves reading the Zohar, the Psalms and prayers, while the groups would disperse in the neighborhood. During the next day, and all the period till the Feast of Weeks (*Shavuot*), the sites of pilgrimage would continue to be animated. During this period alms-giving would be especially practiced, the poor would be invited to join in meals and much time would be devoted to prayer.

Ceremonies such as these indicate the degree of veneration that the tradition-minded Jews of North Africa accorded to their saints and their implicit faith in the saints' powers of intercession. This popular belief has never been systematized by the theologians of traditional Judaism. It would seem to have been a cabalistic belief further developed through especially strong Moslem influences. The cult of the saints and the celebrations of the *Hilula* had at all times been accepted by the rabbis of North Africa,[19] although in Algeria in recent years there has tended to be a more critical attitude especially toward certain manifestations that tended to commercialize the cult and in some way profane it.[20] The rabbis, of course, living in the midst of their community and an intimate part of it, shared the enthusiasm of their congregants' faith. For the congregants themselves there was no question of deep thinking on the subject, no consideration of religious theory. For them, this was a matter of profound faith, a supernatural experience born of an essential purity of spirit.

Centers of Jewish Learning before 1391

Given the close intermingling of Jew and Moslem in the Maghreb, it was only natural that the centers of rabbinic learning were established close to the great Moslem universities at Kairouan, Fez and Tlemcen. However, the Jews, living a precarious existence under the shadow of Islam, were in the main dependent on outside contacts for their cultural accretions.

KAIROUAN

Kairouan, the Arab capital at the edge of the desert, drew many Jewish settlers to the safety of Arab protection. From the eighth century onward, this wonderful city, an oasis of palms and shade, sheltered a large Jewish community devoted to the cultivation of Jewish studies and to the disciplines of the spirit. The city came to play the role of intermediary between the flourishing centers of Jewish learning in the East—Babylon, Palestine and Egypt—and the Jews of the Maghreb. During the Middle Ages, its rabbinical academies were of vital importance for the transfer of Hebrew culture from East to West.[21]

The rabbinical schools of Kairouan had a direct relationship with the talmudic academies of Sura and Pumbedita. The great teachers of the Babylonian universities regarded the Jews of Kairouan with respect because of their combination of sacred and secular knowledge. Among the renowned scholars of Kairouan in the ninth and tenth centuries were Rabbi Jacob ben Nissim ben Josias who founded a rabbinical academy and had many scholars, and to whom at the end of the tenth century Sherira Gaon addressed a famous epistle on the origins of the *Mishna* and the *Gemara;* there was Rabbi Joseph ben Berachia, a scholar of great renown, who was in correspondence with Sherira Gaon's son Hai, and with Rabbi Samuel ben Hophni; there was Rabbi Hushiel ben Elhanan who had been sold as a slave in Kairouan by pirates in the pay of the Caliph of Cordova. Later he founded a rabbinical school in his new home and became the uncontested spiritual authority for the Jews of Africa. In fact, so great was his reputation in sacred studies that he was consulted by Jews from all parts of the Diaspora. Rabbi Hananel was his successor. He was the author of an unusually clear commentary on the Talmud which served as a source for the codifiers of the future, and he also wrote a commentary on the Bible. His theological reasoning was influenced by Saadia Gaon and was based on the attainment of a knowledge of God through the triple agency of reason, Scriptures and tradition. Hananel was assisted by Rabbi Nissim bar Jacob who also wrote a commentary on the Talmud. Both rabbis were imbued with a scholarship whose brightness was diffused throughout the Jewish world. Scholars from Italy and Spain were drawn to Nissim bar Jacob in Kairouan, whom Rabbi Samuel Ha-Nagid of Granada called "The True Light and Glory of Israel."[22] He composed a methodological guide to the Talmud, *Hamafteah La-Talmud*. Rabbi Nissim was also lettered in Arabic and for this was greatly esteemed by the Moslems.

The Jewish community in Kairouan was no less distinguished

for its secular learning. Its head early in the eleventh century, the Nagid Abraham ben Nathan ibn Ata, was a physician of universal fame. The Eschemma family, frequently mentioned in El Kairouani's "Chronicles," produced a number of physicians and historians. Among them was Isaac Israeli, who was physician and advisor to the Caliph Ziyadat Allah l'Agh (903–909) and to the Fatimid ruler Obeid Allah al Mahdi (910–934). His treatises on fevers and diets were translated into Latin in the sixteenth century and taught in the universities of Europe under the title of *"Opera Omnia Isaci Judaei."* His disciple Abu Sahl Dunash ben Tamim was physician to Mansur. He also published a number of works on astronomy which refuted the assumptions of astrology, a commentary on the *Sefer Yezirah,* and a treatise on Hebrew grammar.

At the end of the ninth century the Jews of Kairouan were thrown into a fever of excitement by the arrival of Eldad the Danite who claimed to be a member of the tribe of Dan, one of the Ten Lost Tribes of Israel. Eldad vividly recounted that his tribe was living in an invincible Jewish kingdom beyond the rivers of Ethiopia and was separated from the other tribes by the magical stream of flowing rocks, the Sambatyon, which ceased to flow on the Sabbath. The story of this powerful Jewish kingdom spread to every corner of the Maghreb bringing the light of hope into the darkness of exile; its memories are still a part of Jewish folklore in North Africa.

By the eleventh century, Kairouan reached the peak of its glory. The city was declared a holy site of Islam and Jews were henceforward denied residence there. The exiles moved to Gabès, Djerba and Tunis, and no more than a handful of Jews has ever returned to live in Kairouan even in modern times. The tradition of Kairouan was carried on in Tunis. Among the many illustrious rabbis of that city was Rabbi Solomon Serur who gave a new impetus to Jewish religious studies in the seventeenth century. In 1772, Rabbi Joseph Azulai of Livorno reported that Tunis had over three hundred rabbis and sages.

FEZ

Fez was another center of Jewish learning. At the end of the ninth century, it was the home of Rabbi Judah ibn Kuraish who was a native of Tahert (Tiaret) farther to the west, and was known as the "Father of Hebrew Grammar." He developed a new approach to the study of this subject through comparison with other Semitic languages, and laid special stress on Aramaic, the language of the earliest Bible translations which closely resembled Hebrew in structure and vocabulary. He widened his field of study by drawing on Persian and Berber, and frequently quoted the Koran.

Another grammarian, Rabbi Dunash ben Labrat, lived in Fez from 920 to 990. A student of Saadia Gaon, Dunash ben Labrat did not hesitate to take issue with his illustrious master and firmly established the principle of triple-letter roots for Hebrew verbs to replace the two-letter theory. Abraham ibn Ezra regarded his work as "rational and logical," while the famous grammarian and commentator Joseph Kimhi, who lived in Barcelona in the twelfth century, called him "a scholar with pure linguistic conceptions." Like Judah ibn Kuraish, Dunash emphasized the importance of the study of Aramaic. He was involved in a controversy with Rabbi Menahem ben Saruk of Tortosa which was conducted through the publication of pamphlets in verse and in prose by both sides. Into the exquisite poetry he wrote, Dunash introduced for the first time Arabic styles of rhythm and prosody to enrich the Hebrew. His verses at times matched the most beautiful of biblical passages, and his work inspired the revival of Hebrew poetry in the Middle Ages.

Rabbi Judah Hayudj, living in Fez around the year 1000, analyzed the structure of Hebrew through a comparison with Arabic, with the grammar of which he was thoroughly familiar. His works were widely accepted as authoritative and Jewish scholars such as Samuel Halevy and Ibn Jannah of Saragossa gave them great attention.

But the sage who became in a way the symbol of Hebrew scholarship in North Africa was undoubtedly Rabbi Isaac ben Jacob Alfassi (1013–1103), a native of Fez and a graduate of its Hebrew colleges. He drew up a compendium of the Talmud which was a synthesis of a thousand years of rabbinical teaching. It clearly and lucidly exposed the laws and rulings arrived at by the rabbis of the Talmud and later authorities, without encumbering them by the minutiae of the arguments by which they had reached their decisions. It was an approach to talmudic studies that was later followed by many generations of his disciples. Alfassi taught in Spain where he headed the community of Lucena. His work was studied in Spain, in Provence, in the Rhineland, in Central Europe and in Poland and is still taught in rabbinical schools the world over. His eulogy, composed by his disciple, the famous Hebrew poet Judah Halevi, showed the veneration in which the master was held.

> For thee the mountains trembled on the day of Sinai;
> Then the angels came to thee
> To engrave on the tablets of thy heart
> The Word of the Lord,
> And to crown thy head with His finest diadem.

The tradition of Jewish learning which flourished in Fez during the tenth and eleventh centuries was maintained with varying intensity throughout the subsequent period, and its influence and renown spread throughout North Africa. But, while Fez produced many grammarians, poets, historians, physicians, exegetes, casuists and later Cabalists, it never produced a philosopher. Although Maimonides lived in Fez for a few years, his philosophical works were produced elsewhere.[23] He nevertheless dedicated his *Guide to the Perplexed* (*Moreh Nevuchim*) to a North African scholar and favorite disciple, Rabbi Joseph ibn Aknin of Ceuta, who later settled in Aleppo.

TLEMCEN

Rabbinical academies had been established in Tlemcen since the tenth century.[24] They flourished under the Almoravid rulers in the eleventh century but, with the sack of the city by the Almohads in 1145, Jewish cultural life practically ceased, to be renewed only with the arrival of the first refugees from Spain at the end of the fourteenth century.

As if by unalterable law, the Maghreb was never able to maintain a tradition of great learning except by cross-fertilization from outside. Thus it was that, from the eighth to the twelfth centuries, Babylonian and Palestinian scholarship made possible the renewal of Jewish learning in North Africa. From then till the fourteenth century the Jews of the Maghreb withdrew into partial isolation and were affected by the torpor of their surroundings. During this period, they increasingly devoted themselves to a study of the magic practices which had always been part of the Judeo-Berber world. Maimonides, writing in the twelfth century, had a critical opinion of the Jews of the eastern Berber regions, from Tunis to Alexandria. He described their lack of clear knowledge, their superstitious practices, their unconscious break with sound tradition despite their heightened belief in God; he found the Jews of Tunisia "dry and of a heavy nature."[25] The first refugees who arrived from Spain in the fourteenth century gave a new vitality to Jewish intellectual and spiritual life in the Maghreb and, thanks to them, Algiers and Tlemcen became the principal centers of North African Jewry.

7

Judaism in the Maghreb: The Spanish Component

One of the greatest events in the history of the Jews of North Africa was the arrival of the Jews who were expelled from Spain and Portugal in the fourteenth and fifteenth centuries. The addition to the Jewish communities of the Maghreb of tens of thousands of Spanish Jews in search of a new home served to reinforce and enrich North African Jewish life which, for the preceding two centuries, had been thrown on its own resources and had been greatly affected by the stagnation of the environment.

Spanish influences had predated the expulsion from Spain. Numerous and close ties in the fields of commerce and learning had long connected Iberia and North Africa. For the Jews especially these ties had been exceptionally close for, under the unifying force of Islam, the Jews too had enjoyed a remarkable unity. The ritual, the chants, the liturgy and the traditions of the Jews living in various Moslem countries were very similar, especially in the case of North Africa and Spain which, even after the defeat of the Moors in the latter country, still tended to resemble two provinces of the same country as far as the Jews were concerned. The trade routes from Europe to the Indies passed through the Jewish centers of Spain and North Africa, a commercial link which was strongly reinforced by the cultural relationship. Students from the Maghreb attended the great *yeshivot* of Spain, and the great Spanish scholars, among them

Maimonides, visited North Africa and taught in its academies.

With the decline of the Moslem empire in Spain, contact between Iberia and the Maghreb slackened. However, the traditions of the past made it natural that North Africa should become the principal inheritor of the spiritual, intellectual and cultural wealth of Spain that had been the pride of Jewry for centuries. Thus it was that the largest group of exiles set their faces toward the Maghreb when circumstances forced them to abandon their homes in Spain.

The Expulsion from Spain

The Golden Age of Spanish Jewry was already approaching its end at the close of the fourteenth century. The benevolent policies of the Spanish kings had been unsuccessful and their hope of unifying their kingdoms, including the Jewish and Moorish elements, vanished the more they felt themselves stronger than the decadent Moslem state in Andalusia. Relations between Christians and Jews deteriorated. In 1391, during the reign of the boy-king Henry VII, the first outbreaks occurred. Seventy Jewish communities were pillaged,[1] four thousand Jews were massacred by the mob in Seville, and countless others in Cordova, Madrid, Toledano, Saragossa and the Balearic islands. In Palma de Mallorca alone, three hundred Jews, together with their rabbi, were killed, eight hundred escaped to Africa and the rest were forcibly baptized.[2] The thousands of Jews who fled the mainland and found refuge in North Africa were following the route that had been taken by earlier waves of Jewish refugees escaping the harsh laws of Sisebut in the seventh century, and from oppression by the Almoravids in Andalusia in the twelfth century.

The 1391 massacres were a prelude to the total expulsion of

the Jews from Spain in 1492 and Portugal in 1498—events which marked the final triumph of King Ferdinand and Queen Isabella over the Moors. The Edict of Expulsion was published on March 30, 1492 and decreed that no Jew was to remain in the united kingdom of Aragon and Castille and its dependencies, Sicily and Sardinia, after July 30; those that remained could escape death only by embracing Christianity. The refugees were permitted to take with them their movable property with the exception of gold, silver and wares whose export was forbidden.

One hundred and fifty thousand Jews made their way to the coasts and set sail for more hospitable lands. Those of Andalusia sailed for Africa, where Moors, fleeing from Granada, had preceded them. Twenty vessels were attacked by pirates, three foundered in a sudden storm, others were cast up on the Spanish shore. Five hundred Jews, worn out by their hardships, accepted baptism; the others set sail once again for Fez, where many fell victim to a great fire and a subsequent epidemic.[3] In Arzila and Salé the Arabs and the Portuguese perpetrated rape, robbery and violence against the Jews, but in the rest of North Africa they were well received.[4]

The sultans viewed the new arrivals with approval. The Spanish Jews were more polished than their native coreligionists, they came from a wealthier milieu, and, in settling close to the Arab cities, they founded centers of Jewish life that were thoroughly permeated by Spanish influences. Better educated, more industrious and victims of the same Spanish persecution, the newcomers were welcomed by the Moslems who saw in them an ideal adjunct to the population, and nowhere along the coasts of the Maghreb was anything ever done to prevent the Jews from landing and settling. They founded communities of their own at Fez, Meknès, Debdou, Tangiers, Tetuan, Salé, Arzila, Larache, Rabat, Safi, Tlemcen, Oran, Mostaganem, Miliana, Tenes,

Algiers, Bougie, Constantine, Tunis, Sfax, Sousse, Djerba and even Tripoli.

Jewish folklore in North Africa became enriched by numerous legends about the flight of the Jews from Spain. One tells of the rabbi of Seville who had been thrown into prison and condemned to death along with sixty Jewish notables. While they were praying for deliverance, the rabbi was inspired to draw a ship on the walls of their prison and, when all sixty had touched the drawing, it turned into a boat which carried them all out of the prison, over the rooftops of Seville and to safety in Africa, without demolishing a single wall or causing injury to a single Spaniard. Another legend tells of Torah scrolls that were thrown into the sea in Spain to prevent their destruction by fire. They were washed up on the African coast and the Arabs tried to bring them ashore; but each time an Arab boat approached, it overturned and its occupants were drowned. Finally when Jews came to rescue the scrolls, they managed to draw them out of the sea without difficulty.

The Spanish Jews in North Africa

The Sephardic (Spanish) Jews could bring from their former homeland nothing but their language, their customs, their culture, and the memory of poets and philosophers who had raised the genius of Israel to heights that were never equalled in any other country or era of the Exile. (Indeed, to this day, descendants of the Jews of Spain in many parts of the world remain faithful to their rich spiritual heritage.) After a period of economic and social acclimatization that was at times difficult, the newcomers to the Maghreb were able to offer all their skills and knowledge to help in the revitalization of Jewish life whose degeneration appalled them. They had a profound influence on all aspects of religious and communal life, their scholars bringing about a resurgence of Jewish learning and a reorganization of the communities. It might be said that this period marked Maghrebian Jewry's first real contact with Western concepts and ideas.

The confrontation of the Sephardim, the *Castillanos,* with the native Jews, the *Forasteros,* passed on the whole harmoniously, and equilibrium was established in most cases with a minimum of communal damage. Eventually the two groups achieved a state of amicable symbiosis. However, great prudence and diplomacy had to be employed by the new arrivals to avoid conflicts with the existing Jewish population. The Spanish exiles, or *megurashim* as they were called, brought with them a culture, a mentality and attainments that differed greatly from those of the *toshavim* or indigenous inhabitants, and their superiority in intellectual and commerical pursuits was obvious. The established communities who, living in relative isolation for so long, had adopted Oriental manners, viewed the Spanish, who had been influenced by Christian ways, as if they had come from a different world. (It is not without significance that the local Jews dubbed the newcomers *Roumis* [Romans], in the tradition of the Maghreb which saw all arrivals from Europe as being in some way connected with the ancient overlords of the region, and regarded "European" and "Christian" as synonymous.) The rabbis of the Spanish communities were the first to preach understanding, and advised their congregants not to try to change the customs of the local Jews if they wished to live in harmony with them.[5] Diversity was minimized. The Sephardim, the "wearers of the berets," took to wearing the turban, and Spanish customs, in many ways superior, came to be adopted in the northern regions.

The geographical limits of marked Spanish influence were

noticeable for as long as Jews remained in North Africa. Tangiers and Spanish Morocco were understandably the parts of
Morocco most affected, and it was there that the old Jewish
culture of Andalusia was preserved till recently in its purest
state, free from Arab influence. The streets of the mellah of
Tetuan recalled the streets of Seville or Granada, the houses
looked alike, the passers-by had the same features, the language
was almost the same, slightly mixed with archaisms and
Hebraisms. The manners and customs were those of sober
Seville in the fifteenth century; time had little effect in the
mellah with its long memories.[6] The newcomers to the rest of
Morocco exerted such influence that they soon absorbed to their
ways the native-born Jewish communities in Meknès, Debdou,
Fez, Tangiers, Tetuan, Salé, Arzila, Larache, Rabat and Safi.

The influence of the Spanish exiles tended to lessen and those
of the native *toshavim* to increase with the distance from Spanish
Morocco. The interaction between the two cultures was noticeable and they reached a point of equilibrium that made coexistence possible. Meknès, Fez, Rabat, Oujda, Tlemcen, Oran,
Miliana and Algiers were towns where the harmonious fusion of
the two components was most marked. Many families in these
towns bore surnames indicative of their Spanish or Portuguese
ancestry.[7]

Others who had Hebrew or Arabic surnames preserved a
tradition that their ancestors hailed from Spain. In Morocco and
Algeria and to a lesser extent in Tunisia it was very common for
Jews—above all for Jewish women—to have Spanish first
names: Donna, Bella, Perla, Fortuna, Gracia, Allegra, Reina,
Estrella were very common even in those circles where little
memory of the Spanish past remained. The costume of the
women who wore the characteristic bolero differed substantially
from most of the local population. The Jewish dialect, though it

remained basically Semitic, showed many borrowings from Castillian.

In the south, the home of the *toshavim,* the communities remained faithful to local customs and usage, continuing to live according to standards and traditions which were little affected by Spanish (and later French) influences.[8] Nothing ever succeeded in drawing them out of the isolation and stagnation of the North African milieu.

Friction between *Toshavim and* Megurashim

The earliest known conflict of a serious nature between *toshavim* and *megurashim* was that which was carried on for ten years in Fez over the proper method of inflating the lungs of cattle in the examination of the carcasses after ritual slaughter.[9] The dispute was finally resolved in 1535 in favor of the *megurashim.* But a far deeper misunderstanding between the two groups in Tunisia led to a dispute which exhausted the vitality of Judaism in Tunis for many centuries.

The split, known as the Schism of the Grana, may originally have developed out of deference for the exiled newcomers, or out of a more negative attitude. In any event, the native Jews, on observing that the newcomers had different rites and rituals, seated them in special parts of the synagogue. It was a grave error, for it preserved the basic segregation between the two communities. Eventually, when the newcomers had been reinforced by arrivals from Livorno and elsewhere in Italy and had been able to establish themselves in the local economy, they broke away to form an autonomous community, called Grana. A veritable war broke out between the two Jewish communities. The Grana looked with derision upon the Touansa (Tunisians) who were referred to as "the Turks with the black cap and the violet turban." The Touansa for their part, fired with the ardor of holy war, pressured the Bey to expel these "false" Jews, these "wearers of the perruque," whose religious practices and unbounded conceit were offensive to the dignity of the Jews living under the protection of Islam. The Grana, expelled "outside the Holy City of the Throne," founded a new town at what is now the village of Mélassine while waiting for a more clement Bey to allow their return. They became even more active in commerce; they set up a market, the Souk el Grana, now the main artery of Old Tunis; they became even more attached to their traditional religious practices and set up three new synagogues and two prayer houses, one of them in the Djemaa el Grana in the middle of what was then the Christian Quarter.

The prosperity of the Grana served only to incite further the rancor of the internecine struggle. As the French Consul in Tunis, Saint Gervais, said in 1733, "They hate each other with a perfect hate." Something had to be done to find a *modus vivendi*, if not to establish real peace. On the seventh of *Av*, 5501 (1741), the rabbis of the two communities under the leadership of Rabbi Abraham Taieb, known as the Baba Sidi, signed an agreement according to which the division between the two communities was clearly defined. All Jews whose ancestors had originated in Moslem countries were declared members of the Touansa community; all those whose ancestors had come from Christian lands were declared members of the Grana community. This determined the responsibility for the support of poor wanderers passing through the community; it also decided on which side of a separating wall in the Jewish cemetery the dead would be buried. (This wall was not breached till shortly after the end of the First World War when a joint war monument was erected on the border between the two sections.)

The separation between the two communities enabled the Bey to indulge in capricious acts toward the Jews. Thus the Touansa, who were subject to the status of dhimmis, were compelled to wear a black skullcap without tassel; only the Grana were permitted to wear hats. In 1823, Bey Mohammed took it into his head to administer the bastinado to some Jews who had not worn the black cap, among them a native of Gibraltar and therefore a British subject. Sir Thomas Read, the British Consul-General, delivered a strong protest, to which the Bey replied that he would not tolerate the Jews doing as they pleased in his kingdom. The British thereupon sent the Mediterranean Squadron under the command of Admiral Lord Exmouth to the shores of Tunisia and the Bey backed down. As a result, all Jews of foreign nationality were henceforward allowed to dress as they pleased. Those Grana who were Tunisian subjects were able to purchase permission to cover themselves with the *kbibeshe,* a small white cap of cambric or knitted fabric, and the women were allowed to wear the *sefsari,* a cream-colored peplum striped with orange.[10]

During the eighteenth and nineteenth centuries, the Grana and the Touansa lived side by side without merging. They were separated by their different modes of life and ways of thought, and by their traditions absorbed from the Christian and the Moslem milieux respectively. There were differences of liturgy: the Oriental order of prayers contained some which were unknown to the Sephardic Grana; different psalms were used and the ritual at approaching death differed as did the funeral prayers, the way of preparing the shroud and the customs at the interment itself. There were differences too in the religious prescriptions for the examination of cattle after ritual slaughter. All these were comparatively minor matters. It may well be that the basis of the bitter conflict lay elsewhere, in the comparative emancipation of the woman among the Sephardic Grana, in the virtual abolition of polygamy in that community, in the rights of the widow to a share in her husband's estate. The conservatively inclined Touansa must have looked askance at such revolutionary notions.

The two communities did not finally fuse till the last years of the nineteenth century, when the spread of modern concepts under French influence and the intermingling of the youth in the schools of the Alliance Israélite Universelle facilitated the process. After the death in 1897 of Chief Rabbi Tapia, spiritual head of the Grana community, the French passed a decree in 1899 marking the official unification of the communities with a single Chief Rabbinate for the whole country, a single rabbinical court, a single slaughterhouse, and combined representation in the Community Council and the Government Council. A decree of 1944 completed the unification of the Grana and the Touansa. Nevertheless, down to the present day, there has never been a rabbi of French or Western culture in Tunis.

Community Organization

Upon their arrival in Algeria, Morocco and to a lesser extent Tunisia, the Spanish refugees were generally offered by the sultans living quarters which were usually located in the neighborhood of the royal palaces. From these quarters the mellahs eventually developed, and within them was laid the basic framework of Jewish life and the structure of community organizations which remained substantially unchanged till the arrival of the French in the nineteenth century. The Moslems left all internal arrangements to the initiative of the Jews. Within their mellahs they lived as if within miniature republics, enjoying a

large measure of internal autonomy. They followed their own
religious practices, organized their communities and their system of justice without outside interference. As has been pointed
out in the preceding chapter, Moslem law was more explicit and
more generous toward the Jews in this respect than the legislation of Christian countries.

The link between the separate entity that each mellah formed
and the central state was the *Sheikh el Yahud,* the Prefect of the
Jews—symbol of the ruler's power and authority among the
"Jewish Infidels." He was appointed by the Sultan and, as the
representative of the Moslem administration, was as detested as
he was powerful. His duties included the collection of fines, the
requisition of forced labor and the exercise of vigilance in
watching for any sign of incipient rebellion.

Tsedaka, charity in its widest sense, was at the heart of the
Jewish community structure. The mellah, a closed world, had
the religious and social obligation of caring for its own poor.
The better-off notables of the mellah were entrusted with the
management of the community's finances that were devoted to
religious needs, education, and charity to the poor and sick.
They were also charged with influencing the authorities when
necessary on behalf of their coreligionists; they were both the
community's administrators and its ambassadors to the Sultan's
court. It was a rudimentary system of administration and it
tended to confuse diverse powers and functions.

The community was administered directly by a council of
notables, *Tovei Ha'ir,* the "Quality" of the City. Council members were nominated by the community, their number varying
according to the community's importance. The council saw to
the appointment of rabbis and the proper functioning of all
religious institutions; it supervised the distribution of alms and
presented to the *maksen* (administration) petitions on behalf of

the Jews. The Council of Notables, the *gizbar* (treasurer) and the rabbis constituted the official organs of the total Jewish community. No central body existed to organize or coordinate the separate community organizations. Furthermore, each community was autonomous and had no direct organic ties with neighboring communities.

Under the influence of the Christian civilization of Castillian Spain, the attitude of Spanish Jewry to the rights and position of women had undergone a marked change. The *takanot* (regulations) which had been issued by the rabbis of Castille were introduced to the Maghreb by the Spanish refugee rabbis and thus brought about a change for the Jewish women of the Maghreb as well. The most notable reform was the introduction of a concept akin to the joint ownership of the couple's property.[11] At the death of her husband the surviving widow was entitled to half of the communal property, the other half being shared by the other heirs of the deceased. This reform introduced a principle of equality between husband and wife that had been unknown in Oriental society till that time. The Castillian reform soon predominated in all the communities where Spanish influence was strong and where the populace adopted the customs of the *megurashim,* but in the south and in the interior, the indigenous Jews rejected the reforms and clung to the strict observance of the old talmudic tradition.

Centers of Jewish Learning after 1391

ALGIERS

In 1391, Rabbi Simon ben Zemach Duran, his son, who was to become famous as Rabbi Solomon ben Simon Duran, and

Rabbi Isaac ben Sheshet Barfat, known as the Ribash, settled in Algiers—an event commemorated annually till recent times by Algerian Jews on the Eve of the Day of Atonement. The growth of Algiers dates from this time when the city also received the Jewish refugees from Mallorca, famous for their skill in cartography and in many trades and industries.

The writings of the three famous rabbis of Algiers make it possible to reconstruct a portrait of Jewish life in North Africa in the fourteenth century.[12] They were in close contact with the majority of Jewish communities throughout the region, guiding them and enlightening them on their problems. Their influence was great in all matters of Jewish life, in questions of liturgy, ritual, the teaching of the Torah, marriage, divorce, inheritance and also civil litigation. The learning and reputation of the Spanish rabbis resulted in their opinions prevailing and their customs being widely accepted. Thanks to them, the friction between *toshavim* and *megurashim* in Algeria was minimized. They helped to reorganize Jewish communal life and, with their disciples, brought about a renewed flourishing of Judaism throughout Algeria and also in Tunisia and Morocco.

The works of the Ribash exerted a profound influence on North African Jewry. A native of Barcelona and a disciple of the leading rabbis of his time—Hasdai Crescas, Perez Ha-Cohen and Nissim Gerundi—he had been Rabbi of Saragossa, but his reputation had spread throughout the Diaspora, and he was frequently called upon to arbitrate religious and legal controversies in distant communities. Rabbi ben Sheshet Barfat based his beliefs on the conviction that all wisdom and all knowledge were to be found in the Torah as amplified by the Talmud; the Word of God as revealed to Moses and transmitted to Israel contained all divine and human wisdom, acting as the intermediary between the uncreated Infinity and His creations.

His views resembled those of Maimonides, as did his clear teaching and his penchant for philosophical subjects. He loved the peace of mind, the orderliness and the satisfaction that prayer, meditation and an awareness of God could bring about. "With all my heart and with all my soul and with all my might I labor for the love of the disciples of Wisdom," was one of his sayings. He enjoyed, above all, the search for truth: "Whether it is accepted or rejected, Truth remains Truth." His prayers, devoid of cabalistic or philosophical references, were simple. "I pray with the expectancy of an infant," he said.

Like Maimonides he was skeptical in his approach to the Cabala, and his attitude to dream interpretation was ambivalent. Once, in Spain, when a certain Solomon Matish had warned him that in his dream he had seen the house of the Ribash burn down, the learned rabbi had ignored the advice to proclaim a fast and avert the catastrophe—only to see his house burn down a few days later. When later, in Algiers, he was warned by a certain Hakim ben Abn to proclaim a public fast to avert a catastrophe of which ben Abn had dreamed, he acceded to the suggestion—and was ridiculed by his congregants for his superstitions.

The Ribash was a universally recognized rabbinical authority. He refused to enter into futile and trifling discussions, but helped to impose on North Africa the *Mishneh Torah,* Maimonides' clear and precise codification of the talmudic law that henceforward became the ultimate religious authority for North African Jewry. "We have dialecticians who are capable of making an elephant pass through a needle's eye," Rabbi Isaac ben Sheshet declared. "They move mountains of questions and responses on every iota of the Law and, through their subtleties, they are misled into false conclusions; they permit that which is forbidden and forbid that which is permitted." The Ribash

knew, and frequently cited, the whole of the traditional knowledge of Judaism, both the Babylonian and Jerusalem Tal-
muds,[13] the later writings of the heads of the Eastern academies, the great teachers of Spain, Provence and the Rhineland.
"The Word of God has come to us from France," he would say,
referring to his contemporaries, the rabbis of France, as "stars."
"We live by their words and drink of their sources." This first-
hand scholarship, drawn from the sources of Jewish thought,
was widely disseminated by the Ribash, and its effect served to
nourish North African Judaism for centuries. His admirers
equated him to the greatest minds in Jewry, and for the rabbis
of the Maghreb he served as a model and an inspiration. He was
even claimed as an adept in the Cabala by the Cabalists of the
Maghreb: one of them considered him the reincarnation of the
pure soul of Adam; others saw the three great rabbis of Algiers
as reincarnations of the three Patriarchs, with the Ribash identified with Abraham.[14] To this day the Jews of North Africa
venerate the Ribash as a saint.

The expulsion of the Jews from Spain a century later helped
to consolidate the work of the Ribash and his contemporaries.
The hundreds of rabbis and scholars who descended on the
Jewish communities of North Africa from Agadir to Tunis reinforced the centers of Jewish learning and gave a special impetus
to the study of the Torah and the Talmud, especially in Fez and
Tlemcen.

TLEMCEN

Among the famous scholars who in 1391 found refuge in
Tlemcen—"Pearl of the Maghreb" and "Jerusalem of the
West" as it was called during its most flourishing period—was
the Rab, Rabbi Ephraim ben Israel Alnaqua (who was reputed

by later legend to have arrived from Spain mounted on a lion with a serpeant serving for a bridle.) Other scholars in Tlemcen at that period were Rabbi Judah Kallas, author of *Messiach Ilemim,* a commentary on Rashi's gloss on the Bible; the poet Allal ben Sidun; Jacob Gabison, a physician and student of the Maimonides philosophy, and author of *Derech Hasechel (The Way of the Intellect),* written in defense of his master's *Guide to the Perplexed;* Rabbi Jacob Berab, teacher of the famous author of the code of Jewish laws, the *Shulchan Aruch,* Rabbi Joseph Caro; Rabbi Jacob Kino, a known preacher; Abraham ben Meir Zmiro, poet and philosopher; Moses, Saadia, Elie and Isaac Chouraqui, poets, theologians and philosophers whose writings, largely unpublished, were in part used in the liturgy of the synagogue in the Oran region.[15] Another renowned scholar in Tlemcen in that period was Rabbi Joseph Alaskar who wrote, in addition to poetry and works on moral theology, a cabalistic treatise, *Tzofnat Pa'aneach (Revealer of Hidden Things)* in which he tried to discover a hidden cabalistic meaning in the *Mishna,* so as to establish the existence of a secret concordance between the exoteric teachings of the Talmud and the esoteric traditions of the Cabala. (His tomb, later the scene of reverent pilgrimages, was reputed to have opened up by itself in order to offer refuge to his mother when she was attacked by brigands.)

This double heritage which combined the study and practice of the Torah and Talmud with the mystical study of the Cabala was one of the features of Judaism in North Africa. It is perhaps more than a coincidence that it was a Tlemcen scholar who, in the sixteenth century, proved the need for reconciling the Talmud and the Cabala.

It was the rabbinical academies of Kairouan, Tunis, Algiers, Tlemcen and Fez, and the lesser schools that were founded in other centers throughout the Maghreb, that served as the guardians and propagators of learning and culture among North African Jewry. In them is to be found the inner power that sustained Judaism in the Maghreb through the long centuries of oppression and humiliation which followed.

The Contribution of the Spanish Jews to Intellectual Life in the Maghreb

The infusion of the Spanish refugees into the North African communities brought with it the introduction to Maghrebian Judaism of the great outpourings of Jewish thought whose mainstream was in Europe. The Sephardim succeeded in making the Code of Alfassi, the *Mishneh Torah* of Maimonides, and the *Shulchan Aruch* of Joseph Caro the ultimate authorities on legal and ritual problems; they introduced Maimonides' *Guide to the Perplexed*, the *Kuzari* of Judah Halevi,[16] and other theological works which became part of Jewish spiritual tradition in even the most distant communities of the Maghreb. Published responsa (*She'elot u-Teshuvot*), and weekly sermons by the rabbis and translations into the Judeo-Arabic vernacular helped to spread the new religious and cultural accretion and made it easily accessible to the laymen of the community. The basic work of spiritual theology for the Jews of the Maghreb was the *Introduction to the Duties of the Heart* by Rabbi Bahya ibn Pakuda of Saragossa, which appeared about 1100. (A translation into the vernacular was published in Djerba in 1919). This book inspired many rabbis and, in translation, made the traditional beliefs of the Maghreb's Jews available to all.

The poetry of the Golden Age of Spanish Jewry was another gift to the Maghreb. The chief works of Judah Halevi were incorporated into the liturgy; the great Spanish poet of the eleventh century, Ibn Gabirol, who wrote of the love and the anguish of man smitten with the adoration of his God, became familiar to the humblest Jew in the furthest mellah. His hymns and poems that had become part of the liturgy were known by heart, like the Psalms and many parts of the Bible, among all who attended the synagogue. In recent years, following the decline of Hebrew and Jewish scholarship among the North African masses, the meaning of this beautiful poetry may no longer have been known to many of those who could recite it, but in the farthest villages of the Sahara or the Grand Atlas there were many rabbis who were still writing Hebrew poetry inspired by the Bible and composed in the style and manner of the great Spanish poets.

The advanced culture that the Jews brought with them from Spain was, however, drained of its reserves of vitality in contact with the arid sterility of the Maghreb, and religious knowledge and scholarship tended to get bogged down among the popular superstition of the masses. There remained, moreover, large groups of Jews, rough, unpolished and untutored, known as *Yhud el Arab,* the "Arab Jews" (and by the Jews of Constantine in the ninetenth century as *Bachutzim,* the Outsiders) who had been untouched by Jewish culture. In the 1930's many Jews of the Kabyle region of Souk-Ahras and between Constantine and Khenchela still lived according to standards and cultures that had been affected neither by the influence of the Jews of Spain nor by the hundred years of French influence.[17] But there were many isolated pockets where an authentic culture had nevertheless been created. Foundations had been laid that gave the élite access to the higher spiritual disciplines of Judaism, and it was this contribution of the Sephardim to North African Jewry that enabled the Jews of the Maghreb eventually to participate to the full in the cultural awakening of the twentieth century.

Mysticism

Spain had been the main center of the development of the Cabala from the thirteenth century onward. The esoteric traditions which had been woven into Judaism were taught to an ever-growing circle of initiates by rabbis Solomon ibn Adret, a disciple of Nachmanides, Abraham Abulafia, Joseph Gikatila, Shem-Tov ibn Gaon and, most important, Moses de Leon. These teachers remained faithful to their traditions in opposition to Maimonides' Aristotelian doctrine. All cabalistic tradition was attributed by the Spanish to Rabbi Simon bar Yochai, a disciple of Rabbi Akiba and Rabbi Meir, both second century rabbis. The *Sefer ha' Zohar* (*Book of Splendor*), a basic work of the Cabala to the end of the 13th century, was the venerated book of the mystics, almost equal in sanctity to the Bible, the Talmud and the *Mishna*.

The Cabala gave meaning and importance to the smallest talmudic prescriptions. Between the two extremes of good and evil, between election and rejection, human life was a contest whose stake was the eternal salvation of the soul, of the community of Israel and of the world. Conscious submission to the Divine Order brought about *Dvekut,* a mystic adherence or communion with God in which lay redemption and the source of salvation. Man was created in the image of God and, when freed of the shackles of the world, could become an active collaborator in the great Design of the Eternal; for prayer could bring about the salvation of the world.

The Decree of Expulsion from Spain fell into this mystical world like a searing flame. The theme of exile assumed the appearance of an inescapable and frightening reality. The suffering of the Jews was interpreted not only as it had been formerly, as the punishment for fall and sin, but, in the perspective of an apocalypse, as the final catastrophe in which the world seemed engaged, in which the contribution and the sacrifice of Israel would bring the ultimate redemption. The hour seemed to have struck for the initiates of the Cabala to come out of their reserve and to offer to all Israel the consolation of the Mystery of God. The Cabalists who were among the refugees from Spain, having sacrificed everything for the Sanctification of the Name of God by preferring to apostasy the harshness of exile and the renunciation of all they possessed, arrived in North Africa charged with messianic hope. Their uprooting brought about a spiritual glow which helped them to face the trials of exile and which was diffused among the communities that received the messengers of the new enlightenment.[18] As a result, cabalistic ideas came to exert a profound influence on Maghrebian Judaism.

To Safed in the Mountains of Galilee came many of the sages exiled from Spain, among them some who had passed through the Maghreb and taught there for a number of years. One of these was Rabbi Jacob Berab, a student of Rabbi Isaac Aboab, who had taken refuge in Tlemcen and later had become Rabbi of Fez. He arrived in Safed in 1534 at the peak of the glory he had achieved by his erudition and saintliness. Foremost among the scholars of Safed, he conceived the idea of re-introducing *Semichah,* ordination by the laying-on of the hands. He had himself ordained by a college of twenty-five rabbis with the authority to resume the ordination of rabbis in this way; but the practice was strongly opposed by Chief Rabbi Levi ben Jacob ibn Habib of Jerusalem and did not outlive Jacob Berab. Rabbi Joseph Caro, compiler of the *Shulchan Aruch,*[19] and the Cabalist Solomon Halevi Alkabez, author of *Lecha Dodi* (a mystical hymn recited in the synagogue to welcome the Sabbath) also came to Safed. However, the city did not become the capital of Jewish mysticism till after the time of Rabbi Isaac ben Solomon Luria.

The Ari, as Rabbi Luria was called (from the initials Ashkenazi Rabbi Isaac, Ashkenazi being a cognomen to indicate his German origin), was born in Jerusalem in 1534 and died in Safed in 1572.[20] The Cabala of the Ari was based on a mystical interpretation of the cosmic theme of Exile and Redemption. To escape from Exile to the separate world of God and to achieve *Ein Sof*, the Infinity, the messianic redemption of primordial man, the soul must be cleansed of its impurities. Every practice, every rite, every gesture of man that was inspired by the revelation of the Torah, the *Mishna* and the Talmud was bound to lead to the ultimate ascension of the soul for which the correction of man was a prerequisite. Its practice required a special mental concentration of the intent (*Kavana*) which would direct the spirit of the mystic and every word and letter of his prayer into closer contact with the secrets of Creation. From the salvation for which preparations were thus made, ecstatic joy was realized in the hope of the early coming of the Messiah.

The spiritual heir of the Ari was Hayyim Vital, author of *Etz Hayyim* (*The Tree of Life*). (Vital was also influenced by Moses Cordovero, the author of *Pardess Rimonim,* [*The Garden of Pomegranates.*]) Another disciple, Israel Sarug, dedicated himself to spreading the word of Rabbi Isaac Luria among the Mediterranean countries in the years 1592–1598. These two, together with Rabbi ibn Joseph Tebul, found many ardent disciples who made the cabalistic doctrines of Isaac Luria the foundation of the piety of North African Judaism and succeeded in winning over the masses of Maghrebian Jewry.

The *Haham Kollel,* who was a regular feature of the Maghrebian scene from the fifteenth century down to recent times, did much to spread and propagate the Cabala. The *Haham Kollel* was a rabbi, an initiate of the Cabala, who came from Safed, Jerusalem or Tiberias to make the round of the Jewish communities and collect donations for the support of the schools of sacred knowledge in the Holy Land. In return for the sums he collected and the hospitality he received, he gave freely of his knowledge; he taught, he preached and he cured.* Through the itinerant *Haham Kollel,* the *Zohar* and the teachings of Rabbi Isaac Luria were spread to the farthest Jewish communities, and through him the flame of messianic hope was kept alight; it was he who maintained the unity of the Maghreb's Jews, he who adapted the traditional liturgy to the devoted intent required by cabalistic practice.

Through the *Haham Kollel,* the souls of the Jews were refilled with renewed piety, excited and inspired by the tales of the miracles wrought by the saintly rabbis, exalted with the hope of an imminent return to the Holy Land and the ultimate reintegration of the spirit. The exile from Spain, the fetters of Moslem domination, all the suffering and the misery present in the mellah—all were set free in the abyss of a cosmic necessity. In the soul of every Jew, miserable as he might appear, burned the hope that he might be confronted by the dramatic unfolding of the final destinies of the world which would take place when mankind had reached the required degree of saintliness. Surrounded by pitiless demons who were seeking his downfall, the Jew abandoned himself to the invocation of God and to the

*Healing by the *Haham Kollel* was not something confined to the distant past; the present author owes his life to *Haham Kollel* Rabbi Franco of Jerusalem who cured him as a child in Aïn-Témouchent when all hope for his life had been given up and preparations made for the funeral.

protection of the angels whose names appeared on every page of the cabalistic writings intended for daily devotion; each evening when retiring, the Jew commended himself to the protection of the angels Michael, Gabriel, Raphael and Uriel.

In the synagogues of Morocco and in the majority of those of Algeria and Tunisia, the three daily services of prayer were still preceded, until modern times, by a reading of certain sections of the *Zohar* which sometimes lasted a whole hour. Uttered with great devotion, these cabalistic readings served, like the Psalms, as an introduction to the prayer itself. In the mystery of faith, the mysticism of devotion served as the weapon of combat. All parts of the communal, family and individual ritual were imbued, modified and interpreted in accordance with the message of the Cabala.[21]

Many of the small towns and all the large centers of Jewish life in North Africa maintained a fraternity of readers of the *Zohar,* known as the *Chevra.*[22] In some cases the *Chevra* consisted of old men known for their piety, who were paid by the community to recite the *Zohar* and the Psalms (which had also been integrated into the mystique of the Cabala) according to the tunes of the traditional liturgy. Sometimes teams of *Zohar* chanters would, in relays, be engaged in their devotions day and night. In Casablanca, there were till recently at least five places where the *Zohar* was chanted twenty-four hours a day. In Marrakesh, Fez, Meknès and in the north of Algeria, this custom was less fixed than in the south, but it was maintained with devoted intensity in Tunis. The chanters of the *Zohar* were summoned to every religious ceremony, to marriages and burials and to the donning of the phylacteries by the *Bar Mitzvah*. Like the majority of their audience, the chanters were usually incapable of understanding the Aramaic texts that they read with such fervor; but this was of little moment. The chanting was an exercise in devotion whose observance was its own reward; its efficacy resided in God and His kingdom on which the intent of the soul had to be concentrated.

Pious worshippers frequently joined in with the readers of the mystic works, particularly during the seasons which were especially consecrated to these devotions. Thus it was in the period of *Selichot* preceding the New Year and the Day of Atonement, when worshippers were called from their beds, in the dead of night, to repair to the synagogue where they swayed to the rhythms of the chants till their bodies were themselves forgotten. During the peirod of *Selichot* and the seven days of Tabernacles (*Succoth*), each meal was preceded and followed by a reading from the *Zohar*. The whole night of the Festival of Weeks (*Shavuot*) and of the seventh day of *Succoth* (*Hoshaana Rabba*) were given over to prayer and devotions, to the reading of the Psalms and the *Zohar*.

The *Zohar* was so highly treasured that, even in recent times, it was extremely difficult to purchase a copy, especially in Morocco, despite the publication in Djerba of the first three volumes of a new edition, divided into daily readings. In many places the *Zohar* was venerated as highly as the scrolls of the Torah. Elaborate ceremonials, similar to those which surrounded the reading of the Torah in Jewish communities throughout the world, existed in the Maghreb, especially in Morocco, for the reading of the *Zohar*. In certain communities, at the close of the Sabbath on Saturday evening, the honor of being allowed to return the book of the *Zohar* into the Holy Ark next to the Torah scrolls was auctioned off for the benefit of the community's funds. The women, who were usually excluded from the performance of synagogue ritual, were allowed to share in this bidding for, perhaps more even than the men, their devotions carried them closer to that which they longingly referred to as the *Sod,* the ultimate mystery of God. By extension of meaning, this Hebrew word had come to designate everything that was connected with the knowledge or the practice of the Cabala.

Devotees made use of the *Zohar* as an infallible remedy for their ills; they placed it under the pillow of a sick patient or under the bed of a barren woman. They also employed talismans inspired by the Cabala. These were printed in North Africa and contained Hebrew prayers or cabalistic texts in Aramaic that had been composed by Cabalists of renown, sometimes those who had died in Morocco, preferably those who had come from Palestine. The function of the talismans and amulets was to protect the wearer against the influences of the demons which surrounded him on all sides and to turn away the dangers of the *ayin ha'ra,* the evil eye. The amulets frequently referred to the beneficial influence of the prophet Elijah who had struggled and triumphed against all the demonic spirits. The better to reduce them to impotence, the names of all the demons were listed on the amulet. It was enough to inscribe the names of the spirits near an infant in order to unmask them and thus chase them away. Certain symbolic designs reinforced the efficacy of the amulets: the fish, a symbol of fertility and honor among the early Phoenicians, was one of them,[23] and so was what is erroneously referred to as the Hand of Fatima, a protective symbol dating back to timeless antiquity.[24] Both symbols had been incorporated into cabalistic tradition. The central text of the amulet was usually inscribed all around by the traditional blessings of the Jewish faith that had some bearing on the purpose of the particular talisman. Thus the talisman for a new-born infant contained, like a garland surrounding the central cabalistic text, the traditional blessings that formed part of the regular religious ceremony of the circumcision. The walls of the room in which the child had been born were covered by formulae from the *Zohar* and in the room in which the mother lay during the eight days between the birth and circumcision, the *Zohar* was read with the appropriate ritual. The entire spirit was given over to the mystic combat which was required to break the devastating hold of Lilith, Queen of the Demons, whose demonic influences were the source of the worst evils. The fear of Lilith, so it was believed in North Africa, was part of the beginning of the acquisition of wisdom.

The extent of cabalistic knowledge in North Africa in recent years is difficult to determine, for the adepts of the Cabala understandably talked little about it. Many rabbis devoted themselves to the reading of the mystic works not so much as a science as in order to perform an act of special piety. They were certainly capable of understanding and explaining what they read, as were some laymen. The majority of laymen, however, though they were familiar with the devotional texts in Aramaic, understood only what they had heard from a discourse by their rabbi or what they had learned from a poor translation into the vernacular. It was not rare to find a simple shopkeeper in the mellah or the hara reading from the *Zohar* while awaiting a customer, much as his coreligionist in the ghettos of Europe might have been studying the Talmud.

Both rabbis and laymen were conscious of the sanctity and, one might say, the canonicity of the cabalistic tradition. Nowhere in North Africa was there organized opposition to the diffusion of cabalistic studies similar to that of the Mitnagdim of Eastern Europe, for in the Maghreb rabbis and congregants were too close to each other to allow a conflict to arise between the intellectual piety of the former and the mysticism of the latter. Consequently, though Shabbetai Zvi and his false Messianism raised the masses in North Africa to a state of exaltation more powerful than anything they had previously experienced, Hassidism raised no echoes there. That which in Europe brought about a revolution in the spirituality of Judaism was always accepted as a matter of course in the ardor of the traditional piety of the Maghreb. The sight of the chanters of the *Zohar* sitting in the dimness of their synagogues, groping for the ancient text which they read through almost blind eyes, was highly symbolic of the Jewry of the Maghreb which was groping in its darkness for the ultimate enlightenment it so ardently desired.

8

The Condition of the Jews in the Nineteenth Century

Between the seventh and the nineteenth centuries, North Africa was almost completely cut off from all meaningful contact with Christian Europe. Such attempts as were made by Portugal and Spain during the later Middle Ages to occupy the coasts of Morocco, Algeria and Tunisia usually ended in costly failure and at best resulted in the establishment of isolated enclaves close to the shore which had no contact with the country that was to have been conquered, and which never lasted for any length of time.[1] Though virtually on the doorstep of Spain and only a few days by sea from France or Italy, the countries of the Maghreb—with their disorder and dissension, and, in the case of Algeria and Tunisia, their diminishing ties with the Ottoman Empire—might as well have been on the other side of the moon, so little did they have in common with Christian Europe.

The Jews of the Maghreb, however, maintained closer links with the outside world: there was the influence of the arrivals from Spain and Italy and the bonds that these still maintained with their coreligionists in their former homes or in the other countries to which they had fled; there was, especially from the sixteenth to the nineteenth centuries, the continuous connection with the talmudical schools of Palestine and Jewish communities throughout the world which was maintained by the *Haham Kollel*. The Jews came increasingly to resent the restrictions and discriminations imposed upon them by states that were characterized by the worst features of feudalism, and by a population that subjected them to indignity and suppression.

Eyewitness Accounts

European travellers, merchants, and emissaries who were able to penetrate North Africa on diplomatic missions; Europeans who had been taken captive by Corsair pirates (piracy continued well into the nineteenth century) and sold on the slave markets of Africa and Turkey—all agreed in their descriptions of the misery that was the lot of the Jews under their Moslem "protectors." Extracts from some of these eyewitness accounts go far to explain the welcome that the Jews of the Maghreb extended to the French forces who were to establish peace and justice in North Africa.

ALGERIA

William Shaler, the United States consul in Algiers from 1816 to 1828, had this to say:[2] "The Jews suffer frightful oppressions. They are forbidden to offer resistance when they are maltreated by a Moslem, no matter what the nature of the violence. They do not have the right to bear arms of any sort, not even a cane. Only on Wednesdays and Saturdays are they allowed to leave the city without asking permission. When there is arduous or unusual labor to be performed it falls on the Jews. In the summer of 1815, the country was covered by an immense swarm of locusts which destroyed all growth in its path. Several hundred Jews were given the order to protect the gardens of the Pasha against them; night and day they watched and suffered for as long as the country suffered from these insects. A number of times, when the janissaries revolted, the Jews were pillaged indiscriminately; they are still tormented by the fear of similar occurrences. Even the children run after them in the streets, and the course of their lives is nothing but a fearful mixture of debasement, oppression and outrage. I believe that today the Jews of Algiers are perhaps the most unhappy remnant of Israel."

The French consul, Dubois-Thainville, wrote similarly of an unbelievable degree of oppression and degradation:[3] "There is no abuse to which they are not subjected, no insult of which they escape being the object, no arduous or repulsive labors to which they are not condemned as, for example, burying the bodies of those who have been condemned to death, carrying Moors on their shoulders through the shallow water as they debark from ships, feeding the animals of the seraglio."[4]

The Jews were eternal hostages of ambition and intrigue. Thus, when in 1801 the Caid of Boghni attempted to overthrow the Dey of Algiers, Mustafa Pasha, and replace him by a certain Uwali Khodja, he promised the janissaries, in return for their support, "eight times their pay, white bread, and the right to sack the Jews for three days."[5] Four years later, during a famine for which the Jews were held responsible, the Jewish merchant Busnach was shot by a janissary on the threshold of the Dey's palace. The murder was the signal for a general pillage of the Jewish quarter. The Sarfaty synagogue was desecrated and fourteen Jews who were praying there were done to death. The death toll among the Jews reached forty-two besides countless injured during the three-hour-long massacre. Two hundred Jews found refuge in the residence of the French consul, M. Dubois-Thainville. After the massacre, a hundred Jewish families fled to Tunis and two hundred to Livorno.[6] The follow-

ing year, to avoid a revolt by his janissaries, the Dey offered them
the lives and the property of the Jews: three hundred were
killed within a few hours. In 1813, the Jewish paramour of
Mohammed Bou Kabus, Dey of Oran, was cruelly done to death
with her five sons after the Dey had been defeated by Omar
Agha in his struggle against the central government in Algiers.[7]
In 1815, Chief Rabbi Isaac Abulker of Algiers was decapitated
during another massacre of the Jews.[8]

The decadent Moslem rulers, wishing to hide the extent of
their debaucheries from their coreligionists, forced the Jews to
supply them with their women, their drink and their other illicit
desires. In 1818, the Dey of Constantine, Kara Mustafa, a lewd,
self-indulgent, licentious man who had surrounded himself with
a following of Jews who were compelled to serve his extrava-
gant passions, was defeated by Ahmed el Mameluke. It seemed
only natural to the victor to vent his revenge on the community
from which Kara Mustafa had drawn his unfortunate accom-
plices. Seventeen young Jewish girls were carried off from Constantine and presented to the Dey of Algiers. They were released eventually by the Dey's successor, Hussein.[9] Even as the
French troops were marching toward Algiers, in 1830, the
houses of the Jews of that city were pillaged. The Bey of Titeri,
to whom the Dey had entrusted his soldiers, claimed that he was
unable to punish those responsible without causing defection
among his troops.

MOROCCO

Life in Morocco in the nineteenth century was far different from
that of the countries of the Maghreb that had come under the
leavening influence of Turkish suzerainty. Tunisia was tranquillity itself by comparison, and even turbulent and anarchic

Algeria was relatively peaceful. From the seventeenth century, isolated pockets where Jews could breathe in relative peace and security had become progressively rarer in Morocco as the noose of the Alaouite dynasty tightened around the Sherifian Empire. The chroniclers of the reign of Mulay Ismael early in the eighteenth century expressed their astonishment that during a peaceful interlude of twenty years "a woman or a Jew could travel in safety from Sous to Oujda."[10] The acts of monarchs such as Mulay Yazid, whose two-year reign was inaugurated with the pillage of the mellah of Tetuan in 1790, and of a multitude of major and minor tyrants, gave to the Jews and the mellahs of Morocco the abject appearance that so impressed the many European travellers who wrote about them.[11]

Charles de Foucauld, a young French officer who spent two years (1883–1884) travelling through Morocco in the disguise of a rabbi to gather information for his government, wrote of his mission in his *Reconnaissance du Maroc*. He divided the Jews of Morocco into two groups: the Jews of the Bled Makhzen who lived in the territories ruled by the Sultan, and those of the Bled Siba who lived in the regions outside his rule—

The Jews of the Bled Makhzen are protected by European powers and supported by the Sultan who sees them as necessary for the commercial prosperity of his empire and for his own wealth. They are helped by the corruption of the magistrates to whom they speak arrogantly even while kissing their hands. They amass large fortunes, oppress the poorer Moslems, respect the wealthy, and succeed in resolving the difficult problem of gratifying at the same time their avarice, their conceit and their hate for all who are not Jews. They live on the fat of the land, are lazy and effeminate and have all the vices and all the weaknesses of civilization without having any of its refinements.

The Jews of the Bled Siba are no less despicable, but they are more unfortunate. They are attached to the soil each one with his own Moslem seigneur whose private property he is. Bled white without restraint, seeing that which they have earned with great pain taken away from them each day, they enjoy security neither for their persons nor for their belongings; they are the most unfortunate of men. Lazy, avaricious, gluttons, drunkards, liars and thieves, lacking both good faith and kindness, they have all the vices of the Jews of the Bled Makhzen excepting only their cowardice. The perils that menace them at all times have given them a vigorous disposition that the others lack, which often degenerates into bloodthirsty savagery.

Every Jew in the Bled Siba belongs body and soul to his seigneur, the sid. If the family of the Jew had lived in the area for a long time, he came into the sid's possession through inheritance, as part of his personal belongings under the rules of Moslem law or of the custom of the *Imazirs*. If he had settled only recently in the place where he lived, then immediately on his arrival, he had to become some Moslem's Jew. Once having rendered homage, he was bound forever, he and his descendants, to the one he had chosen. The sid protected his Jew against strangers as someone would protect his own property. He treated his Jew in the same manner as he administered his patrimony, all according to his personality. If the Moslem was wise and thrifty he took care of his Jew, never taking more than the interest on his 'capital': an annual fee calculated according to the profits made is all he would demand. He took care not to demand too much so as not to pauperize the Jew, nor to take from him his wife or his daughter lest he try to escape from his bondage as a result. In this way the 'property' of the sid increased steadily like a wisely managed farm.

If, however, the sid was headstrong and a spendthrift, his treatment of his Jews was like the squandering of an inheritance. He demanded excessive sums from the Jew: the Jew would say he does not have more and the sid would take the Jew's wife and keep her as a hostage till he was paid. Before long there was another order and further violence. The Jew led an utterly impoverished and miserable existence, unable to earn a cent that was not immediately snatched away. Then his children were taken from him, and finally he was himself put on the market, put up for auction and sold. (This was done in certain localities in the Sahara, but not everywhere.) Or else he was robbed of everything, his house was destroyed and he was chased forth with his family. One could see villages where an entire quarter lay deserted: the astonished passer-by learned that here there was once a mellah and that the sids had one day, by concerted action, stripped the Jews of everything and then expelled them. Nothing in the world protected the Jew against his seigneur: he was entirely at his mercy. If he wished to absent himself temporarily, he had to obtain permission; it was not refused because travelling was necessary for the Jew to enable him to trade. Under no circumstances, though, might he take his wife or children; his family had to stay behind under the sid to assure his return.

De Foucauld went into minute details. He described the black slippers that Jews were forced to wear as a sign of differentiation, the special taxes levied on assimilated Jews, the special tolls levied on them on the highways and at the gates to the cities, the taxes on their beasts of burden; how they were compelled to walk barefoot in the cities, how their hovels were crowded together in the mellah. He described the trades to which they were limited: goldsmiths, shoemakers, leatherworkers, workers in iron, itinerant traders, town criers, money changers, domestic servants, traders, usurers. He wrote, too, of the Oriental tranquillity of the homes of the wealthier Jews. De Foucauld explained that "since, in the eyes of the Moslems, the Jews are not considered human, they are forbidden to bear arms or to own horses." He mentioned the desire of all Jews to acquire foreign protection, usually through a real or fictitious sojourn in Algeria. The Jews spoke Arabic or Tamazirt, and all could read and write in Hebrew characters which they frequently employed for writing Arabic. One in every five or six adult males was a rabbi; each town had a number of synagogues, and every village, in which even only six or seven Jewish families lived, had its synagogue and rabbi. Those who lived where there was no rabbi to slaughter animals according to ritual requirements did without meat; those whose trading caused them to travel in isolation through Moslem villages often went without meat for six or eight months.

De Foucauld had harsh things to say even of the religious observances of the Jews:

The Jews of Morocco meticulously observe the external practices of their faith, but they do not conform to the moral requirements prescribed by their religion; not only do they not follow them, they even deny them. Trickery, falsehoods and the violation of their oaths they call wisdom; vengeance, hate and calumny they call justice; avarice they call prudence. Cowardice, idleness, gluttony and drunkenness they regard as fortunate qualities bestowed on mortals to make the difficulties of life bearable. The Jews believe themselves to be the beloved children of the Lord: when they render Him the homage that is His due, when they pray and fast, observe the Sabbath and the festivals, eat only of permitted foods, wash and bathe when commanded, they will always be God's beloved. In other matters they may permit themselves to do as they please, for the rest of mankind is detestable. . . . My observations apply to the mass of the people: there are happy exceptions to the general scene, but these examples are rare and seldom imitated.

De Foucauld was a keen observer, and the harshness of his judgments adds weight to his reports. When reading them, however, it is important to bear in mind the conditions under which this young viscount worked. His sudden transformation from officer in the French Army to disguised rabbi, forced to share the life of a people who certainly lacked the graces of Parisian salons, filled him, uncompromising as he was, with impatience. During the entire course of his mission, de Foucauld had to endure the most abject miseries which in his eyes were utterly degrading. His irritation was such that he forgot even the courtesies that, as a guest, he should have extended to the Jews. He did not take into consideration the debt he owed them for the grave risk they ran in harboring a false rabbi, and for the help they gave him in the fulfillment of his perilous mission. No Jew could have been taken in for a moment by his disguise, though no Moslem suspected it. As he wrote himself: "They (the Jews) kept the secret which they had discovered religiously; nothing leaked out of the mellah. They were discreet even with me; nothing changed in their manner except that they became even more obliging and more disposed to furnish me with the information that I required."

No doubt de Foucauld later regretted the sharp opinions he expressed on the Jews, and especially on his fifty-three-year-old guide and travelling companion, Mordecai aby Serour who, though he contributed greatly to de Foucauld's success, was hardly mentioned by him in his reports. De Foucauld later made amends for this unjust omission and, in the notes published by René Bazin, he gave credit to the man who suffered with him all the dangers and rigors of his travels and who in his own way was also something of a hero.[12] It is sad to compare de Foucauld's opinion of the Jews who sheltered him with the warm and glowing memories that these retained of the wise and mysterious stranger long after he had left.[13]

The failings that de Foucauld saw among the Jews of Morocco, and which blinded him to their good qualities, were the inevitable result of the degradation to which they were subjected by their Moslem overlords. His own reports are the most telling evidence of this. Had it not been for their guile, which enabled them to thwart the manifest greed all around them, the Jews would most certainly have perished; deceit was a necessary defense mechanism; alcoholism, as de Foucauld himself said, was the gift of God "to make the difficulties of life bearable." In any event, the testimony of this least sympathetic of witnesses proves beyond all doubt that the lot of Morocco's Jews was not an easy one to bear.[14]

The Mellah and the Hara

By virtue of their status as dhimmis, the Jews of North Africa had been forced to live in special quarters outside the pale of Moslem society almost from the outset of the Arab conquest. In Tunisia, these quarters were known as the *hara,* an Arab word meaning simply "quarter" which was used instead of the original *Harat el Yhud,* the "Quarter of the Jews." In Morocco, the Jewish quarter was called *mellah.* The origin of this name is obscure and has given rise to many popular traditions. The most widely accepted version is that the name derives from the Arabic word for salt, the Jews having been given by the Sultan salty, non-productive land near the city on which to build their quarter. The first mellah in Morocco—and for a long time the only one—was at Fez.[15] Prior to its establishment, the Jews had lived in a section of the present medina which still bears the name Fonduk el Yhudi. They were transferred to a new quarter close to and under the protection of the Palace by the reigning sultan, in order to restore order after a pogrom had broken out against them.[16] This event is variously dated at the end of the thirteenth century—during the reign of Abu Yussuf Yakub (1269–1286)[17] when the Jews were accused of having filled the sacred lamps in the mosque with wine—and at 1433.[18] The earliest title-deed in the mellah is dated 1438. In Algeria, the Jews lived in special quarters which had no particular name. Although they were predominantly Jewish, the segregation was not as absolute as in Tunisia and Morocco.

The mellah or hara was a city within a city; no two were alike and they differed as much from each other as did the Moslem cities in which they were situated. In their diversity there were, however, certain common traits which makes it possible to paint a general picture of the condition under which the majority of the Jews of North Africa lived both prior to and to some extent following the arrival of the French in the area.

The mellah generally nestled close to the casbah, under the symbolic protection of the authorities: in Fez it was close to the Sultan's palace, in Tunis near the Mosque of Sidi Mehrez. The mellah was a typically African agglomeration of buildings closely packed against each other to provide shade. Houses were built in the manner of the country, their exterior walls presenting a closed aspect to the world. The narrow alleys climbed and twisted haphazardly. Their impermeable surface flooded under the slightest rain, and a nauseating smell arose from the rubbish strewn about them. The misery common to all social prisons was evident here too, where feverish activity could not hide the underlying despair. The windowless houses, the poor construction, the misery which oozed from the very stones and the expression on the faces of the mellah's inhabitants, attested by their ugliness and their vulgarity to the fact that happiness, security and living itself were rare pleasures in these surroundings. Rot and decay infested the houses in time; only the wooden or iron beams which shored them up kept them standing. But the doors were always open and the traveller was accorded a royal welcome.

MOROCCO

The mellahs in certain parts of Morocco were perhaps the worst. Many startling descriptions of them have been given, among them one by Charles de Foucauld:

In the mellah, the Jew is at home. On entering it he puts on his shoes—as a dhimmi he was forced to walk barefoot in the Moslem quarter—and behold, he disappears in a labyrinth of dark and dirty alleys. He trots among the refuse and stumbles against rotting vegetables. He collides with a sick donkey that blocks his path. All the bad odors rise to his nose, discordant noises assail his ears from everywhere. . . . He arrives at the market: some meat, some vegetables, lots of brandy, a few commonplace wares. These are the objects which he finds; the fine things are in the Arab town.

The splendor, the colors, the rich aromas, the Arabian-Nights world that existed in even the poorest medina of North Africa was absent from the Jewish mellah.

Pascal Saisset, author of *Heures juives au Maroc,* had this to say:

To proceed by describing the innumerable alleys that keep hidden their nameless crowds would doubtlessly be a way of showing one of the aspects of the misery and degradation. The houses are leprous, the ground is muddy, the filth in the dark and narrow lanes is repulsive. Long lines of beggars fill the streets, assailing the passers-by with their wailing, displaying their clothes in shreds, their sores covered in vermin, or asleep dressed in their torn burnouses in the dust and refuse which have accumulated alongside the houses.

In Marrakesh and the mellahs of southern Morocco, especially in Demnat and Taroudant, there was the same state of desolation. "They are only one sphere removed from Dante's Inferno," Saisset wrote. The infernal may not be exactly appropriate, but no horror could be more frightful to observe than this living death of men adrift, drowning in their misery, with no longer even a human form under their rags. The daily struggle simply not to die of hunger took up all the energies of those who had not fallen completely on the welfare of the community through blindness or infirmity. As will be seen in Part Three, these conditions persisted substantially unchanged until the mid-twentieth century, the administration having been powerless to alleviate them to any appreciable extent.

In other parts of Morocco the situation was not so desperate. In Meknès, for instance, a new mellah was built, allowing the old one to be emptied and permitting at least a temporary normalization of life. In Fez, the affluence of the town gave rise to a level of activity which tore through the atmosphere of stagnation. In Tetuan and Tangiers, old-established and noble Jewish communities had maintained the traditions of mutual help. But the extreme conditions that have been described above were also to be found even in the most fortunate of mellahs.

TUNISIA

Here the situation was very much the same as in Morocco. In Tunis, whose immense hara sprawled under the white domes of Sidi Mehrez, in Sousse, in Sfax and in Gabès, the same warren of streets, the same insanitary conditions, the same decay and the same way of life were to be seen. A few smaller details showed that Tunisia was in some ways more privileged: the walls were usually whitewashed, the buildings better constructed, the rooms larger and, on the whole, not so overcrowded. It was rare in Tunisia to see beaten earth serve as floor, bed and table. However, the unpaved streets full of excrement and refuse turned the welcome showers into a curse for the hara.

The streets of the hara, like those of the mellah, hummed with activity: traders and craftsmen crouched in their stalls selling and making everything imaginable. Occasionally an old man with flowing white beard would appear, like some apparition from the Bible—a mendicant holy-man—trudging along and chanting ancient hymns with an absent look of beseeching reverie on his face.

In southern Tunisia, one could observe the strange civilization of the troglodytes. A dozen villages, all in the neighborhood of Matmata, had no hara, for here the Jews, like the Berbers, lived in caves scooped out of the limestone. The caves were in the form of pits, from whose depths a staircase led to huge "rooms" arranged according to the needs of the family. A large cave in the center of the village served as a synagogue. Another was used as a stable. When a home was no longer habitable, the family simply moved into some other cave that had been hollowed out by special teams of workers. These caves looked clean and healthy, incomparably superior to the hovels of Casablanca and Tunis. This region of Tunisia was the only one in the whole of North Africa where housing problems were unknown.

The island of Djerba was another special exception. Here the splendor of an oasis was combined with the charm of a Mediterranean fishing port. This important Jewish community of close to five thousand souls lived in two villages a few miles apart. It was, one might say, a Jewish community in a pure state, preserving its old traditions and customs almost completely untouched by either Moslem or European influences. The two villages, Hara Kbira and Hara Shgira, struck visitors by their atmosphere of freshness and cleanliness; here the open air could be breathed and the sky was visible from everywhere. There was less misery, and what there was was more discreetly hidden; the occasional rags, which seemed to contrast surprisingly with the exceptional beauty of the island, were worn here with the dignity that is characteristic of the great nomads of the south.

ALGERIA

In northern Algeria, where there was neither mellah nor hara, the main concentrations of the Jewish population were in

Tlemcen, in three of the quarters of Algiers and in the Jewish quarters of Oran and Constantine. In these, the Jews made up the overwhelming majority of the population. As will be seen in Chapter Thirteen, the social emancipation which the Jews enjoyed under the French led eventually to their almost complete integration within the general population.

The only true mellahs in Algeria were in the south. In Ghardaia, Messad, Laghuat, Bou-Saada and Colomb-Béchar conditions were similar to those of Jewish communities in other parts of the Moslem world. In Ghardaia, the Jews were subjected to certain Mozarabic laws such as one which forbade Jewish (as well, incidentally, as Moslem) women to leave the oasis, since it was their presence which ensured its continued existence. In these towns of the south, however, the misery was less extreme than in the mellahs of Morocco, and the conditions of life were relatively normal considering those of the surroundings.

Health, Sanitation and Popular Medical Practice

The state of health and hygiene among the Jews of North Africa was the result of a long history of poverty, inadequate means and belief in the occult powers—all of them conditions shared by the Jews with their Moslem neighbors. Before the advent of the French, epidemics and disease ravaged the Maghreb. Tuberculosis, syphilis and infectious diseases had so depleted the town and village populations that, despite an extremely high birth rate, the number of deaths was often higher than that of the number of births, and spontaneous abortions were more frequent than the number of babies carried to term. Infants were brought up according to the customs of the country, with infant mortality reaching frightful proportions.[19] The way of life and popular beliefs of the population, even until quite recently, were still conducive to the spread of disease, and the congestion of the mellah did nothing to alleviate the situation.

Much of the population was completely ignorant of personal hygiene, washing only as much as was necessary to conform to Jewish ritual. In poorer areas, particularly during the dry season, the public bath was not always as clean as it might have been, owing to the great shortage of fresh water. Only the wealthy could afford to visit the *hammam* (Turkish bath). The religious rites requiring the washing of hands before a meal and the general cleansing on the eve of the Sabbath had only modest effects on general hygiene. Since there was no running water in the homes of the mellah, a vat at the entrance to each street served as a communal source of water. Weekday clothes were seldom cleaned.

Dietary habits were also hardly conducive to good health. Food, especially in the south, was characterized by the almost complete absence of vegetables. A good meal was considered to be a succession of greasy and highly spiced meats accompanied by couscous, all washed down with the deadly brandy, *mahia* or *bokha,* distilled to the highest proof from dates and figs. The bottle that promised oblivion from misery was on every table within reach of all—even children.[20]

Medicine in North Africa was more concerned with magic than with science. Jew and Moslem shared a common popular system of pseudo-medical beliefs and superstitions for the diagnosis and cure of disease. Numerous popular books on these, written in the Judeo-Arabic dialect, used to circulate in the mellah, the most influential of which were *The Method of Pharmacopoeia of Si Abi el-Muna ibn Nazr the Jew* and *The Treatise of Sidi Chaarani.*[21] For the Jews of the Maghreb, steeped as they were in local superstitions, sickness had no natural causes but was a sign of God's displeasure. God had withdrawn his protection and allowed the *djnun* to inflict their punishments. The people felt themselves at the mercy of sinister, omnipresent forces that had to be placated to avoid sickness or to effect a cure.

Fear of the *djnun* was the principal factor in ensuring cleanliness inside the home and respect for the ritual requirements for washing, cleaning, preparing food and whitewashing houses. *Mardh men taht idehum,* maladies from under their (*djnun's*) hands, were the results of the vengeance or malevolence of the *djnun,* and included snakebites, scorpion stings and accidents. The worst sicknesses were those brought on by God Himself, the *mordh Allah:* trials and sufferings which were proof of a violation of divine law. Epidemics were believed to be caused by non-observance by women of ritual purity, by shamelessness, adultery, prostitution, and by violation of the Sabbath and religious proscriptions. Drought and floods were likewise attributed to human inadequacy as regards the divine order.

A whole arsenal of counter-spells and practices offered protection against the *djnun* and the evil eye. The figure five was considered a sovereign remedy and the number would be slipped incongruously into any conversation, to the surprise of the uninitiated listener. Good-luck charms in the form of a hand or a fish were painted on the exteriors and interiors of houses. The extent to which these could be seen was often a good indication of the degree of cultural development of a particular neighborhood. "Preventive medicine" in North African popular practice took the form of talismans obtained from a *marabout* or a rabbi; the latter, being rarer, were considered in the eyes of the Moslems to have greater value. Each type of talisman was believed to be invested with special powers—one against the evil eye, one against curses, another against *djnun,* those that were supposed to be effective against God-inflicted sicknesses, against scorpions and other dreaded evils. Garlic was considered to have special protective and curative powers in most cases, and was perhaps intermediate between a talisman and a popular herbal remedy.

When pious ritual, magic formulae and all else failed, recourse was had to healers, sorcerers, and fortune-tellers. It was of little importance whether these were Moslem or Jewish: all that mattered was the ability of, and powers attributed to, those healers who were believed to be endowed with divine inspiration. Those in search of cures flocked alike to *marabout*, dervish, *f'quih, oulis, muadeb,* rabbis and *refafas.* Some would visit the miracle man five or six times a day so that he could foil the tricks of the evil eye. Moslems and even Christians frequented the Jewish healers in the mellah, and it was not rare to hear of Jews making a pilgrimage to Lourdes in search of a cure. This situation persisted right down to recent times, and miracle men were consulted when doctors had failed.

Popular medicine was a strange mixture of traditional folk remedies based on plants—olive oil was most widely used in cures—and the most unlikely magic cures. For sunstroke, for instance, the roasted head of a goat was applied, fiery hot, to the patient's head with the appropriate magic ritual. Paralysis was cured by thrusting the patient into the still-steaming stomach of a freshly slaughtered ox. Ringworm was believed to be a proof of intelligence. Pascal Saisset thought that all the children in the mellah of Amizmiz in Morocco were wearing caps on their heads—till he discovered that this was the ringworm that had spread all over their scalps. Magic had its own homeopathic traditions: thus, when the cause of a disease was not known, the staircase or the passage leading to the sickroom was washed and the patient was given to drink the water which had been carefully mopped up. The *djnun* or the person who had cast the evil eye were believed to have left their traces in the dust at the entrance to the room and by drinking this the patient would gain the power to fight back against them. The pharmacopoeiae in general use among the healers of North Africa reflected all known magic systems: oral traditions of the Persians, the Greeks, the Egyptians and of medieval Jewish and Arab doctors were all jealously preserved.

Economic Life

Under Moslem domination, the Jew had not only to try to earn enough to keep alive; he had also to provide sufficient to purchase his right to live from the Moslem prince. The economic role of the Jews was to do that which the Moslems would not, or could not, do. With rare exceptions, the Jews were allowed neither to own nor to work the land which was the principal source of wealth in the Moslem world. This left them with the choice of being either traders or craftsmen. The social ladder was short: at one end were the mass of miserable beings who toiled to keep starvation at bay and who lived in a state of penury which made the poverty of the Western world look like luxury. Then there was a class made up of traders and of ingenious workmen who could turn the most worthless objects to good use. Thanks to their skill, they could provide satisfactorily for their needs. At the top were the merchants, only a few of whom rose to riches.

The army of Jewish peddlers who acted as intermediaries between Jewish importers and wholesalers on the one hand, and the Moslem consumers on the other, formed the central commercial network of the Maghreb, bringing all essential requirements to the furthest Moslem village. The peddler trotted everywhere with his donkey bringing cottons, silks, needles, thread, manufactures of France, Germany and Japan, hardware, glass trinkets and jewelry to arouse the jealousies of the Moslem women who could not do without the wares of the despised Jew.[22] For centuries the Jews of the Maghreb had practiced the art of being indispensable. Moslem society, reflecting the Arab spirit, is more concerned with the past and the present than with the future. It is based on the conservation of wealth and the satisfaction of present needs, and is closely related to agriculture.[23] The Jewish spirit, on the other hand, is directed outside its misery into the future (the present tense is skeletal in Hebrew), an attitude which might explain the readiness of the Jews to speculate. Indeed, living in Moslem society, the only way they could amass wealth was by speculation on the future. Had the Jews not made themselves indispensable by their preparedness to meet the Moslems' future needs, they might well have disappeared. The Moslems recognized and prized the Jews' function but always retained the upper hand so that if the Jews became too wealthy they could easily be robbed.

All contemporary accounts picture the mellah as a veritable hive of activity. Merchants, craftsmen, day laborers—all strove hard to satisfy their wants. The mass who failed—begged. In Meknès, where the Jews were relatively best off, there were about 6,000 Jews living in the mellah in 1900—just over 1,000 families living in 260 houses. Those who had an occupation were employed mainly as lace and button makers, druggists and hardware mongers, tailors and dressmakers, gold, silver and tinsmiths, shoemakers and cobblers, flour merchants, and in a host of sundry trades—there were clock and bellows makers, embroiderers, sellers of silk thread, public criers, scribes and many others as shown in the statistical breakdown in Appendix I.[24]

Above the mass of abjectly miserable Jews, and at times on its ruins, lived the class of wealthier dealers, the most affluent of whom, living in the port cities, brought to the Maghreb the riches of the wide world. They imported marble from Italy, silk from France, rare woods and hides; they organized the export of cereals, tobacco and eggs. At Meknès they developed rice cultivation, and when that became unproductive as a result of competition from cheaper sources, they turned to the cultivation of carvi, a plant with uses similar to aniseed. They were always on the lookout for new ideas or methods,[25] contenting themselves with modest profits to ensure a rapid turnover, and using imagination and careful calculation to earn their profits. Jewish merchants wandered as far as the ports of the English Channel to buy up salvaged goods from ships that had been stranded.

When the Jews had amassed a fortune, they often agreed to act as bankers for the Moslems but were forced to charge usurious rates in view of the known improvidence of their masters and the uncertainty of the future. The consequences were disastrous for both parties; the Moslem became enslaved to the person whom he despised but without whose services he could not manage, and the Jew risked ruin by putting himself at the mercy of future vengeance. It has been suggested that usury was one of the principal causes of the material deterioration in which the Jews were enmeshed at this period.[26] Real wealth, however, was rare among the Jews of North Africa. At the end of the nineteenth century, there were perhaps three wealthy families in Marrakesh—the Corcos, the Drakis and the Trudjmans—and the situation was similar in all parts of the Maghreb.

Education

The old type of Jewish schools, corresponding somewhat to the *cheder* of Eastern Europe, gives an indication of the type of education that was available to Jewish youngsters before the advent of the French. The schools were variously called *Beit Midrash* (House of Study), *Em Habanim* (Mother of the Sons), *Etz Hayyim* (The Tree of Life) and *Sla* (The House of Prayer), or by the Arabic name for school, *ḳutab*. The school was usually housed in a nondescript little room in the mellah[27] whose only ventilation and light came through the refuse-strewn doorway. Ragged children were squeezed together on the stone benches that ran around the walls, and on the makeshift seats in the center of the room. Thus, listening attentively to the voice and the stick of their teachers, countless generations had carried out the biblical commandment: "And thou shalt teach them (these words) diligently unto thy children ... (Deut., I, 7).

The *ḳutab* took children from a very tender age, sometimes even infants below two years (thus serving also as a kind of day-care center). This was in conformity with the teaching of Rabbi Elisha ben Avuya who said that teaching a child is "like ink written on new paper" (Ethics of the Fathers, IV, 25). As soon as he could stand on his feet, the Jewish boy was taught to read Hebrew characters; soon he was reading the weekly portion of the Torah and the corresponding portion from the Prophets. The important consideration was to imprint the Holy Scripture on his memory and to mold it deeply into his consciousness. The text was recited in chorus to an Oriental chant which was supposed to make memorization easier. Reading from the Torah was accompanied also by the singsong recitation of ritual prayers.

These liturgical exercises encompassed all spiritual needs: the children were taught neither grammar nor history. As they progressed in their studies, the teacher translated the texts into their mother tongue, Judeo-Arab. At thirteen the young boy was considered to be ready for the *Bar Mitzvah,* when he put on the phylacteries for the first time and entered into the community of which henceforward he would be a responsible member.

The ablest students proceeded to the *yeshiva* where they received a deeper talmudical education. Their studies schooled them for the most abstruse intellectual exercises; they entered into a dialectic which broke through all the barriers of the intellect, freeing it for the accomplishment of its great vocation. Through the Talmud the young men were initiated into the mysteries of the Will of God as revealed in His Torah, and, as rabbis, they eventually became the teachers of that Law.[28]

In this sacred, more spiritual world, the miseries of material existence were not resented with the same force and urgency as they came to be in modern times, for the spirit was orientated toward the inaccessible perfect knowledge of the God Who fulfills all the expectations of man. The rabbi of the Maghreb who satisfied the necessary requirements and delved into the study of the Cabala was thereby initiated into the ultimate mysteries of human destiny and acquired the respect due to a *Baal Sod,* Master of the Mystery. Those who for some reason had to break off their studies had nevertheless learned enough, if only by osmosis, to make their way in life, and to order their lives in accordance with biblical precepts.

As early as 1862, the Alliance Israélite Universelle, together with the Anglo-Jewish Committee, took the first step toward improving Jewish education in the Maghreb. In that year, the first modern school for Jewish children was opened in Morocco. As will be seen in the following chapters, the educational activities of the Alliance were to become a significant factor in the evolution of North African Jewry during the period of French influence.

The Jews as an Elite

The condition of Maghrebian Jewry before the arrival of the French, dire and destitute as it was in absolute terms, takes on a different aspect when regarded both in the perspective of the feudal Moslem milieu and in relation to the Jews of Eastern Europe before their emancipation. Unlike that of their European coreligionists, the right of the Jews of North Africa to their lives and possessions was legally protected by the Charter of Omar, and although this statute was at times abused, its provisions nevertheless retained their immutable basis in Moslem law. The internal autonomy of the Jews was likewise legally recognized, thus enabling the communities to establish and maintain a solid communal structure.

One of the direct consequences of Jewish communal solidarity in the Maghreb was that Jewish children were given at least a basic Jewish education, if not a secular one. All Jewish men were not only literate in Hebrew (in which it was also possible to write Arabic) but were familiar with some elements of Jewish culture. Among the Moslems, 98 per cent of the male population was totally illiterate. Small wonder then that the Jews regarded themselves as superior to their Moslem neighbors and that, paradoxically, the Moslems regarded the despised dhimmis as a cultural élite.

The importance and prosperity of the Maghreb as a commercial center on the great international trade routes declined abruptly at the beginning of the sixteenth century with the discovery of the sea route to India. The adverse effect this had on the Maghreb was compounded by the opening up of the New World which led to a shift in the center of world civilization from the Mediterranean basin to the shores of the Atlantic

Ocean. Henceforth Europe was to face West. During the ensuing centuries of isolation, stagnation and penury which enveloped North Africa, the Jews of all classes, precisely because of their Judaism, were able to maintain their status of an élite in relation to the corresponding strata of the Moslem population. By virtue of their history and heritage, they possessed cultural and commercial links with both East and West which enabled them to serve as a bridgehead in both directions. Since the Moslems did not possess such a network of international connections, they were totally dependent on the Jews in all matters of foreign enterprise. The Jew was therefore a vital and indispensable element in the life and economy of the Maghreb, a position which might well have been the envy of the less fortunate European communities. The overseas contacts which the Jews maintained undoubtedly served to reinforce their already existing cultural advantages over the local population and endowed them with a relatively more secure economic basis. There are degrees of poverty just as there are degrees of affluence, and if life in the mellah appeared at first glance as a drama of destitution, it was prosperous by comparison with the utter penury of the Moslem milieu.

Well before the advent of the French, the beginnings of change in the degree of subjugation of the Jews could be discerned. In the towns of the north, especially in Tunisia, where European influences had penetrated and protection was extended by foreign consuls, the Jews enjoyed wider liberties relative to conditions elsewhere. Thus at the end of the nineteenth century, the Jews of Meknès could own the houses in which they lived, and were allowed to visit the Moslem city without being forced to walk barefoot. But further south, Moslem overlords had changed little, and the Jew was little better than a slave. In Marrakesh, the Jews were compelled, well into the twentieth century, to wear a blue, white-flecked kerchief on their heads and to walk barefoot, hugging the walls, when they entered the medina.

The arrival of the French in North Africa marked the beginning of the Maghreb's emergence from its isolation from world currents. For the Jews, it signified the end of second class status, and the commencement of the movement of emancipation—a gradual process which had not yet worked itself out when the Jews departed in the middle of the twentieth century from the countries that had been their homes for two millennia.

Part 3

The French Period

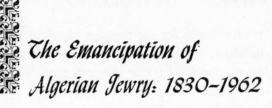

9

The Emancipation of Algerian Jewry: 1830–1962

With the French occupation of Algeria in 1830—an event which marked the beginning of profound French influence throughout the Maghreb—and the subsequent establishment of French protectorates in Tunisia and Morocco in 1881 and 1912 respectively, North Africa could no longer be regarded as an historical and political unit. Henceforth, its development proceeded along national, rather than regional, lines, each country with its own distinguishing characteristics. Similarly, the progressive emancipation of the Jews evolved in accordance with the prevailing conditions in each country.

The French Occupation of Algeria

It is ironic that the final incident that sparked off the French conquest of Algeria was the intervention of the Dey of Algiers in the affairs of the Jewish merchant company of Bacri and Busnach. The Busnach family, originally of Livorno, had established itself in Algiers in 1723 and, in association with the Bacris, formed a consortium that was responsible for the major part of the Algerian principality's foreign trade.[1] (It was the murder of a member of this family that set off the 1805 massacres. The Dey intervened to seek the settlement of a debt of several million francs for the payment of wheat owed to the Jewish merchants by the French Government since the end of the eighteenth century, a matter in which even the intervention of Talleyrand and other French notables had been ineffective. The Dey's interest and vehemence were due in no small measure to his hope of gaining personal profit from the collection of the debt. On April 30, 1827, the fateful interview between the French Consul and the Dey which was to have settled the question, was held. The French offered to pay the debt, but with certain reservations. It was these reservations which aroused the unbridled anger of the Dey who struck the Consul with his fly whisk. The repercussions of this insult to the French Government led directly to the French occupation of Algeria in 1830.[2]

Although in 1541 and 1775 the Jews of Algeria had fought alongside the Moslems to repulse the Spanish invaders, in 1830 the opposite was the case. The invader now was not Catholic Spain with its record of persecution and expulsion of Jews, but France, with its message of liberty for the prisoners of the mellah, equality for the "second class" citizens of the Maghreb, and fraternity for those whom the Law of Islam had condemned to humiliation.[3] The arrival of the French marked the end of the oppression of which the Jews had been the chief, though not the only, victim, for the Moslem population too had suffered from the anarchy which had reigned under the capricious, all-powerful sids.

The welcome that the Jews extended to the French was stimulated by the anger of the Turks who held the Jews partly responsible for sparking off the French occupation as a result of the Bacri affair. Bacri and Duran immediately offered their services to the French commander-in-chief, and among the mass of the Jewish population throughout Algiers, joy knew no bounds. "The Jews who were in the streets knelt down and kissed the hands and feet of the [French] soldiers—proud and triumphant, they walked through the streets in vivid clothes, beating the Turks whom they met, and crying 'Viva les Franchais!' to the accompaniment of ironic cheers from the crowd. Their sudden emergence into liberty was intoxicating; it was an extraordinary adventure, like a tale they had heard from their story tellers which had come to pass."[4] Because they sided with the French, the Jews had to follow the French army to avoid Moslem vengeance when Blida and Macara were temporarily abandoned in 1830 and 1835 respectively. When Oran was besieged in 1833, they took an active part in the defense of the city alongside the French.[5]

The Act of Capitulation of July 5, 1830, stipulated that "The liberty of the inhabitants of all classes, their religions, their properties, their trade, their industry, will not be violated; their women will be respected. The commander-in-chief assumes this obligation on his honor." This text implied the abolition of the traditional relationships between Moslems and Jews. Nevertheless, a distinction was maintained between the two based, not on religion, but on the concept of nationality.

The Jews were considered members of the Jewish nation, subject to French rule but having the right of separate administration.[6] Jacob Bacri was nominated head of the "Jewish nation" and invested with the power to police and supervise all the Jews in the city, to execute the judgments of the courts and to collect taxes. He thus replaced the *Sheikh* or *Caid el Yhud,* with the important difference that his power derived directly from the French administration through the commander-in-chief. A new head was chosen annually from a list of three candidates put forward by leading figures in the Jewish community. In June 1831, a Jewish council was formed to assist the head of the Jewish community. It consisted of three members chosen, like the head of the Jewish community, by the commander-in-chief from a list of nine submitted to him. The council was independent of the head of the Jews and was charged specifically with the collection of taxes.[7] The rabbinical courts were entrusted with the administration of justice. Jews were also incorporated into the new legislative and administrative bodies that were set up. The decree of January 9, 1831, according to which the new municipal council of Algiers was organized, made provision for the inclusion of seven "Moors" and two Jews; a chamber of commerce, in charge of economic affairs, was composed of five Frenchmen, one "Moor" and one Jew.[8]

The Beginning of Legal Emancipation

In 1833, a commission of enquiry was sent to Algeria by the Government of Louis-Philippe. Aaron Moatti, the head of the Jewish community, informed it that the Jews would willingly submit to the civil and economic laws of France, "provided only that nothing in them be contrary to the Law of Moses."[9] In accordance then, both with the wishes of the Jews of Algeria and the views of the Duc de Dalmatie, France's Premier and Minister for War, the autonomous community structure was abolished and a new policy of integration was introduced.

The commission of enquiry considered the rabbinical courts unsatisfactory, viewing their methods as more degrading than those which obtained in the Moslem courts. The first inroad to be made on Jewish autonomy was therefore the restriction of the rabbinical courts' competence in matters of marriage and divorce; and the provision that the parties to such cases would be allowed to choose the courts in which to settle their disputes. The ordinance of August 1834, which effected this reform, met with no opposition, not even from the rabbis whose powers it affected.[10] Henceforward the Jews had recourse to the French courts for all civil and commercial litigation. In 1836, the position of head of the Jewish community was abolished and its powers were transferred to special Jewish aides who were appointed to all municipal councils,[11] together with a Moslem and a French aide. Jewish autonomy was finally abolished by two ordinances of 1841 and 1842, which entrusted all juridical powers concerning the Jews to French courts. Jews were judged in these courts according to Jewish law, (just as Moslems were judged according to Moslem law till the end of French rule) and reference was made to the written opinions of rabbis in matters of personal status.[12]

The desire of the Jewish population to emerge from this intermediate status was supported by the General Consistory of the Jews of France,[13] and as a result emancipation was carried a stage further by the ordinance of November 9, 1845, which laid down a new French policy for the Jews of Algeria.[14] The ordinance created an Algerian Consistory which sat in Algiers, and provincial consistories at Oran and Constantine—a system modelled upon that of France, but independent of it. The chief rabbi and the lay members of the Consistory of Algiers were nominated by King Louis-Philippe on the recommendation of the Secretary of State for War, who also nominated the members of the provincial consistories on the recommendation of the Governor General and in consultation with the Consistory of Algiers. Salary and housing for ministers of religion were provided by the state.[15] The chief rabbi and the lay members of the consistories together were responsible for the administration of the synagogues and the nomination of synagogue officials. They were to foster the emancipation of their communities by encouraging members to send their children to modern schools, and by orienting them toward agricultural occupations. The consistories also took charge of the communities' financial and philanthropic affairs. The setting up of the consistory in Algiers in 1847 marked the end of the old system of Jewish life in Algeria. Henceforward Algerian Jewry became completely assimilated to French Jewry, whose organizational structure it copied. The consistories through their struggle against poverty, and their promotion of the integration of the Jews through modern education, were the basic factors in, and the respected guides of, the movement toward emancipation.[16]

The Crémieux Decree and the Granting of French Citizenship

The fall of the French monarchy and the proclamation of the Second Republic (1848) at first provoked much apprehension in Algeria, a feeling which was dispelled by the declaration of the new Minister of Justice, Adolphe Crémieux, himself a Jew: "The Republic desires the assimilation of Algeria with France." It is in the light of this declaration that the subsequent development of Algerian Jewry must be regarded. With the full support of their coreligionists in France,[17] the Jews of Algeria requested that they be accorded full French citizenship as soon as possible. The idea of mass naturalization of the Algerian Jews had probably first occurred to Crémieux in 1843 when he was one of the most active members of the Commission which drew up the 1845 ordinance. The principle was first ratified in a draft decree drawn up by the legal adviser of the Ministry of War in May 1848,[18] and was referred to whenever the question of the reorganization of Algeria, or Algerian Jewry, was raised.

By the decree of August 1848, both Jews and Moslems were

granted the right of suffrage for the election of municipal councillors, subject, however, to very strict conditions of age, residence and property. They had to be over twenty-one years of
age; to have been resident in Algeria for two years, and in the
district for at least one; they had to possess civil rights in Algeria;
be property- or lease-holders in the district or to have paid rent
there of over 600 francs for at least six months; or to have a
commercial or a third-class license.[19] On November 14, 1858,
the Jews were accorded the right to elect one Jewish councillor
by each province.[20] When, two years later, Jews became eligible for compulsory military service, they regarded the obligation
as a signal honor and a mark of confidence and esteem on the
part of the French authorities.[21]

But the piecemeal nature of the legislation affecting the Jews
only made their legal situation more complex. For thirty years
they had been adapting themselves with incredible speed to the
language, customs and culture that France had introduced, with
the result that they had become increasingly assimilated to the
French population of Algeria. Yet, although for offenses committed in the military zones which covered large areas of Algeria they were subject to French law,[22] they remained under
rabbinical jurisdiction in the rest of the country. This created
the utmost confusion, and it was never clear which law was
applicable. In matters of civil status the ill-defined position of
the Jews created the most difficulties for both judges and administrators. Since in practice the Jews contracted their official
marriages before civil registrars, this raised questions of
whether their marriages were subsequently subject to French or
Jewish law, whether they could be ended by rabbinical divorces,
whether the property of the spouses was deemed to be held
separately or jointly. There was further confusion when a person contracted one marriage before a rabbi and another one

before a registrar. To these complications were added a host of contradictory legal decisions: at times the Jews were considered natives and at times French. The latter seems to have been the more common case and it gave rise to a government circular of 1856 which stated emphatically that no legislative measure had ever conferred on the Jews the status of Frenchmen.

The desire of the Jews for full French citizenship became stronger. It was supported by the French colons in Algeria, many of whom had been deported for their liberal leanings after the uprisings of 1848, and who continued to strive for wider democracy in Algeria.[23] Christians[24] and liberals[25] added their voices to those of French[26] and Algerian Jews,[27] in advocating that the rights of French citizenship be extended to all the Jews of Algeria.

In 1865 a petition signed by the majority of the heads of Jewish households in Algeria was presented to Napoleon III during his visit to Oran. It called for collective naturalization of all Algerian Jews to avoid the anomalies of the law and of the legal decisions concerning their status. It led the Emperor to declare, "The Jews of Algeria will soon be French." The Senate decree of 1865, however, did not mention collective naturalization, but only individual change of status for which it was necessary to obtain a special decree from the Emperor. Article Two of the decree, identical to Article One which referred to the Moslems, read:

The indigenous Jew is French; nevertheless he will continue to be regulated by his own law of personal status. He may be accepted for service in the forces on land or at sea; he may be called to perform public office or to accept civil employment in Algeria. He may, on demand, be admitted to exercise the rights of a French citizen. In this case he will be regulated by French law.[28]

These provisions served to complicate further the status of the Jews.[29] Families of whom certain members had been naturalized found themselves divided; in questions of marriage and of inheritance there were interminable conflicts.[30] Moreover, the process of naturalization was so cumbersome that during the following four years, only two hundred and eighty-nine Jews took advantage of it.

In March 1870, Émile Ollivier, Minister of Justice and an influential member of the government, presented to the *Conseil d'État* a draft law providing for the collective naturalization of the Jews of Algeria. Adolphe Crémieux, who had meanwhile become president of the Alliance Israélite Universelle, redoubled his efforts to have the measure adopted. On July 19, 1870, Crémieux presented the draft from the rostrum of the legislative Chamber. It was favorably received by Ollivier and the only remaining question seemed to be whether the legislation should be in the form of a law or decree. Article One of the law read: "All Jews indigenous to the territory of Algeria are admitted to exercise the rights of French citizens through the application of the Senate decree of July 14, 1865." Article Two made provision for any Jew who so wished to renounce French citizenship.[31]

The war with Prussia, the fall of the Empire and the proclamation of the Third Republic considerably affected the passing of the law. The French army was defeated and the effective seat of Government was transferred to Tours. There, Adolphe Crémieux, Minister of Justice and in charge of Algerian Affairs by virtue of his many journeys to that country,[32] was entrusted with the full authority of the Government of National Defense to carry out the long-awaited reforms. On October 24, 1870, Crémieux laid before the Cabinet nine decrees for political, administrative and legal reforms in Algeria. The seventh, which alone is called the "Crémieux Decree," read:

The Jews indigenous to the departments of Algeria are declared citizens of France. In consequence their civil status and their personal status will be regulated according to French law, effective with the promulgation of the present decree: all rights acquired to this day remain inviolate.

Every legislative provision, decree, rule or ordinance contrary to this decree is hereby abolished.

> Enacted at Tours, October 24, 1870
> Signed: Ad. Crémieux, L. Gambetta,
> A. Glais-Bizoin, E. Fourrichon.[33]

Thus, after a twenty-seven-year effort, Crémieux achieved his goal and fulfilled his duty as a Frenchman and a Jew.[34] Henceforward, the Jews of Algeria were French citizens.[35]

However, a distinction was made between the Jews who lived in the three departments of Algiers, Oran and Constantine and those of the southern regions. This left the Jews of the south in the same predicament in which those of the northern departements had been before the Crémieux Decree, and, through typical bureaucratic bumbling, their civil status was in fact reduced despite the grant of universal suffrage by 1947.

Anti-Semitism

The new dignity, and the accretion of political and economic strength that the Jews acquired as a result of the granting of French citizenship backlashed, upsetting their relative tranquillity and leading to a wave of anti-Semitism that persisted till the end of French rule. Conflicts of a political nature fed the passions engendered in the individual ethnic groups which, instead of developing in harmony, became even more rigidly separated. The Jews began to suffer from an anti-Semitism that rapidly degenerated into obscene and frequently criminal hatred.[36]

The first anti-Semitic campaign was provoked by the 1871 insurrection in the Kabyle, an area in which very few Jews actually lived. The anti-Semites deliberately ignored the true reasons for the insurrection, and the fact that the local population could have had little knowledge of, or interest in, the repeal of the Crémieux Decree.[37] The affair came before the French parliament, where an attempt was made to abrogate the Decree.[38] Though an eloquent defense by Crémieux succeeded in saving the principle of it, French citizenship was henceforth not to be granted automatically. A supplementary decree was passed in 1871 which stipulated the conditions according to which a Jew was to be regarded as a native of Algeria and as such eligible for the rights granted by the Crémieux Decree. Every Jew was obliged to make a "declaration of citizenship" before a Justice of the Peace which entitled him to registration on the electoral roll.[39] As a result of an anti-Semitic outbreak in 1838, when three hundred and eighty Jews were struck off the electoral roll of Sidi-Bel-Abbès on the pretext that their parents had not made the requisite declaration in 1871, a further supplementary decree was issued in 1939 which affirmed the voting rights of all Jews whose paternal ancestors had in any previous year been included in the electoral rolls.[40]

Opposition to the Jews and to the Crémieux Decree continued unabated and, particularly after 1878, frequently erupted into violence, especially around election time. Radical and socialist supporters were frequently in the forefront of the fight for repeal of the Crémieux Decree because the Jews tended to vote for the rightist parties; not that the Jews got any thanks from the equally virulent rightists.[41] In connection with the alleged influence of the Jews on the elections, it is interesting to note that in 1871 Crémieux, candidate for Algeria, was decisively defeated by Vuillermoz. The impassioned anti-Jewish polemic of Edward Drumont[42] further hardened the feelings between the ethnic groups which had by now become enemies. Political passions turned the existing religious and cultural differences between Europeans, Moslems and Jews into intense segregation, whereas with time and goodwill these might so easily have been bridged by understanding. Anti-Jewish campaigns were conducted in the press. Jews were black-listed; there were street demonstrations and deliberate provocations. Synagogues were desecrated; Jews were robbed and even assassinated.[43] The Dreyfus Affair brought fresh outbursts in Algeria, instigated by Max Régis and his followers, and in 1898 there were anti-Jewish riots in all the principal towns of Algeria.

In the small town of Aïn-Témouchent, one of the leading Jewish personalities, Abraham Meyer, devised an original method to put a stop to the anti-Semitic outbursts. He assembled his large domestic staff which was composed mainly of Moslem agricultural laborers who worked his land. He taught them the basic anti-Semitic slogans and then led them through the streets chanting the most virulent of them at the tops of their voices. In this case, humor triumphed over hate.

A number of factors finally led to the defeat of the anti-Semitic party in Algeria and to its disappearance in 1902. These included the vindication and rehabilitation of Dreyfus, the lessening of anti-Semitic agitation in France itself, the prudence of the Jewish community in Algeria, the skill of the French administration, the moderation shown by a large proportion of the European settlers, and the end of the economic crisis which had been exploited by the agitators. Most important perhaps was the refusal of the Moslems of Algeria to allow themselves to be drawn into the anti-Jewish manifestations, thus confounding the hopes and plans of the agitators. This phenomenon is a telling proof that the assertions regarding the so-called axiomatic hatred of the Moslems for the Jews were utterly unfounded.[44]

The evolution of the Jewish community continued with gigantic strides despite the restraining effects of its opponents. The war of 1914–1918 brought a new spirit of dedicated unity to all segments of Algeria's population, raising hopes that an end had come to the old bitterness and conflicts. Algerian Jews played a heroic part in the war: over 1,350 gave their lives, 39 won the cross of the Legion of Honor, 113 won military medals, some 850 were awarded the Croix de Guerre, and 1,000 were mentioned in dispatches.[45]

Yet an undercurrent of hate persisted:[46] in 1921 Dr. Molle's Neo-anti-Semitic Party came to power in the Oran municipality. Reckless and irresponsible agitation filled the columns of the *Petit Oranais*. The rise to power of the Nazis in Germany gave further impetus to the anti-Semitic movement. The swastika appeared everywhere, especially in Oran. A campaign of vilification in a Constantine periodical provoked the 1934 massacre in Constantine which left twenty-five dead, scores injured, and homes, shops and property pillaged. The Moslems who had been involved in the massacre were tried the following year and it became clear that the riots had been made possible through the almost criminal ineffectiveness of the local authorities. Responsible leaders of the three faiths joined after this massacre to form the *Union des Croyants Monothéistes* whose aim was to protect the rights of each religion and to prevent future misunderstandings. (This was one of the first such interdenominational committees ever to be established.)

The accession to power of the Popular Front in France and the appointment of Léon Blum, a Jew, to the premiership, led to a "general mobilization against the Jews" in Algeria. Again a scurrilous press poured out its hate, Algerian anti-Semites drawing their inspiration from Nazi Germany. A young Jewish soldier and war-orphan, Leon Kalifa, was killed in cold blood in Algiers in 1936 as he tore down an offensive placard. On June 18, 1940, the French government surrendered to the Germans. On October 7 Marshal Pétain, head of the puppet government in Vichy, abrogated the Crémieux Decree, deliberately disregarding the principle of the non-retroactivity of French laws. The Jews of Algeria though deprived of their nationality remained subject to French law in matters of property and personal status. Their disenfranchisement caused them untold suffering: they were expelled from the schools, excluded from all public life and subjected to a new law, that of October 2, which made them veritable pariahs and threatened them with concentration camps.[47]

In working for the resistance, the Jews found an outlet for their desires and frustrations by helping to hasten the downfall of National-Socialism.[48] An insurrection in Algiers on November 8, 1942 neutralized the capital and facilitated the landing of Allied forces. Generals Darlan, Châtel and Giraud, who were entrusted with civilian administration immediately after the landings, did all in their power—with the silent complicity of certain local American representatives—to keep the Jews subject to the German-inspired laws. Incredible measures were taken by General Giraud: they included the setting up of internment camps for the Jews and an ordinance of March 14, 1943, which abrogated once again the Crémieux Decree to an extent that went even further than Pétain's measure: not only did it deprive them of their citizenship, but it also denied them their legal right to be judged under French law in matters of personal status. Furthermore, it included war veterans who had been exempt under the Pétain decree.[49]

It required the intervention of the French Committee of National Liberation in London,[50] the protests of the rabbis and consistories of Algeria, of leading political and intellectual figures in Algeria,[51] of the leaders of the major Jewish organizations throughout the world (notably Stephen S. Wise representing the World Jewish Congress; Edward de Rothschild; Judge Proskauer, President of the American Jewish Committee; Henry Torrès, President of the Committee of the Jews of France) and finally the personal intervention of President Roosevelt, to right this injustice. Even Moslem leaders in Algeria, among them Ferhat Abbas, joined in the opposition to the anti-Jewish policies, and resisted all attempts made by French anti-Semitic groups to draw them into the conflict—further proof of Judeo-Moslem solidarity in Algeria. The French Committee for National Liberation, which was created through the merging of Charles de Gaulle's National Committee with the North African administration, assumed civil government in Algeria on September 1, 1943. André Philip, Commissioner of the Interior, and René Cassin,[52] President of the Legal Committee, were responsible for the communiqué issued by the F.C.N.L. on October 20 which declared the nullity of all laws containing discrimination against Jews, and confirmed that the Crémieux Decree would henceforth be fully enforced.

The new Algerian constitution in 1947 declared: "All French nationals in the departments of Algeria shall enjoy the rights inherent in the quality of French citizenship and shall be subject to the same obligations, without distinction of origin, race, language or religion."[53] This declaration of principle which had been imposed by General de Gaulle, at that time Prime Minister of France, remained ineffectual in practice. It was opposed by the mass of French colons in Algeria and by the local administration, but even without the personal prejudices of these against the emancipation of the Moslem masses, the cost of granting full equality would have been beyond the capacity of the French economy. The great misery of the majority of Algeria's Moslem population added fuel to the nationalist movement in that country and led, after a prolonged and costly civil war, to the setting up of an independent Moslem state in Algeria in July 1962.

The Jews in Algerian Political Life

During the period of their influence in North Africa, the French had neither the desire nor the ability to eliminate the discrimination of the past with one short blow. Such a desire, had it existed, would have been opposed with equal vigor both by the tradition-bound Moslems and the anti-Semitic element among the European colons. Following the 1870 decree, the Jews of Algeria were at last able to enter the public life of their country in which many of them were to play an important part. The transition of the Jews from their marginal position in the Moslem society in which they had had no civic rights, to the assumption of the responsibilities inherent in their new civic equality, was extremely rapid.

The Jews held significant political power in Algeria, the more so because the Moslems had no right of suffrage. Frequently the outcome of electoral contests depended entirely on the Jewish vote. The proportion of Jews elected to office at the local, regional and national levels was always higher than the proportion of Jews in the total population. The individual political parties in Algeria were therefore anxious to initiate the Jews into political affairs as rapidly as possible in order to win their votes at the polls. The Jews tended naturally to the more democratically inclined parties, especially the Radical-Socialist and

Socialist parties. Moreover, the anti-Semitic elements, of which the bourgeois parties were never able entirely to divest themselves, more or less compelled them to turn to the left-wing parties. Indeed, many of the rightist parties in fact promoted the spread of anti-Semitism among the European colons. It became an issue which decisively influenced a number of elections at the end of the nineteenth century as well as during the period of Nazi ascendancy. It is not without significance that it was the same group of colons who twenty years later supported the Secret Army Organization (O.A.S.) in its opposition to the granting of Algerian independence.

Algerian Jews were one of the rare groups in the Moslem countries of Africa and Asia who were able to go through an apprenticeship in democratic life. The role that some of them later played in political and public life in France itself is some indication of their aptitude for it. A special example is that of René Moatti, a Jew of Algerian origin, who was for many years President of the Municipal Council of Paris, later a member of the Chamber of Deputies, and President of the Foreign Affairs and National Defense Commission of the French Parliament.

Even after the outbreak of the civil war in Algeria, the Jewish community there retained its stability. Not until the last few weeks preceding the granting of independence in July 1962 did it suddenly and almost completely pull up its roots and disappear.

10

The Status of the Jews in Tunisia (1881-1956) and French Morocco (1912-1956)

TUNISIA

Throughout its history Tunisia, at the junction of international land and sea routes, had been more exposed than either Algeria or Morocco to foreign influence, European as well as Turkish. Although the French Protectorate was established only in 1881, the occupation of Algeria in 1830 exerted a profound influence on Tunisia's rulers and on the life of the Jews there. The accession of Ahmed Bey to the throne in 1837 marked a turning point in the evolution of Tunisia, and during his eighteen-year reign the Jews had a foretaste of the security and freedom that they were to enjoy under the Protectorate.

Ahmed Bey and Mohammed Bey. An intelligent ruler and admirer of the West, Ahmed Bey saw himself as something of a Peter the Great of Tunisia. He sought to emancipate himself from Ottoman control, and strengthened his country's ties with Europe, especially with France. In the Bey's service were Jewish administrators, physicians and officials whose influence secured for their coreligionists a tranquillity which was the envy of the Jews of Algeria and Morocco. The official tradition of hospitality toward Jews fleeing from other countries[1] was maintained, and the Bey even included the Jews in his regular distribution of alms.

Ahmed Bey's cousin, Mohammed Bey, who succeeded him to the throne in 1855, was an Oriental ruler of refined tastes.[2] Immediately after his accession, he abolished the corvée duty to which Jews were still subjected under the old laws for the dhimmis, and he made the Jews subject to the same fiscal laws as Moslems. This meant above all the abolition of the special customs duties which had been levied against merchandise belonging to Jews and, in consequence, the end of the collective responsibility of the Jewish community for the collection of these taxes. The Bey's attitude to the Jews was probably influenced by the advice of the caid of the Jews, Joseph Scemama, who was also paymaster to the Bey's army. Rather than true reforms, these new regulations are to be seen as the first radical departure from the ancient structure of Islamic public law with its insistence on the dhimmis' inferior status.

The Trial of Batto Sfez and its Consequences. Progress, however, was accompanied by reaction. During the very period the Bey was announcing his liberal policies, he issued a decree, on November 15, 1856, to set up a tribunal "to promulgate the law and to regulate religious affairs." This all-powerful commission had to judge Batto Sfez, a Jew who had been accused by a Moslem of the traditional charge of uttering blasphemies against Islam. Since, as we have seen in Chapter Five, the oath of the Jew was invalid against that of a Moslem in the Moslem court, the accused in such a case was liable to receive the death penalty. In general, every effort was made to settle disputes of this kind in a less extreme manner, but this was not so in the case of Batto Sfez who was condemned to death by the powerful tribunal. Even the protection of foreign powers, which since 1823[3] had been fairly effective in cases of arbitrary persecution, was of no avail; neither were the monies freely paid to judges and accusers, the representations to the Bey, the interventions on the part of the representatives of Christian states, notably that of the French Consul, Léon Roches, nor the pleas of the princesses and other highly placed persons who were interested in the case. Whether out of blind fanaticism, because he had taken an unshakable oath or through fear for his popularity, the Bey could not be moved and the innocent Batto Sfez was decapitated.

Passion ran high. Jews and Christians in Tunisia sent a joint delegation consisting of one Christian and two Jews[4] to Napoleon III to present him with full details of the case and to request French protection for the non-Moslems who no longer felt safe in Tunisia. The European colony in Tunis was in favor of the firm application in Tunisia of the *Hatti Sherif* Edict of Gulhane by which Abdul Medjid, the Sultan of Turkey, had in 1839 abolished all discrimination among his subjects and guaranteed their equality without distinction of race or religion. Léon Roches, feeling that Tunisia was ripe for the beginning of similar modernization, worked together with the British Consul, Mr. Wood, and the Tunisian General Kheireddine, for the granting of a liberal constitution; but the Bey was unyielding. The arrival of a strong French naval squadron under the command of Admiral Tréhouart at the port of La Goulette caused a sudden change of mind on the part of the Bey and he returned to his earlier devotion to liberal ideas. On September 9, 1857, he promulgated, under the name of "Fundamental Pact," a document which brought about a veritable revolution in the classical concept of traditional Moslem law. With that Tunisia emerged into the nineteenth century Western world.

The Fundamental Pact. The preamble to the Pact declared the obligation to follow the commands of God and to prevent injustice or contempt toward all His creatures. The Bey was determined that nothing would be spared to guarantee to all his subjects the effective exercise of their rights, and pointed out that the reform introduced by the charter had been foreshadowed by the liberal measures he had taken after his accession to the throne. The Pact itself consisted of eight articles followed by four chapters of commentary. Article One formally guaranteed full security for all the Bey's subjects, without distinction of race, nationality or religion; this security was to extend to the person, the property and the dignity of his subjects. It was, in a way, a restatement of the ancient rights of the dhimmis with the important difference that no discrimination was to be made henceforth between Moslems and non-Moslems: the rights of citizenship were not to be limited to a Believer.

The second article proclaimed the equality before the law of Moslem and non-Moslem. The fourth article dealt specifically with the Jews. It guaranteed respect for their religion, swept away all repressions and pressures aimed at obtaining their conversion to Islam, granted them the right freely to practice their rituals, and promised full protection for their synagogues against desecration. Article Six was a direct consequence of the preoccupation of the day: it made obligatory the appointment of a Jewish assessor to every bench that judged a Jew in a criminal matter. Article Seven reiterated the benevolent provisions of the Moslem law with regard to the dhimmis. Article Eight abolished special privileges, since all were equal under the new law.

The commentaries to the Pact recognized not only the rights of every individual freely to practice his chosen religion, but also to change it, though no compulsion was allowed to be exerted in order to induce this, or to prevent it. This last measure is of considerable significance for the law of Islam punishes its apostates with death, and even in modern days the Arab states have refused to endorse the Universal Declaration of the

Rights of Man at the United Nations because these include a clause on the right to change one's religion. The last three chapters of the commentaries expatiated in flowery style on the underlying intentions of the Charter, confirming the personal, religious and material security of all. They guaranteed the right to possess real estate, a reform which broke with tradition, and declared the inviolability of both movable and immovable property. The principle of forced labor at the command of the government was henceforward abolished. With direct reference to the case of Batto Sfez, assurance was given in the commentaries to all the subjects of the Bey that "their honor would be respected and that no criminal sentence would be pronounced against them based on an unsupported accusation alone, whatever the power or the station of the accuser, for all men are equal before the law."

Article Seventy-eight of the constitutional laws made provision for the freedom to enter state employment of any qualified person irrespective of his religion, provided only that he was a Tunisian and had not been condemned to the loss of his civic rights. Article Ninety-nine made military service obligatory for all Tunisians of eighteen years of age who had been born within the kingdom.[5] Article Ninety-four stated that any non-Moslem Tunisian who changed his religion would, despite his conversion to Christianity, remain a Tunisian subject and liable to the jurisdiction of the country, without the right to claim foreign protection which would free him from the regular payment of taxes.[6]

The proclamation of the Fundamental Pact was accompanied by the setting up of a *Conseil Suprême* which was to be the guardian of the constitutional laws and to serve as the national High Court of Justice. It was celebrated with great solemnity at the Bardo Palace in the presence of Admiral Tréhouart and officers of the French fleet, the entire consular corps and all the high

officials of the country. The Ulemas blessed the noble disposition of His Majesty the Bey. All of Europe was moved by this
event, which was considered a stroke of political genius; it won
for the Bey the *Grand Cordon* of the Legion of Honor. Indeed,
it was a peaceful revolution worthy of all the attention it received for it marked the first attempt in the Maghreb to dissoci-
ate the spiritual from the temporal, and to regulate the temporal
state on a solid and equitable basis which distinguished between
the status of the individual, the citizen and the believer.

Repercussions of the Pact. The mass of the people was not
prepared to accept the revolutionary concepts that Mohammed
Bey had adopted at the prompting of the French. It was not
enough to proclaim the laws in order to make the citizens and
even the judges respect them. (The following remark made by
Mohammed Bey on the advantages of proportional taxation is
indicative of the mentality of the time: "Proportional taxation is
certainly more equitable; but if I were to introduce it, the rich
would bribe the caid to have themselves registered as poor, and
the poor, who would be unable to buy off the caid, would be
registered as rich.") The unexpected reversal of long accepted
values and of the deeply entrenched establishment incited strong
discontent in the feudal mentality that directed the country, and
the most fantastic rumors regarding the new laws were rampant
throughout Tunisia. Mohammed es Sadok Bey, who succeeded
to the throne in 1859, swore to maintain the Fundamental Pact
which was to be the source of Tunisian sovereignty to the exclu-
sion of all outside interference, and incorporated it into the state
constitution. But it was swept away by the Tunisian revolt of
1864.[7] As this revolt spread, a grave sense of insecurity was felt
by the population, most of all by the Jews, who placed themselves under the protection of the European diplomatic mis-

sions. Caid Nessim Scemama, State Treasurer, sailed for Italy taking his treasure with him.[8] Foreign settlers started to emigrate. When order was restored, Mohammed es Sadok Bey hastened to revoke the liberal laws for which his people were still unprepared. This measure, however, was not taken specifically against the Jews.

Henceforward the Jews were still able to find effective protection for their rights and their security either through the Tunisian authorities or through the foreign consuls. In 1897, when France, on behalf of the Bey, was revising the treaties that had been concluded prior to the establishment of the Protectorate, some hundreds of Tunisian Jews were found to be under Italian, Spanish, Dutch, Belgian and other protection.[9] Even France extended a special form of protection to certain privileged categories of Tunisians. In 1875, it was the consular corps headed by the British Consul General which, at the request of the French Consul General, intervened with the Bey when a Jew was murdered in broad daylight by a Moslem who took refuge in a religious institution to escape punishment. Following the intervention of the consular corps, the Moslem was taken from his place of sanctuary, tried and, though he belonged to a Sherifian family, eventually executed.[10]

In 1863, a committee of the Alliance Israélite Universelle was set up in Tunisia, affiliated with the central committee of the Alliance which had been established in Paris three years earlier. The educational work of the Alliance had a more lasting effect on the development of Tunisia's Jews than the much-hailed Fundamental Pact, as will be seen in Chapter Twelve. The committee was reorganized in 1877 and intervened effectively whenever an official measure was taken that might have discriminated against the Jews. In 1877 it succeeded in having an order given to the Governor of Tunis that the bastinado was no longer to be administered to Jews though all sections of the population were submitted to it.[11] When a third of the Jewish community of Tunisia fell victim to the epidemics and famine that swept the country in 1866, 1867 and 1868, funds were raised for them throughout Europe through the Alliance Israélite Universelle and the Board of Deputies of British Jews in London. In 1878 a modern school was opened in Tunis, largely supported by the Alliance and the Anglo-Jewish Association.

The Situation under the Protectorate. The French Protectorate over Tunisia was established following the signature of the Treaty of Bardo on May 12, 1881, and was confirmed by the Convention of June 8, 1883. But for the Jews of Tunisia it did not signify the revolutionary change which the 1830 conquest had meant for their Algerian coreligionists. It served, rather, to confirm and safeguard through the French presence the existing liberal tendencies which had characterized the Regency since the reign of Ahmed Bey. The avowed intention of the Treaty was to ensure the independence of the Bey and his sovereignty over Tunisia, even against Turkish claims.[12] In conformity with this principle, and no doubt also out of a desire to avoid a repetition of the Algerian experience, the French administration intervened as little as possible in Jewish affairs.

The Jews remained subjects of the Bey and continued to have their own separate community organizations.[13] Since the basic theocratic nature of the Moslem state and its religious law was maintained, the Jews continued to be judged in all matters of personal status, as well as in all civil and commercial disputes between Jews, in the rabbinical courts. Only criminal cases were tried by the French public authority. Matters which involved a Jew and a Moslem were tried in the Moslem court, in which the Jew appeared in his status of dhimmi and was judged according to koranic law. Between 1881 and 1898, the only laws that related specifically to Jews were concerned with minor matters, such as the organization of Jewish welfare funds, the regulation of religious life, and questions of ritual slaughter and the manufacture and sale of unleavened bread; all these were noncontroversial issues.[14] A slightly more daring step was taken in 1898 with a law reorganizing the rabbinical court of Tunis. Together with a further beylic decree of 1922, this law replaced an earlier one of 1872 and reshaped the rabbinical court into the form that it retained till the end of the French Protectorate. The court was composed of a chief rabbi who acted as honorary president, a presiding rabbi, two rabbinical judges, two surrogate rabbis and one registrar. Two unpaid surrogate judges could be called on to replace judges unable to attend. But this reform was minimal and was restricted to reorganizing an already existing institution.

The Jews had hoped that more positive measures for their political emancipation would have been taken by the authorities at the prompting of the French, but only a few timid steps had been made in this direction. Decrees passed between 1884 and 1903 which regulated the organization of various municipalities reserved two seats for Jewish councillors in the municipality of Sousse,[15] and provided for one Jewish representative on each of the councils of La Goulette,[16] Tunis,[17] Souk-el-Arba,[18] Bizerta[19] and Gafsa.[20] No provision was made for the election of Jews to other municipal councils but neither were there any explicit laws which would have prevented this. The representative institutions in Tunisia were at this time still in their early formative stages and the Jews were able to play only a minor role in them. Apart from their seats in the municipalities, the Jews had no representation. At the 1907 Conference which preceded the formation of the *Grand Conseil* of Tunisia, there was only one Jewish representative as against thirty-two French-men and fifteen Moslems.

Nationality and Jurisdiction. Since the inequality inherent in the Moslem Statute persisted, the Jews felt themselves to be living on the fringes of both European and Moslem society, excluded to all intents and purposes from public life. Before the establishment of the Protectorate, they had found in diplomatic protection a remedy for discrimination against them, but the patents of protection were personal and non-transferable and eventually disappeared completely. Just as the Jews had voiced through their élite their desire for foreign protection, so now they wished to acquire French nationality.

A series of public campaigns to this effect were carried out. They aimed, not at mass naturalization on the Algerian pattern which, by removing so many subjects from the Bey's jurisdic-tion, would have caused the Protectorate to degenerate into a virtual annexation, but at extending to the Jews of Tunisia the same privilege that was granted to all foreign residents in Tuni-sia, namely that of acquiring French citizenship after three years' residence in the Protectorate.[21] The Jews also demanded equality with French subjects in matters of jurisdiction. They claimed the right to opt for the laws under which they were to be judged in the same way as an Algerian law of 1889 gave such an option to the indigenous population in matters of civil and personal status; Tunisian Jewry hoped to see such an op-tion extended to include also criminal law. In effect, the Jews wished to be judged in French courts rather than Tunisian or Jewish ones, thereby enjoying the same rights as Frenchmen. Their appeal was supported by the Bar Association of Tunis which in 1898 asked the French government to place the Jews under the jurisdiction of French courts, in which they would be

judged according to Jewish law, on the pattern of Algerian procedure. Tunisian Jewry addressed a petition to the Parliament
in Paris: "We beseech Parliament to make us subject to the
jurisdiction of French courts, which alone can give us impartial
justice. . . . The treaties of 1881, 1883 and 1896 permit France
to act thus in the interests of justice and humanity. . . . The
fulfillment of our wishes cannot but strengthen French influence
in Tunisia."[22] The French League for the Rights of Man and of
the Citizen[23] and various political parties[24] added their voices
to these continuous demands during the first decade of the twentieth century; they fell on deaf ears. The presidential decree of
1899 continued to preclude the Jews, more thoroughly than the
Moslems, from aspiring to French citizenship.[25] Such was the
procedure for naturalization that from 1891 to 1910 not a single Tunisian Jew was able to acquire French nationality despite
the strong desire that the Jews expressed to this end. (Ninety-
seven Moslems did succeed in acquiring French nationality during this period.)

A decree of 1910 made it possible for the first time for a
person to renounce his allegiance to the Bey and accept French
nationality. Till the establishment of the Protectorate, Tunisian
nationality had been regulated, as in all Islamic countries, on
the principle of irrevocable allegiance. Article Ninety-two of the
Constitution of 1861 had provided that every Tunisian who
left his country for whatever reason and whatever length of
time, whether he had adopted foreign nationality in his absence
or not, would, on his return to Tunisian soil, return to his status
of Tunisian citizen. A major exception to this principle was now
made in favor of French nationality which could be acquired
under special circumstances. However, these special conditions
could rarely be met. In view of the pressure brought to bear by
the growing number of foreigners (mainly Italians) in Tunisia,

the French government recognized its obligation to give early consideration to its policy on nationality in Tunisia.

The war of 1914–1918 intervened before the problem could be solved. Some hundreds of Jews enlisted under the French flag. In 1917 there were grave disorders in Bizerta, Tunis, Sousse, Sfax, Kairouan and Mahdia, when the rabble attacked the Jewish quarters leaving death and destruction in their wake. After the war it was again possible to give realistic consideration to the question of nationality in Tunisia. A decree of the Bey in 1921, modifying an earlier decree of 1914, prepared the way for the law of 1923 which remained in force till the end of the Protectorate. The law of 1923 eased the conditions and the formalities required for the acquisition of French nationality. A promise was given during the debate in the French Parliament that "the former French protégés . . . need only submit to the Resident-General their request for naturalization. It will be investigated immediately. . . . How could it be otherwise when it is a question of Tunisian subjects who have affirmed their affection and their love for France even when the French flag was not yet flying over Tunisia.[26] Between 1911 and 1923, 299 Jews had acquired French nationality under the 1910 decree. In the five-year period from 1924 to 1928, 4,126 Jews were naturalized, constituting approximately 35 per cent of the total naturalizations for that period.[27] Another 2,334 were naturalized in the next five years.[28] Thereafter there was a slackening off, due perhaps to the slowness of the bureaucratic process, perhaps to a reaction of the Jewish community to the rise of anti-Semitism in Germany which tended to distort the Jewish outlook and caused a withdrawal of the community into itself. From 1934 to 1938, only 180 Jews were naturalized— about 5 per cent of the total[29]—and in the next five years which covered the period of the Vichy régime and the German occupation, 147 Jews acquired French nationality.[30] During the four-year post-occupation period, another 156 were naturalized.[31] Altogether, 7,311 Jews were granted French nationality in Tunisia between 1911 and the end of the Protectorate. These, with their descendants, eventually made up one-third of the Jewish population of Tunisia, and until the country gained its independence in 1956, the community remained divided into two groups—those who had opted for French nationality and those who had retained allegiance to the Bey.

The tranquillity of Tunisia was interrupted by its occupation by the German army following the Allied landings in Algeria on November 8, 1942. The first act of the Germans on November 23 was the arrest of leading Jewish personalities and the presentation of the first demands by the *Kommandatur* to the Chief Rabbi of Tunis and the president of the community. Two thousand, then three thousand, Jews had to be delivered to the Germans for forced labor under pain of reprisals.[32] The French and Tunisian authorities made the Jewish notables responsible for collecting the men and facing up to the German demands. A recruiting committee had to be organized, a dozen labor camps were set up for thousands of workers, mostly Jews. There were many victims; some were slain in the line of duty. The six months of Nazi occupation lay heavy on the Jews of Tunisia, and at times it seemed that they would be submitted to the same fate as their coreligionists in occupied Europe.[33] Fortunately the rapid Allied advance did not give the Germans the time to carry out the atrocities which they had planned.

The Tunisian Community during the Post-War Period. At the end of the war, the Jews of Tunisia still formed a well-organized group, not having lost their community structure which predated the Protectorate as had their neighbors, the Jews of Algeria. The rabbinical court was still a very active force. In 1950, for instance, it dealt with six hundred and sixty civil, personal and commercial cases.[34] The court, whose judges were appointed by the Bey, had its seat in Tunis and its jurisdiction extended over Tunisian Jews throughout the country. (The Jews of French nationality were, of course, subject only to French law.) A beylic decree of 1935 had provided the rabbis of provinces outside Tunis with the authority to determine alimony payments; these were subject to appeal in the rabbinical court in Tunis.[35] Since the rabbinical court based its judgments in matters of personal status on Jewish law, its decisions frequently caused grave unhappiness when a Tunisian Jewess, fully emancipated in society, was subjected to a law that provided for an inferior status for women. This question will be discussed in more detail in Chapter Fourteen.

The Jewish community was directed by a council which was established by a decree of 1921. It was formed, in effect, of two bodies representing the "Tunisian" and the "Portuguese" sections until the 1944 decree united them.[36] A further decree of the Bey in 1947 reorganized the council which henceforth consisted of ten members elected for four-year terms by forty elected delegates. The election of the delegates was usually the subject for widespread public interest and debate. Twenty-three communities outside of Tunis were organized into "religious and welfare funds," while a twenty-fourth, the committee of the synagogue of Ghriba on the island of Djerba, was concerned solely with the religious interests of the Jews of the island. The officers of the funds were appointed by the government with the exception of those of Sfax and Sousse who were directly elected. The income of the communities was derived from income from the cemeteries, taxes on Kosher meat, on wine and on *bokha*. This, in a typical year (1950), accounted for some three-quarters of the expenditure. It was supplemented from government grants that covered the support of the Chief Rabbinate and the School for Rabbinical Law, and grants from public funds for the support of welfare projects.

The Jews in Tunisian Affairs. Besides their own community structure, the Jews of Tunisia were also represented as a separate group in the country's representative bodies. They composed a separate electoral college which elected three delegates to the *Grand Conseil* of Tunisia: one representing Tunis, one northern Tunisia and one central-and-south Tunisia. As has been noted, they were also separately represented in the municipal councils of those cities where they formed an important element. Provision was also made for Jewish representation in the chambers of commerce; six Jews were elected to the Chamber of Commerce of northern Tunisia, three to the Chamber of Commerce and Agriculture of the central region and two to the Chamber of the southern region.

The division of the Tunisian Jewish community into French and Tunisian subjects did nothing to simplify their position when the Néo-Destour under the leadership of Habib Bourguiba commenced the struggle for complete independence from France. Placed where France and Islam faced each other and interacted, the Jews were caught unprepared for this national conflict which, starting in Tunisia, was to spread throughout North Africa.

FRENCH MOROCCO

During the nineteenth century, the desperate situation of Moroccan Jewry had come to the attention of the Jews of Europe who, in 1863 and 1864, made official representations to the

Sultan of Morocco. Sir Moses Montefiore, president of the London Committee of British Jews, then already seventy-nine years old, made a long journey to Morocco in an attempt to bring relief to the sufferings of his coreligionists there. In Tangiers and Safi he was instrumental in freeing Jewish captives. He was received twice by the Sultan with great honors, and succeeded in obtaining from him the Dahir of February 5, 1864.[37] This decree, couched in words of eloquent benevolence, stated "Every man has in our eyes, an equal right to demand justice" —though which justice and from whom, it did not stipulate. For all its fine but ambiguous words, the decree remained a dead letter. Soon the Jews were being accused of arrogance and of exclusiveness and a second Dahir annulled the first.[38]

Moroccan Jewry's only hope at this time was the Alliance Israélite Universelle, which set up a network of schools in the main cities, the first of which was opened in 1862 at Tetuan. As will be seen in Chapter Twelve, this intensive school system helped to bridge the gap of centuries by bringing modern education to the mellahs of Morocco. Through the schools, moral and material assistance was made available to the whole community.

The French presence came to Morocco with the treaty establishing the Protectorate, on March 30, 1912. It was followed almost immediately by a frightful massacre in Fez on April 17–18: sixty Jews were killed, some fifty seriously injured, women were raped before being done to death, the entire mellah was sacked and a third of it burnt down, leaving ten thousand people homeless.

The Consequences of the Protectorate. Throughout the period of French protection, the situation of the Jews remained similar to that of Tunisian Jewry at the turn of the twentieth century.

Though freed by the French presence of their worst disabilities, the Jews became a monolithic block poised between Europeans and Moslems, not fully accepted by either group. From the outset, the French administration committed the fatal error of allowing the separate development of the ethnic groups instead of striving for their cultural and economic fusion. The equilibrium in which the Jews and Moslems had lived, for better or worse, for twelve centuries was upset by the introduction into Morocco of the third and henceforth most powerful force—the French.

Under the Protectorate, two superimposed jurisdictions were created in Morocco: that of the Sultan, the nominal sovereign of the country and chief of the Makhzen (Moroccan) administration, and that of the Protectorate headed by the Resident Commissioner-General, in whose hands the real power lay. From 1912 to the end of the Protectorate in 1956, the Moslems were in the position of subject colonials, while the Jews were placed between them and the French. Liberated from their traditional position of inferiority, the Jews became an important link between the two groups and took an active part in diffusing European influence among the native population. But in the absence of effective constitutional guarantees for their theoretical rights, Morocco's Jews found themselves, at the end of fifty years, alienated from both societies on whose perimeters they lived. The Protectorate did nothing to destroy the fundamental theocratic character of the Sherifian Empire which continued to exclude the Unbeliever from all possibility of equality within its borders. While his rights as a dhimmi were recognized, the Jew could not aspire to civic equality with his fellow-citizens and was thus excluded from the state of which he was a subject. In Morocco, France did not take the Jews under its protection as it took virtually all of Algerian Jewry and a large part of the

Tunisian community. Thus, while the Jews of Morocco had been plucked from their generally inferior position, they were not granted guarantees for, or opportunities to exercise, their theoretical liberty.

The Legal Position of the Jews. The marginal position of the Jews in relation to both the societies which surrounded them led to the creation of a unique and complex juridical system. In accordance with the religious nature of the Sherifian legal system, the Moslem was judged in the Moslem court according to the Law of Mohammed, and the Jews in the rabbinical court according to the Law of Moses in all civil, personal and commercial disputes between Jews. (For details of the workings of these courts, see Chapter Fourteen.) As in Tunisia, all criminal cases were tried by the French authorities, and suits involving a Jew and a Moslem were tried in the Moslem court. Frequently, therefore, the Jew would be judged according to the Koran by Moslem judges, *cadis,* who represented the canon law of the *Shari'a* (Moslem legal code). Beside the cadis there were the caids, who represented the central power and also had certain rights of jurisdiction in torts and in equity as representatives of Makhzen justice. The situation of a Jew, facing judgment by cadi or caid, was not without difficulty for he appeared before his judges as an inferior being. (Moslem law itself, it will be remembered, confirmed this inferiority by fixing the "blood price" for the death of a Jew as half that of a Moslem.) Furthermore, according to Malekite law which was the only one applicable in Morocco, the Jew could not benefit from the law of retaliation; in the majority of cases, this made it impossible for him to have his rights recognized. The principal, if not the only, means of proof permitted by Moslem law were the oath and the evidence of a witness but, as we have seen in Chapter

Four, the oath of, or evidence presented by, a Jew or an Unbeliever were practically worthless against those of a Moslem.

The Protectorate, instead of bringing about a clarification of this difficult legal situation, only complicated it further. The French legal system, superimposed on those already existing, reinforced the compartmentation of justice into Moroccan, French and rabbinical systems. Each one functioned in isolation and there were no higher courts of appeal to unify or resolve the justice rendered by the three different jurisdictions. French law and French courts had no say in the law dispensed in the Sherifian or the rabbinical courts. This evolution of three separate legal systems paralleled the three separate societies who lived in the same country with hardly a point of contact. Despite all efforts, the problem was never solved. It was eased somewhat when, at the end of French rule, both the French and the Jewish communities were considerably reduced and their importance diminished. The principal fault of Sherifian jurisprudence remained the lack of proper codification, a problem which must ultimately be solved in the process of the country's modernization.

The Nature of Moroccan Nationality. The legal position of Moroccan Jewry was largely dominated by the question of nationality. As in Tunisia, France had only the rights of a protecting power. Sovereignty, at least in theory, remained in the hands of the Bey and the Sultan respectively, and the Jews remained their subjects. While in Tunisia provision eventually was made for the Jews to opt for French nationality, no such possibility existed for the Moroccan community.

The Jews of Morocco had always lived on the margin of public life, subject to their own legal jurisdiction and their own community organization. Insofar as nationality may be defined as the political link between the individual and the state, the Jew, deprived of political rights, was not strictly speaking a subject of the Sultan. This was so widely admitted that when the European powers first became actively interested in the Mahgreb, many Jews sought and obtained foreign protection. The problems created by the policy of foreign protection in Morocco gave rise to an international convention in Madrid in 1879, subscribed to by Morocco, the United States, Great Britain, France, Denmark, Spain, Portugal, Italy, the Netherlands, Belgium, Sweden and Norway. The Convention ruled *inter alia* that any former Moroccan subject who had obtained foreign nationality while abroad without the consent of the Sultan would automatically, after a certain period of residence in Morocco, become once more a Moroccan subject unless he chose to leave Morocco permanently. The concept of Moroccan "nationality" appeared for the first time in this text; till then there had been no such thing as a "Moroccan," only Jews and Moslems.

The new status of nationality to which the Jews of Morocco now became subject was more rigid than that obtaining elsewhere, for it could be relinquished only by the acceptance of permanent exile. By superimposing the Western concept of nationality on the old Oriental principles of Moslem law, the Convention of Madrid served only to complicate the issue further. The Jews, who had formerly been simply protégés of the Moslem state without any real ties or obligations to it, were suddenly made part of the body of the Sultan's subjects without, however, having extended to them the same rights. From the point of internal politics the Jews were outcasts; for the outside world they remained Moroccan subjects. The conflicts of law and jurisdiction became even more acute when the French left the newly independent Morocco in 1956.

In effect, however, the principles which determined the status of Moroccan nationality had gradually been eased over the years through a slow evolution in Moroccan jurisprudence that discarded historical concepts in favor of the principles of modern international law. Eventually, Moroccan nationality was determined principally according to paternal nationality. By virtue of this evolution, for which French judges and legislators were responsible, Moroccan nationality was no longer a concomitant of the adherence to Islam of a Moslem resident in Morocco, but was acquired exclusively by the application of the *jus sanguinis*. Moroccan nationality which had been acquired through the *jus solis* was considered solely as an interim status. It is for this reason that since the country gained its independence, the Moroccan authorities have systematically refused to grant citizenship to Christians who wished to settle permanently in Morocco.

A further complication is the principle of perpetual allegiance which was recognized by the Madrid Convention of 1879, confirmed by the Act of Algeçiras of 1906 and is still in force today: it is impossible for a Moroccan to renounce his nationality without royal consent. In this respect it differs from the law obtaining in countries such as France and the United States, where citizens automatically lose their nationality when they accept foreign nationality, or from that in other countries where citizens can choose either to retain or to renounce their former nationality when accepting a new one. Thus the Jews of Morocco now living in Israel remain, in the eyes of the Moroccan authorities and, in principle at least, of the signatories of the Madrid Convention, Moroccan subjects. This legal paradox is fortunately of little importance at the moment, but it can again cause difficulties when normal relations between Israel and Morocco are established.

The severe restrictions imposed by the principle of perpetual allegiance caused Jews to seek an escape from it whenever possible. Before the French Protectorate was established, they tried to gain the protection of one of the Capitular Powers or to gain foreign nationality while abroad. (A large number of wealthy Moroccans travelled on British passports.) After 1912, many Jews tried to establish their Algerian descent in order to claim French citizenship. Frequently, too, Moroccan women arranged to be delivered in Algeria so that their children at least would have French nationality. The present Moroccan regime will eventually have to repudiate the principle of perpetual allegiance in its nationality laws, and it will have to abolish the last vestiges of religious discrimination if it is to live up to its official undertaking to grant legal equality to its Jews, and if it is to fulfill its obligations under the Charter of the United Nations.

During the fifty-four years of the French Protectorate, the Jews of Morocco were almost completely excluded from the country's political life, embryonic as it was, despite the best intentions of the Sultan and of the French administration. The Government Council which was created in 1919 did not have any Jewish members till 1947 when six Jews, representing the communities of Casablanca, Fez, Marrakesh, Meknès, Oujda and Rabat were elected by the community councils which had been reorganized under a Dahir of 1945. This was the first time that Jews were able to play even a modest role in the political life of Morocco. Following the proclamation of Morocco's independence a Jewish physician, Dr. Benzaquen, was included in the Cabinet as Minister of Posts after much bickering and horse-trading. A short time later, under cover of a Cabinet reshuffle, Dr. Benzaquen was replaced by a Moslem.

The Moroccan Jewish Community Structure. From the fourteenth to the twentieth century, the community structure in Mo-

rocco remained unchanged. While in Algeria the Crémieux Decree led to the organization of the Jewish communities on the
model of those in metropolitan France, and in Tunisia, where
one-third of the Jewish community was French, the protecting
power exerted a decisive influence, in Morocco the French presence did nothing to change the situation.

Only in 1918 was a Dahir promulgated that gave legal existence to the community councils and enumerated their functions.
A regulation by the Vizier in 1919 created a new post, that of
Inspector of Jewish Institutions. Following repeated complaints
by the Jewish community, a Dahir of 1945 reorganized the
community councils which were then endowed with social and
religious functions and made responsible for the administration
of ritual religious matters, provision of help to the poor and the
administration of religious endowments. The income from these
endowments, known as *hekdesh* in Hebrew and similar to the
habbous of the Moslems, was dedicated in perpetuity to the
upkeep of the poor and the maintenance of religious buildings.
These included certain tombs which were the centers of Jewish
veneration, most important of which was the tomb of Rabbi
Amran ben Divan of Ouezzane.[39] The community councils
remained under the supervision of the Protectorate administration and were never entirely emancipated. Even this, the sole
field of public activity in which the Jews were able to play any
part, was severely circumscribed from all sides, as were all aspects of life in this country where the Jews were never fully
emancipated.

The reform of 1947 was more benevolent insofar as it permitted the federation of the separate community councils into
the Council of Communities which met annually at Rabat under
the supervision of a French official who presided over the meet-
ings. Thanks to the initiative of some of the leaders, this annual

assembly of the presidents of Jewish communities in Morocco underwent a transformation and assured a permanent and general representation of the Jewish communities with the authorities. The National Council of Communities tried in vain to obtain a ratification of its competence from the new independent regime. The legal position of the Jews and of their community organizations in Morocco remained ambiguous till the end and only the emigration of the majority of the country's Jews served in some way to resolve the problem.

The Beginning of Emigration to Israel. With the creation of the State of Israel, the traditional peace between the Jews and the Moslems could be maintained thanks to the equilibrium created by the French presence. The two communities had a tacit understanding that the conflicts which plagued their co-religionists in the Holy Land were to be avoided, though each side expressed its sympathies unequivocally in the Jewish and Moslem press. The French authorities and leaders of the Jewish and Moslem communities kept a vigilant watch to avoid plunging the country into an irretrievable disaster. On May 23, 1948, scarcely a week after the proclamation of the State of Israel, the Sultan of Morocco made an appeal to his subjects in which he reminded them of the protection that Morocco had always accorded to the Jews. He asked the Jews to refrain from all Zionist manifestations, and the Moslem population to prevent any disturbance of the peace.

However, despite all precautions, bloody riots broke out against the Jews in northern Morocco, close to the Algerian border. Anti-Jewish propaganda, probably from foreign sources, had been disseminated among the Moslems of Oujda since the end of May. Finally, on June 7, the crowd, sparked off by a minor incident, poured into the Jewish quarter. In the three hours that passed before the army could control the mob, five people (including one Frenchman) had been killed, thirty had been severely injured, shops and homes had been sacked. The same night an even more serious riot occurred in the neighboring mining town of Djérada where the Jewish population, consisting of about a hundred souls, had been surrounded by an uncontrollable mob and attacked with outrageous savagery. Neither children nor old men were spared; thirty-nine Jews lost their lives, thirty were severely injured and others less severely so.

Similar massacres occurred a few days later halfway across North Africa, in Libya, which at the time was still under British control. There had previously been anti-Jewish massacres in Libya, shortly after the end of the war, when a Moslem mob had unexpectedly attacked the Jews of Tripoli on November 4, 1945, killing one hundred and twenty Jews, injuring hundreds and desecrating synagogues. The disorder had spread also to other towns. In 1948 everyone was warned and the Jews secured assurances from the British authorities and the Moslem notables. But despite these assurances the same scenes as three years earlier unfolded on June 12, 1948: the Moslem gangs poured through the hara of Tripoli killing young and old, women and children, hacking to pieces the bodies of their victims. The Jews, prepared this time for such a contingency, fought back bravely; it took the British three hours to restore order. The next day fresh disorders broke out as the excited mobs were once more egged on to pillage and murder.

The 1948 massacres severely undermined the confidence and security of the Libyan community, which at the time comprised thirty-five thousand Jews, five thousand in Cyrenaica, some eight thousand in small communities in the interior of the country[40] and the rest in the hara of Tripoli, one of the most vibrant centers of Jewish life in the entire Maghreb. Two thousand young Jews stole away from the Libyan shore in sailing boats during the following year. Following the United Nations decision of 1949, according to which a united Libya was to become independent by 1952, the mass exodus of Jews began, this time with official approval. By September 1951, nearly 27,000 Libyan Jews had settled in Israel. By the time Libya gained its independence on January 1, 1952, only a few hundred Jews still remained in Tripoli, the majority of them holders of foreign nationalities.[41] Elsewhere, in Cyrenaica and the interior of Tripolitania, the Jewish quarters were entirely deserted, the synagogues locked and abandoned: a history of more than two thousand years of Jewish settlement had come to an end.

The events at Oujda and Djérada in Morocco were not followed by such an extreme reaction. That year, however, marked the beginning of mass emigration of North African Jews to Israel. Those who remained behind continued to suffer the contradictions which are the lot of the Jew living in the Diaspora, aggravated by the special conditions of life in a Moslem country. The Moroccan fight for independence was followed by policies which deeply affected the tranquillity of the Jewish community and eventually caused an ever-growing wave of Jews to follow in the steps of those who had gone before them in 1948, to settle in the land of their forefathers.

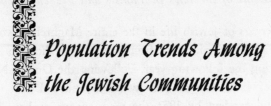

11

Population Trends Among the Jewish Communities

Definition of the North African Jew

The Jews of North Africa could not be defined as a racial entity but rather as a community bound together by religion, culture, history and tradition. The successive waves of conquerors and colonizers from all parts of the Mediterranean basin and beyond obliterated and intermingled all separate racial traits among the inhabitants of the region, Jews as well as Moslems and Berbers. To the original Semitic strains of Israelites and Phoenicians were added considerable numbers of Berber converts to Judaism; the later influx of Jews from Spain and Italy introduced European racial strains into the Jewish community. Thus, while the Jews of North Africa were predominantly dark-haired and dark-eyed, blue eyes and blond or red hair were not at all uncommon; on the other hand, a casual observer would have been hard put to it to distinguish, by facial features alone, a group of Jewish children in North Africa from a group of Moslems or even Christians.

In the absence of physical or documentary criteria for determining the racial antecedents of the Jews of North Africa, it has been necessary to fall back on family names. A survey, conducted in 1936 by the late Chief Rabbi of Algiers, Maurice Eisenbeth, which was based on 4,063 Jewish family names in

North Africa and traced back to 1,146 name origins, showed that over 10 per cent of the names were of Hebrew or Aramaic origin, nearly half of Arabic or Berber origin, just under 20 per cent of romance origin, 3.5 per cent of Teutonic origin and the rest of indeterminate origin.[1] The high proportion of Arabic and Berber names suggests a preponderance of Berber and Arab converts to Judaism among the Jewish population, a hypothesis reinforced by the fact that the Berber surnames are generally traceable to tribal and geographic appellations.

Despite the diversity of racial factors and the absence of anthropological characteristics, the Jews of North Africa retained a distinct and tangible ethos that may well have been based on the collective experiences of twelve centuries of oppression and cultural isolation under Moslem rule. The semi-Oriental milieu of the Moslem period imposed on the Jews a language, a mode of dress and a place of residence that largely influenced their way of life and patterns of behavior. These exterior influences were so marked that outsiders would claim to be able to recognize a Jew simply by his deportment.

The definition of "Jew" in North Africa must thus fall back on allegiance to Jewish faith and traditions, for it was that which determined, throughout the centuries, the fact that a person was a Jew; once a person had broken all religious, cultural and traditional ties with Judaism he was in all respects lost to the Jewish community. A sizable portion of North African Jewry thus disappeared during the centuries of Moslem rule by conversion to Islam. Once adopted into their new faith and its ways, they gradually lost all traces of their former Jewishness. (In Fez, however, where the number of Jewish apostates—especially in the sixteenth century—was considerable, their descendants still retained a number of distinguishing characteristics.) The sense of belonging to the community was preserved among the Jews of North Africa with great vigor, reinforced both by a common faith and by shared oppression and suffering. Jewishness, as defined through allegiance to the Jewish community, makes it easier to delineate a demographic study of the Jews of the Maghreb.

The North African Communities and World Jewry

In regard to Morocco and Tunisia, separate statistics are by-and-large available for the Jews; in Algeria, where the Jews were officially integrated into the French community, there were no separate listings of Jews in later decades. As an official publication of 1934 pointed out,[2] the only factor that set Jews apart from other Frenchmen in Algeria was their religion and their history, and to have listed them separately would have been resented by the Jews. Through the painstaking efforts of Chief Rabbi Maurice Eisenbeth, who scrutinized the lists of inhabitants of all Algerian localities on the basis of the census of 1931, a practically complete and precise record of all Jews in Algeria was nevertheless obtained and this fortunately made possible the future determination of statistics on the Jewish community. Statistics are particularly liable to error in countries such as those of the Maghreb. At best one may draw on all available sources in order to determine, with careful reservations, certain group characteristics and to make certain valuable comparisons.

According to the Palestinian sociologist, Arthur Ruppin,[3] there were 130,000 Jews in Algeria, 70,000 in Tunisia and 175,000 Jews in French Morocco in 1927. They formed, at the time, 30 per cent of all Jews living in Moslem countries including Palestine and 2.25 per cent of Jews throughout the world. The upheaval of the Second World War, the murder of six million Jews, and the creation of the State of Israel changed the ratio considerably during the next decade and a half. By 1951 the number of Jews throughout the world was estimated, according to the *American Jewish Year Book* of that year, at close to eleven and a half million.[4] The Jewish population of Algeria was then estimated at 140,000,[5] that of Tunisia at 105,000[6] and that of Morocco at 255,000[7]—making a total of half a million at a time when Israel's Jewish population was one and a quarter million. The Jews in North Africa thus made up 4.35 per cent of the world Jewish population—nearly twice their pre-war proportion—and they represented no less than 60 per cent of all Jews then living in Moslem countries. They formed the fourth largest Jewish community in the world after the United States, Soviet Russia and Israel, and were well ahead of the communities in Great Britain, Argentina, Rumania and France.

Important as their proportion was in world Jewry, the Jews of North Africa formed only a very small minority of the populations in their respective countries: 1.75 per cent in Algeria, 3.23 per cent in Tunisia and 2.5 per cent in Morocco. Their importance was quite out of proportion to their relatively small numbers because of the role they played as intermediaries between the French colonizers and the local Moslem population. Where the proportion of the French element in the population was highest, the proportion of Jews to "Europeans" was lowest. In Algeria the Jews constituted 12.7 per cent of Europeans, in Tunisia 31.8 per cent, and in Morocco a hefty 70 per cent.[8] When studying this period, it is essential to bear in mind the social upheavals in the Maghreb at the time which were caused by the interaction of the ever more powerful élite formed by the European minority, whose size and importance varied as a direct function of the length of French domination, and the underprivileged masses. The Jews were caught between the two.

ALGERIA

Population Increase. The Jewish population in Algeria was numerically midway between that of Tunisia and Morocco and proportionally smaller than either. The hundred and twenty years of French supremacy in Algeria and the eighty years of political emancipation and integration into the French populace which Algerian Jewry enjoyed placed them in a more favorable position than the communities of the neighboring countries.

Early figures for the size of the Jewish community in Algeria are fragmentary. The first useful estimate was a census taken in areas under French rule in 1851 which gave the total number of Jews as 21,000. After that, growth was steady and phenomenal, and by 1921 the Jewish population had reached 74,000. Statistical details of the population growth during this period can be found in Appendix II. The 1931 census, for which the number of Jews was meticulously extracted from the rolls throughout the country by Chief Rabbi Maurice Eisenbeth, gave the figure of 110,127, an increase of nearly 50 per cent[9] over ten years. The figures obtained by Chief Rabbi Eisenbeth, and cross-checked with the local Jewish communities in each doubtful case, are probably the most accurate ever obtained for the Jewish population in Algeria. In 1941 after the Crémieux Decree had been abrogated under the Vichy regime and the Jews of Algeria deprived of their French nationality, a new census of the Jews was ordered by the authorities, to be coupled with a forced declaration of property and capital. Despite the special circumstances in which the census was taken, it may be assumed that the majority of the Jews complied with the order. The total then given was 117,646.

The increase of only about 7,500 over ten years[10] is extremely low in comparison with that of the previous century. However, it should not be assumed that considerable numbers of Jews simply refused to be listed as such, for the atmosphere of terror and the warnings of serious penalties for misstatements were such that few would have dared to "cheat." The Jews were still blissfully unaware of the infamous purposes to which the Nazis could have put the listings of all Jews in the country. Other factors account for the sudden drop in the rate of increase. These were the economic depression that followed thirteen years of boom conditions, the uncertainties about the future engendered by the increasing vehemence of Nazi propaganda, the increasing Westernization of the Jews of Algeria that was reflected in a falling birthrate among its most assimilated sections and, finally, an ever-growing rate of emigration to France. Figures for Constantine, generally regarded as the most "traditional" of the large Jewish communities, show the trend most clearly. In 1931, 33 per cent of families with children had either one or two children, 47 per cent had three, four or five, 20 per cent had six or more; the comparable figures for 1941[11] were 40 per cent, 40 per cent and 20 per cent. Despite these tendencies, the Jewish population remained predominantly young, 30 per cent being under fifteen years old. The statistics thus reveal the stability of the Jewish family unit and the high birth rate which maintained it at close to the minimum of three infants per family prescribed by the Talmud.[12]

From 1830 to 1931, the Jewish population of Algeria had increased well over fivefold. Thereafter it remained fairly stable, largely due to assimilation to European social habits. The limited rate of increase shown in later surveys does not tell the full story, for a significant number of Jews had migrated to Algeria from Morocco and Tunisia.

Geographical Distribution. The Jews were spread throughout Algeria, though the greatest concentration was in the north. In 1936 they were to be found in 257 separate towns and villages; five years later in 237, excluding the sixteen oases in the southern territories. It was the drift to Algiers that brought about the abandonment of thirty centers in the departments of Oran and Constantine and the establishment of ten new ones in the department of Algiers. In 1931, some 51,000 Jews were living in the department of Oran where the influx from Morocco was most marked, 34,000 in the department of Algiers, 25,000 in Constantine, and some 4,300 in the south.

Like the Europeans, the Jews tended toward the urban areas, and three-quarters of the total Jewish population lived in the eleven largest towns. By this time, Oran and Algiers each had some 26,000 Jews, Constantine half that and Tlemcen 4,000, Sidi-bel-Abbès, Sétif and Mascara had between 2,000 and 3,000 each. There were smaller communities in another thirty-seven towns and centers. These figures are indicative of the search for communal security that could be found only in the larger communities. From 1881 when the first reliable statistics became available, until 1931 when the counting of the population by community was stopped, the growth of the Jewish population in the three main cities paralleled that of the Moslem and European communities, though, as can be seen in the statistical analysis in Appendix III, the rate of increase was greater where the European element predominated. By 1941, the Jewish population in Oran, Algiers and Constantine was over three times larger than it had been a century earlier.

But the Jews were not drawn exclusively to the settled life of the great cities: the Jews of Miliana, ideally and comfortably situated in every respect, were willing to leave their community to settle in the plains where they contributed significantly to the agricultural and economic development of the newer towns of Affreville, Duperré, Orléansville, Les Attafs, Rouina and Oued-Fodda. The Jews of Tlemcen and Constantine were also factors in the growth of other newer towns to which they migrated. In general the growth or decline of the Jewish population in any town was a reflection of the economic life there for the Jews lived almost exclusively by commerce. In the town of Tiaret, for instance, a growing city situated where the fertile north bordered on the arid south, the Jewish population grew from about 100 in 1921 to 3,000 in 1931. It then dropped abruptly, following a disastrous slump in the cereal trade, and reached some 1,500 in 1941. Part of this fluctuation may however be attributed to the patterns of migration of Jews from the Sahara regions who tended to settle in towns like Tiaret before moving further north.

Despite the national and civic discrimination which was practiced for so long against the Jews of the south, especially in the M'zab region,[13] the Jewish communities there also increased greatly. In 1931, according to Rabbi Eisenbeth, they totalled 3,650, living in twenty-three towns and villages. The most important center was Ghardaia, capital of the M'zab, where the Jewish community numbered 1,361 souls. At the last census in 1941, the distribution of the Jews in the south had changed considerably owing to the economic development of the region through the exploitation of its mineral deposits. The number of Jews in Colomb-Béchar rose from 186 to 1,936, in Djelfa from 168 to 848, and increased markedly in other centers. The Jewish population of this region was largely itinerant. The bread-winners—peddlers, jewellers, shoemakers, butchers and tinsmiths—travelled to the surrounding oases or even to the towns of the north to make their living, adopting the nomadic heritage of the people among whom they lived. Thus the full Jewish population was to be found in these areas only during the spring Passover festival and the Jewish High Holidays in the autumn.

Remarkably, almost no Jews were to be found in the Berber speaking regions of Algeria, where there were altogether scarcely 3,000 Jews. This phenomenon was traceable to historic factors that had led to the concentration of Jews in coastal centers far from the Kabyle mountains. There was also a powerful economic consideration stemming from the fact that the Jews and the Berbers generally competed in the same trades. There was certainly no inherent antipathy between the communities, for in neighboring Morocco they lived together in close harmony.

TUNISIA[14]

Population Growth. In 1921, when the Jews were first counted separately in the census, their precise number was fixed at 48,436. In the next twenty-five years, the population grew by almost 50 per cent, to reach 70,000. This figure included only Jews of Tunisian nationality. If to them are added the 32,000 of French nationality, the Jewish community is seen to have made up over 3 per cent of the entire population, a proportion that was considerably higher than that in Algeria (1.75 per cent) or Morocco (2.5 per cent). Details of the expansion of the population can be found in Appendix IV, Table I. Table II shows the number of births and deaths registered in the community between 1914 and 1945.

With the rise in the rate of natural increase which took place over the next five years due to improved physical and sanitary conditions, and taking into account the Jews who were listed in the census under their European nationalities, the Jewish community was calculated in 1951 at 105,000 souls—a doubling of its number in thirty years. It was estimated that in 1951 the Jews constituted nearly one-third of the non-Moslem population which was midway between the 12.7 per cent they made up in Algeria and the 70 per cent in Morocco.

Birth and Mortality Rates. The birthrate among Tunisian Jews was the highest of any ethnic group in the Regency. Between 1919 and 1938 the average annual birthrate was 335 per 10,000 population and was well over that of the Moslem and European populations, as the figures given in Appendix V, Table I, clearly show. However, by 1938 the birthrate in all groups had fallen due to the influence of Western ideas, and tended to equality around the 290–300 per 10,000 mark. By way of comparison, it is interesting to note that the birthrate in North America and Western Europe is 170 per 10,000.

Mortality rates showed a similar trend during the same period. That of the Jews was considerably higher than among the other groups during the first decade (an average of 200 per 10,000 for the Jews compared with 170 for the Moslems and 160 for the Europeans). By 1938 it had dropped to 166 which was lower than the Moslem 170 but had still not fallen to the European level of 141. In North America and Western Europe the comparable figure is 110. Appendix V, Table II, gives details of the mortality rates in the different ethnic groups.

The war years had a devastating effect on the Tunisian Jewish community. Food shortages, anti-Jewish measures and, following the Allied landings in 1942 when the Germans applied even more discriminatory measures, economic sanctions, forced labor and confinement in concentration camps—all were reflected in the community's decreased birthrates and rising deathrates as detailed in Appendix V, Table III. By 1945 the situation was again normal with almost 1,350 births and less than 600 deaths registered. Infant deathrates per 1,000 live births are equally revealing for the war years as Appendix V, Table IV, shows. In 1943, the rate among the Jews reached over 260—more than double that of previous years, and for the first time higher than the rate registered in the Moslem community. In normal years, the number of infant deaths per 1,000 live births was a good third lower than that among the Moslems and slightly higher than among the Europeans. The sharp drop in infant mortality among the Jews during the post-war period was due to improved living conditions and to the introduction of European standards of hygiene. Whereas the average annual excess of live births over deaths per 10,000 between 1929 and 1938 was 144, it rose to 221 during the period 1945–1947. This was intermediate between the figure of 299 for the Moslems and 128 for the Europeans.

Geographical Distribution. The distribution of the Tunisian Jewish population followed a unique pattern. In the north, the Jews lived in the urban agglomerations where Europeans were to be found in large numbers. Out of the total Jewish population, 61 per cent (65,000) lived in Tunis and its surroundings. A similar proportion of the European population was likewise concentrated in Tunis. Other important centers of Jewish population in the north were Sousse with a community of 6,400 and Sfax with just on 5,700. Nabeul, Bizerta and Grombalia each had around 2,500 Jews. In all of these towns there were large concentrations of Europeans.

In the south the pattern was reversed. The Jews dwelt in the towns that they had traditionally inhabited for some two thousand years and where they continued to lead a way of life that had changed little since the Middle Ages. There were almost 4,500 Jews on the island of Djerba where there were only 600

Europeans; nearly 4,000 in Gabès whose European community numbered 17; 2,000 in Ben-Ghardane and 1,000 in Gafsa. Altogether there were twenty-six major Jewish communities throughout Tunisia, but in addition to these there were some seventy localities where nearly 4,000 Jews lived in virtual isolation in groups of no more than family size. After the end of the Second World War, the tendency was for the Jews to escape their isolation by moving into the larger communities where they felt more secure.

An analysis of the official census figures (for details see Appendix VI) which included only Jews of Tunisian nationality reveals that nearly 45 per cent of Tunisian Jews were under 20 years of age. The comparable figure for the Moslems was 50 per cent and for the Europeans (including Jews of French nationality) 30 per cent. Just over 7 per cent of Jews were over 60—more than the 6 per cent for Moslems but less than the 9 per cent for Europeans. These and the other demographic patterns were a reflection of all aspects of Tunisian Jewry's existence in which they held a position between the Moslems and the Europeans. Having formerly led a way of life that was not very different from that of the Moslem population, they began, with the advent of the French, to adapt themselves to European ways, and the figures quoted in this section are a measure of the extent to which they approached European standards.

MOROCCO

Accurate statistics for Morocco are hard to come by. The French did not arrive till 1912, and the population surveys they made in 1921, 1926 and 1931 were incomplete because of the civil unrest which still prevailed in certain areas. The 1936 survey applied to the whole country but, like earlier ones, was based on figures furnished by local authorities who fulfilled their task with varying degrees of precision. Only the 1947 census, based on the scientific interpretation of the information collected for the purposes of food rationing by the Food Department,[15] can be regarded as reasonably reliable. It is thus extremely difficult to get an idea of the growth of the Jewish population in Morocco.

Estimates of the Jewish Population. Charles de Foucauld[16] estimated the Jewish population of Morocco in 1883 at about 7,200 families. They were scattered throughout the country, though the larger concentrations were in the ports and large towns of the Bled Makhzen, in the Grand Atlas and along the water courses draining its southern slopes westward to the sea. There were few Jews in the eastern region. The distribution of the Jews throughout Morocco had changed little since the sixteenth century[17] and it remained basically unaltered well into the twentieth. However, as the following paragraphs will show, there was a tendency in the later years, before the mass exodus of the Jews from Morocco, to move from rural to urban concentrations, from smaller mellahs to larger ones and from the Oriental south to the European north.

The only accurate statistics available are those of 1947, and according to them the Jewish population was 203,800—2.3 per cent[18] of the total and 38.5 per cent of the non-Moslem population. The rate of natural increase was calculated as 2.1 per cent annually, an indication of the tremendous vitality of Moroccan Jewry when compared with the United Nations worldwide average figure of 1–1.1 per cent.

Population Distribution. The 1947 census showed that the Jews were well distributed in 112 communities throughout the seven administrative regions of Morocco. One-third of the total Jewish population was concentrated in Casablanca, a quarter in Marrakesh, and a third was divided almost equally between Fez, Meknès and Rabat. The rest were in Oujda and Agadir. As in Algeria and Tunisia, some 80 per cent of the Moroccan Jewish community were city-dwellers.

CASABLANCA REGION

Between 1945 and 1949, the population of the city of Casablanca itself increased by a hefty 25 per cent to reach 63,000.[19] While a third of this growth can be attributed to natural increase, the remainder was due to the influx from the towns of the interior—Marrakesh, Mogador, Safi, Demnat and others—of men seeking a livelihood. It is interesting to note that in Casablanca males outnumbered females in the ratio of 7:6, the men having left their wives and daughters behind when going in search of work. This general movement of Jews from the country towns to the large cities provided the latter with their small traders, artisans and clerks. From the smaller communities in the south, particularly from the Tafilalt region, came a different type of Jew which formed the most impoverished part of the dank, overcrowded mellahs in the cities. By 1951, the total Jewish population of Casablanca was around 80,000. There were twelve other communities in the Casablanca region, the largest of which were Beni Mellal and Mazagan, each with some 3,000 inhabitants.

MARRAKESH REGION

In this region there was the greatest concentration of Jews after Casablanca, where the community was of comparatively more recent creation.[20] Its 50,300 Jews lived in twenty-four communities and the predominance of women in the population, particularly in Marrakesh itself, revealed the tendency among the men to leave the region to seek a living elsewhere. There were over

18,000 Jews in Marrakesh itself, the next largest community of 5,000 being in Mogador. There were between 2,000 and 4,000 Jews in each of another nine towns, including Safi and Demnat, and the rest were widely scattered around the more important centers. Life here was intense; this was Berber country which enjoyed the great vitality of the south.

FEZ REGION

Here too there was a tendency for the migration of men away from the region. In 1947 there were twenty major Jewish communities with the largest at Fez itself which counted 14,140 souls,[21] two-thirds of the total for the region. There were nearly 2,300 Jews in Taza, and the rest were dispersed in other centers.

MEKNÈS REGION

With its 22,200 Jews in a score of communities, this was also a region from which men tended to migrate. However, in Meknès itself, where the Jewish population was 13,670, the sexes were well balanced. Other communities of between 1,000 to 2,000 souls were Erfoud, Ksar-es-Souk which formed the gateway to the south, and Midelt. The immense Tafilalt area, which had only 6,500 Jews in 1947, was the source of much of the migration to northern Morocco and Algeria. The ratio of women to men there, 5:4, is an eloquent indication of the migratory tendencies away from this area.

RABAT REGION

Jews had been living here for a very long period, and it was a center of attraction for migrants from the south and the interior, second only to Casablanca further down the coast. The sexes were more balanced, however, men outnumbering women only slightly. Rabat itself, administrative capital of Morocco and seat of the Central Council of Jewish Communities, had a population of about 11,800. Jews in this region were essentially town dwellers; there were only ten Jewish communities here, only four of which were of any consequence: Salé, Ouezzane, Port Lyautey and Mechra bel Ksiri.

OUJDA REGION

This easternmost area, bordering on Algeria, had only 6,884 Jews in a dozen communities, of which Oujda (3,000), Debdou[22] and Touarirt (1,000 each) were the largest. There were four more communities of over a hundred Jews each.

AGADIR REGION

This newly developed area had 4,850 Jews[23] in a dozen main centers. The oldest of these was Taroudant where nearly 2,000 Jews were crowded together in a mellah of frightening misery. In Agadir itself there were 1,100 Jews.

SPANISH MOROCCO AND THE INTERNATIONAL ZONE OF TANGIERS

The 1947 statistics applied only to the Jews living in what was then French Morocco. There were another 25,000 living in Spanish Morocco and the International Zone of Tangiers. In these two areas the Jews constituted 7 per cent of the total population. The largest concentration was in Tangiers where 10,000 Jews, holders of Moroccan, French, Spanish and other nationalities, lived. The next largest community of over 7,500 souls was in Tetuan, while Larache and Alcazarquivir each had some 2,200 Jews. The rest were scattered in twelve other towns in Spanish Morocco and in rural areas in the Riff mountains and the Quert territory.

Age Structure.[24] The age structure of the Jewish community of Morocco was very similar to that of the Tunisian community: one-third of the Jews in the 1947 survey were under fifteen, 8.0 per cent were over sixty. In the Moslem community, the figures were 42.7 per cent and 5.9 per cent respectively.

Among both Jews and Moslems there was a particularly high proportion of young people, caused principally by an exceptionally high birth rate coupled with a similarly high mortality rate, typical of backward and underdeveloped societies. However, the so-called age-pyramid among the Jews showed a healthier distribution than among the Moslems, indicative of a lower birthrate and of a much lower mortality rate.

The average Jewish family in Morocco counted five members. Allowing for young families, for the many that broke up early through death, desertion or divorce while the wife was still in her prime, it is clear that six children per family was normal, ten or twelve not exceptional. Overcrowding, hunger, misery and unemployment were no deterrent. The arrival of a new mouth to feed was not regarded as a calamity. On the contrary, it was the infant itself that was the bearer of a hope that in its generation at least, conditions would improve. Each new-born child was an expression of faith, a reflection of the dynamism in the soul of the Moroccan Jew.

French Influences on the North African Communities

Wherever the Jews lived in North Africa they formed a very small percentage of the population. They had survived as a separate entity only by virtue of their internal cohesion, their faith and their traditions and by the outside pressure of discrimination and persecution that had reinforced their will to retain their identity, even at the price of martyrdom. The liberating influence of the French presence eased this external pressure and gradually allowed the demographic and social structure of the Jews to change and approach those of the European colonizers. It was a change that became gradually apparent in habits, in clothing, in housing, in occupations, in culture and ways of thought.

Inevitably, as the following chapters will show, the assimilation to the powerful and enlightened European culture gave rise to mixed marriages between Jews and Christians. (Cases of Jews and Moslems marrying were rare.) In Algeria, the most "integrated" of Jewish communities, there were just over 2,000 mixed marriages on record in 1941.[25] Over half the couples lived in the department of Algiers, the most "Europeanized." Of the remainder, 650 lived in the department of Oran and 280 in the most traditional region of Constantine. In Tunisia, 850 mixed marriages were registered between 1939 and 1945. This intermarriage was a recent phenomenon: from 1830 to 1877 only 17 unions between Jews and Christians were recorded and 124 from 1884 to 1896.

From all the statistics that have been presented and interpreted in this chapter, one fact stands out clearly, as it does whenever the three main communities of North Africa are compared: the Jews were everywhere in a position midway between the Europeans and the Moslems. The Moslems, vastly greater in number, offered more solid resistance to the new ideas; the Jews, on the other hand, embraced them warmly, and absorbed them with remarkable speed and enthusiasm.

12

Facing West

The French administration in North Africa set up a new ethos of power, wealth and prestige alongside the two separate but hitherto complementary worlds of the Moslem medina and the Jewish mellah. Perhaps the most outstanding characteristic that North African Jewry acquired as a result of the French presence was its position at the meeting point of the traditional, culturally underdeveloped Moslem world on the one hand, and the highly developed modern civilization of the West represented by France, on the other. The Jews, out of their ardent desire for progress, were the first to be drawn to the European way of life. The spirit of the new civilization reached into the depths of the furthest mellah, giving rise to hopes, doubts and aspirations. Eventually, initial hesitations would be resolved and the first tentative step taken toward the new world that France had opened up. Once the knowledge of French had been acquired, new patterns of speech and thought opened up, which in turn rapidly led to new customs, new interests, new attitudes, new manners, new values and, finally, to a new society.

The traditional social framework of the Jewish community tended to lose ground in the face of the new culture with its frequently contradictory ideas. The closed society of the mellah began to open up through the contact with French influences and, for the first time, the Jews were able to leave its physical and spiritual confines without arousing its wrath. The presence of the French gave the Jews a chance to become acquainted with the modern world, to learn from and adapt to it, and to find those who would guide and help them to put to good purpose the exceptional faculty for adaptation which characterized the Jews in all the ghettos of their dispersion.

The French administration, grafted onto the existing realities of the Maghreb, made possible and encouraged the accelerated integration and assimilation of North African Jewry, a process that gathered momentum as French influence became more deeply entrenched. As the colonial society became wealthier and better organized, offering increasing opportunities for the education of wider sections of the native population, so did the integration of the Jews into French society, culture and economic life become more rapid. By the eve of the Maghreb's independence from France, the process had become a large-scale flight from the material, and frequently spiritual, poverty of the mellah.

The degree of advancement which the Jews attained was not uniform throughout the Maghreb, being greater where French influence had been deepest and most prolonged. Thus, while the Jews of the northern departments of Algeria had reached a standard of living which approximated that of the European element in the population, those of the southern territories had hardly progressed from the position they had held in Moslem society. Southern Tunisia was likewise more backward than the north of that country. In Morocco, emancipation came much later than in Algeria or Tunisia, and though it proceeded more rapidly, conditions there were decidedly worse than in the rest of the Maghreb.

Inevitably, the new society and the powerful drive for emancipation brought with it new problems. The weaker elements in the population who, under the old order, had managed to eke out a precarious existence, were quickly dragged down to utter destitution in the face of competition from the newer forces. The influx of Jews from the south in search of economic and social betterment swelled the mass of the miserable urban proletariat which itself had not succeeded in escaping from the mellah, and made living and sanitary conditions even more pestilential than they already were. There were attendant social evils, the result of abject poverty and degradation. And there was the alienation from Judaism and its traditional values. The following chapters will describe the degree to which the cultural and economic life of the Jews evolved toward Western standards, and the social and spiritual maladjustments which were the product of the sudden confrontation of two eras.

Education

Modern secular education played a decisive role in the mass evolution of North African Jewry. It was in the new schools that succeeding generations assimilated the ideas and customs that France had introduced and there that they learned French, their passport to a new civilization. As was pointed out in Chapter Eight, the rabbis had maintained a monopoly of Jewish education until the arrival of the French, yet strangely enough, they put up little resistance to the new requirements of secular instruction. From the outset, the French government (in the case of Algeria) and the major French Jewish organizations undertook the task of facilitating the rapid transition of the native population from their mediaeval way of life to nineteenth and twentieth century conditions. "By working on the young generation one may regenerate the Jewish people," wrote Claude Martin, a leader of French Jewry, in 1840.[1]

ALGERIA

The first special school for Jewish boys under the directorship of a French Jew was opened in Algiers in 1832 as the result of the efforts of the Jewish organizations in France led by the consistoire. Shortly afterward a girls' school was opened. The number of pupils at the schools rose from forty in 1832 to one hundred and forty in 1840. At this point a certain opposition on the part of the rabbis, who saw themselves about to be deprived of their prestige and part of their meager income, led to a sharp drop in the number of pupils.

The French Government then set up a Study Commission headed by the orientalist Albert Cahen, to investigate the reform of education. The findings of this commission resulted in the ordinance of Saint-Cloud of 1845—a major event in the evolution of Algeria's Jews. The law stipulated that all education for Algerian Jews was to be taken over by the state, guarantee being given that Jewish children would be assured of their religious instruction. In return for certain concessions, the rabbis undertook not to accept in their schools any pupils who did not also regularly attend the state-operated schools. This was the beginning of the integrated education of Algeria's Jews.

By 1858, 1,700 Jewish children, boys and girls, were attending the new schools. It is indeed remarkable that in this quasi-Oriental milieu, no opposition was raised to the education of girls who had till then been deprived of any sort of instruction. In 1860 a Jewish girl carried off second place in the final schoolteachers' examination, and in the same year a group of young Algerian Jewesses performed Racine's Esther.

The evolution among the men was even more rapid. "With some imponderable exceptions that have their importance, the Jew in Algeria has become indistinguishable from the Chris-

tian," wrote Émile Félix Gauthier in 1937.[2] "It requires an
effort to recall that he too is a Maghrebian, as deeply rooted in
its soil as the others. . . . For fifteen centuries it has been shown
that the Jews have been in the Maghreb and it has not been
proved that they ever came there from somewhere else. They
were not strangers; they simply represented minds that had been
trained and selected from among the minds of the Maghreb." In
1860 a young Jew whose father was illiterate in French was
awarded the first prize in Oran for rhetoric and Latin verse; the
second prize was also taken by a Jew. An increasing number of
Jewish children completed their primary and secondary education and, from 1861, took their baccalauréat and went on to
obtain their higher education, preferably in France, source of
the new culture.

As from 1870, when they were granted French citizenship,
the Jews were educated in the French state schools and from
then on their cultural evolution was rapid. By 1941 when the
Vichy laws against the Jews were introduced, there were just
over 19,000 Jews of whom nearly half were girls in the primary
and middle school system in Algeria. Nearly half of them were
in the department of Oran, the remainder being divided almost
equally between the departments of Constantine and Algiers.
The Jews made up an average of 7 per cent of the total primary
school attendance in Algeria. Among those receiving secondary
education, the 1,400 Jews made up 13 per cent of the total.
More than a third of them were girls, a remarkable indication of
the degree of their emancipation. The proportion of Jewish students at the universities was even higher—37 per cent at the
Faculty of Medicine, 26 per cent at the Faculty of Law, 17 per
cent in Pharmacy and the Sciences and 10 per cent in the Hu-
manities. The figures for 1941 were unusually high because they
included students who but for the war would have been studying

in France. Nevertheless, they indicate the large number of Algerian Jews who embarked on a university training, mostly in the free professions. (In the technical colleges, there were only 66 Jewish students.) It is interesting to note that the proportion of Jews increased from the primary schools, through the high schools to the universities where it was greatest.[3]

The secular nature of French education was inevitably accompanied by a strong tendency toward assimilation and a loss of Jewish identity. The fact that Jewish religious education at the end of the nineteenth century was still given according to the old methods did nothing to counteract this process. In the words of A. Confino, a delegate in Algeria of the Alliance Israélite Universelle who tried from 1912 to reform the system of Jewish education in Algeria: "Till then the Jewish children had been gathering under the thumbs of old-fashioned rabbis who satisfied themselves with teaching them the rudiments of reading Hebrew and chanting the Torah—nothing else. Neither grammar nor translation nor Jewish history nor real religious instruction." The last phrases outline the type of reform that the Alliance tried to introduce in the schools it set up in Algiers, Constantine and Oran and which it continued to operate till 1940. But despite the courageous and enlightened efforts of the consistoires, the process of assimilation and loss of Jewish values continued, a problem which arose wherever the Jews burst free from their ghettos. In the process of turning away from a discredited past the infant was often thrown away with the bathwater. While enough of tradition was preserved to fill the synagogues on the High Festivals, religious life for the younger generation seemed to be cut off from its sources. In Algiers only five hundred young students attended the Talmud Torah in 1951 out of a Jewish population of thirty thousand; only 165 boys celebrated their *Bar Mitzvahs* that year. To cope with this situation the Jewish communities in Algeria sent some of their students to France for rabbinical studies but unfortunately, attracted by the advantages offered by France, none of them returned to their homeland. For this reason the Federation of Jewish Communities in Algeria set up a rabbinical school in Algiers in 1949 but it closed before it had time to have any effect.

Despite the French success in wiping out illiteracy among most of the Jews of Algeria in less than a century, isolated pockets remained in the south of the country. In Ghardaia, especially, a large proportion of Jewish youth was deprived of education because of a lack of buildings. The community disappeared in 1962 before the situation could ever be rectified.

TUNISIA

In Tunisia—as also in Morocco, but unlike Algeria—private agencies and not governmental bodies were behind the schools that sparked the emancipation of the Jewish masses. Before the creation of the Alliance Israélite Universelle in 1860, the first French school open to Jews in Tunisia had been started by a Christian, the Abbé Bourgade. Following this some of the Catholic teaching orders and English Protestant missionaries opened schools in the hara, some of which existed till recently. (In Algeria, too, Christian missions had opened schools which admitted Christians and Jews indiscriminately and which were frequented by the children of prominent Jews.) This initiative helped to create an air of amity between Christians and Jews which persisted despite the strains of political turmoil. In the Maghreb there were no memories of Christian persecution to affect these relations, and the Jew of the Maghreb was therefore more receptive to the new influences from Christian Europe.

The new era in education really opened in 1878 when the Alliance Israélite Universelle opened its first school in Tunis. Times had changed since 1832 when the first modern school for Jewish youth had opened in Algeria, and the Algerian example had its effect on the Jews of Tunisia who had at all times been more exposed to modern influences. Within its first year, the school had 1,025 pupils. Four years later a school for girls was added in Tunis. The movement spread rapidly in answer to the demands of a population avid for education. In 1883 schools were opened in Beja, Mahdia and Sousse; that in Sfax was not opened till 1905. Because of a certain resistance on the part of the Jews of southern Tunisia, especially in Gabès and Djerba, the schools did not spread further; instead the Alliance developed and broadened its educational network in Tunis, Sousse and Sfax. A trade apprentice school was opened for boys in Tunis in 1881 and one for girls in 1895. In 1901 an agricultural school was opened in Djédeida.[4]

The establishment of the Protectorate in 1882 further accelerated the pace of emancipation for the Jews. In 1883 they were given the right to attend the public schools of the Protectorate, and in 1889 the government started subsidizing the work of the Alliance Israélite Universelle. The combined efforts of the government and the Alliance showed rapid results in the education of Tunisian Jews: in 1915, just under 9,000 Jewish children attended schools; in 1945, their number had reached 14,000. At all times the number of girl pupils was equal to that of boys. In 1951, two-thirds of the Jewish school children attended French primary schools which included the schools of the Alliance; over 1,000 attended secondary schools and 105 were receiving a university education. These figures do not include those who went to France or Algeria for higher education. There were in addition some 1,350 Jewish pupils in Franco-

Arab primary schools, private primary schools, private and government trade schools and in private establishments for higher education. In 1946, as the result of an agreement between the State and the Alliance, a further agreement between the Alliance and the Organization for Technical Rehabilitation (O.R.T.) was signed in 1950, according to which two new schools for teaching manual skills to Jewish youths were opened.

But despite the great achievements, the haras still swarmed with ragged children who did not enjoy the benefit of a modern education. Their number was estimated at four thousand, of whom the majority lived in Djerba, Gabès and other towns of the south.

Jewish education, as such, was more widespread in Tunisia than in Algeria. This was due partly to the political structure which gave less scope for French influence, partly to the existence of the Alliance network of schools which had well over 3,000 pupils in 1954, and partly to the lesser degree of emancipation granted to the Jews. The fact that the legal jurisdiction of the rabbis was maintained helped to preserve the attachment of Tunisian Jewry to its religious traditions. Nevertheless, and despite a number of adequately trained teachers, Hebrew education still left much to be desired. The *kutab* dispensed its traditional lessons, depending more on memory than on the child's intelligence, without having advanced much beyond the earlier system. Grammar or history were rarely taught and religious instruction, as such, usually took the form of a weekly sermon (*drash*) by the rabbi which was beyond the children's comprehension. They were, moreover, confused by the gulf between the lessons learned in their modern elementary school and the preaching of the rabbi in Judeo-Arabic. Less so than in Algeria, the sudden awakening of the old society into the modern world, the conflict between the beliefs of the hara and of the world around, gave rise to attendant problems and tensions.

MOROCCO

As in Tunisia, the start of modern schooling for the Jews of Morocco was a privately initiated affair. In December 1862, fifty years before the establishment of the French Protectorate, the Alliance Israélite Universelle opened its first school in Tétuan. One hundred and ten pupils were accepted for the first year and two hundred had to be turned away for lack of room and teachers. The influence of neighboring Algeria, where Jews had been benefiting from French schooling for thirty years, no doubt had much to do with the prestige that the schools attained in Morocco. In 1865 a school was opened in Tangiers and after a period of consolidation others were opened between 1883 and 1900 in Fez, Mogador, Monastir, Casablanca and Marrakesh. By 1901 the Alliance Israélite Universelle was operating eight groups of schools in Morocco which were attended by 2,500 boys and girls. That year schools were opened in Meknès and Larache. By 1912 when the French arrived, there were also schools in Rabat, Mazagan, Safi and Settat and the total enrolment was almost 4,500.

By the 1950–51 school year there were 69 Alliance primary schools in the three zones of Morocco (French, Spanish and International) with a total of 25,000 pupils. In addition, there were continuation classes leading to the school-leaving certificate examination in the six major towns, and trade schools in Casablanca, Rabat, Fez and Marrakesh where courses were given in woodworking, metalwork, electricity, plumbing, shoe-making and tailoring. In conjunction with O.R.T., agricultural training was given at Marrakesh and Meknès, and there were dressmaking workshops for girls in Casablanca, Fez, Mazagan, Safi, Marrakesh, Boujad and Midelt and a bookbinding workshop in Mogador. A further 4,000 Jewish children attended modernized Talmud Torah schools and public schools.[5]

The isolation of Morocco made the conditions under which these advances were achieved incomparably worse than those in Algeria or Tunisia. The reports of the directors of the Alliance school system were full of startling descriptions of their struggle against the misery, filth and destitution of the mellahs;[6] children had to be washed, clothed and given a desire to persevere. There was also the opposite phenomenon which had to be coped with: at one time, the daughters of certain well-to-do Jews in Marrakesh arrived at school arrayed in the shrillest colored garments, bedecked with the family jewels and crowned with immense feathered hats specially obtained from Tangiers.[7] It was as important to teach the new language and culture as it was to instill a sense of proportion and good taste. The success that the Alliance Israélite Universelle achieved within the space of a few decades far surpassed anything that might have been dreamed of.

Nevertheless, thousands of Jewish children in Morocco were unable to go to school for lack of facilities; each year the same scenes were repeated as children had to be turned away at the doors of the schools. Every child that was rejected helped to swell the army of abandoned children that roamed the alleys of the mellah or crowded the benches of the kutab. In Casablanca there were more than four thousand of these unfortunate children. Half of them roamed the streets in search of alms or adventure, and the rest were crowded into forty-two kutabs, where half of the teachers were either blind, consumptive, albino, suffering from trachoma or decrepitly old. In minute, airless, leaking, filthy, shockingly-overcrowded classrooms, some 2,700 children between two and fourteen years received what, with all due respect, cannot possibly be called education. Many of these unfortunate little ones suffered from ringworm, blindness, rickets and the various other diseases which were rife in the mellah. After the Second World War, the American Joint Distribution Committee, which reported on these conditions, saw to the construction of a block of classrooms to finally eliminate the scourage of the *kutab*.

In 1951 a modern training college for Hebrew teachers was set up in Casablanca by the Alliance Israélite Universelle in response to the desire of Morocco's Jews to maintain their Jewish traditions and heritage. This was accompanied by a widespread reorganization of Hebrew and religious teaching; from this a symbiosis of past and present was created in Morocco and emancipation, for once, did not mean the disappearance of the ancient values and disciplines.

Though in Morocco modern education had come last and had suffered under the severest handicaps, it progressed faster and more fully than in the other countries of the Maghreb. By the attainment of Morocco's independence in 1956, all Jewish children in Morocco were receiving a proper education through the various efforts of the French authorities, l'Organisation pour le Secours de l'Enfance (O.S.E.), the Alliance, O.R.T. and the American Joint Distribution Committee. This widespread education much simplified the mass emigration of Morocco's Jews and overthrew the old order of Jewish history in the Maghreb.

Jewish Intellectuals in the Maghreb

The fact that, despite the sad and heavy heritage of the past, a widespread layer of educated Jews with a growing and important core of intellectuals was created in the Maghreb is by any standards an exciting and creditable achievement that is unparalleled elsewhere. By the end of French rule, almost all children were receiving a modern education, and the number of Jews with a post-primary education was completely out of proportion to the size of the Jewish community. It has been estimated that an unprecedented 20 per cent of the current generation of North African Jews completed their studies (the more wealthy among them in France) with at least a baccalauréat, a standard equivalent to approximately two years of college in the United States. The creation of this class of educated people was in clear defiance of the usual laws of evolution, for the leap was made almost without any transitional period from the most backward stage imaginable to the forefront of modern knowledge.*

A number of factors explain how the backward Jewish society in North Africa could so rapidly furnish a percentage of academically trained people which was not only higher than that of any other society in Africa or Asia but also exceeded that of many Western countries. Firstly, the Jews constituted a favored minority that was able to take advantage of the special conditions inherent in the presence of the French and the consequent cultural and economic revolution. As will be seen in the following pages, the Jews were able to take advantage of the

* The University of Paris alone has eighty-five Jews of North African origin among its instructors and lecturers, more than twice as many as the number of students from North Africa that the Hebrew University in Jerusalem counted in its student body in 1962, before the campaign for the higher education of the North African immigrants was commenced. Some of these professors have acquired an international reputation in their specialities, and include the designer of France's first atomic pile and the inventor of the first system for photographing the movements of the heart. Special mention should be made of the eminent urologist Pierre Aboulker who operated on General de Gaulle in 1964.

wealth that the colonial system offered to its colonists, and their position between the colonizers and the colonized in North Africa enabled them to set up a relatively well-off middle class with astonishing speed, one which was fortunately able to develop also an intellectual élite. Their minority status and their traditional desire for learning combined also to make the young Jews feel a particular urge to excel in studies; one was always finding Jews bunched at the top of their class at all levels of the educational system.

No less significant to the intellectual development of the Jews were the methods and virtues of the French educational system. Its democratic and universalistic nature enabled everyone, Jew or Moslem, black or white, to feel at ease within its culture and its academic world. The French teachers were dedicated to the cause of widening the intellectual horizons of their charges, of instilling in them a desire for knowledge, and of ensuring their progress in the academic world. Furthermore, no student was hindered by lack of means: education, from nursery school to university, was entirely free, and deserving students were given grants that enabled them to pursue their studies without financial want, and that often even helped them to support their families. The Jews of North Africa—especially those of Algeria —benefited fully from these privileges which changed the course of their destiny, their outlook and their culture within the space of only a few generations.

Economic Life

The rapid development of North Africa during the period of the French presence profoundly affected the traditional economic activities of the Jews and modified somewhat the functions they fulfilled in society. With the crumbling of the old order, the Jews acquired new needs which the conditions of the modern administration enabled them to attain. The benefits of peace and tranquillity, of impartial justice, of a degree of political emancipation and of a modern education gave the Jews the opportunity to develop their economic potential which had lain dormant under the earlier economic system.

Functions which had once been the exclusive preserve of the Jews came to be fulfilled by large European corporations and by a growing class of the Moslem élite. A microcosmic reflection of this process can be seen in the change in the structure of the money market in the Maghreb. In former days, because the lending of money at interest was forbidden to Moslems by the Koran, Jews exclusively had been engaged in the practice of moneylending. The introduction of large banking firms, of an economic policy based on the wide extension of credit, of provident societies, mutual loan funds and mutual aid societies considerably reduced the dependence of the fellah on usurers. The former Jewish money lenders, now deprived of much of their former clientele, also had to compete with European capitalists, Frenchmen, Spaniards, Italians and Maltese. Moslems, too, began to compete in this activity, often assuaging their religious scruples by resorting to some legalistic stratagem—such as charging vastly higher prices for goods sold on extended credit.

Conversely, the Jews became progressively integrated into the modern economic life of North Africa, with the result that Jewish society lost its former character of a body parasitic on or symbiotic with the main economic structure. A class of large-scale traders developed; there was a growth in the number of constructive industrial workers especially among the youth. Jewish farm laborers increased; and a class of university-trained intellectuals who filled the professions and served the administration grew up rapidly. This process was accompanied by the gradual disappearance of the petty craftsmen who had been ruined by the competition of large-scale manufacture, and also of some of the wealthy old families who could not adapt to the new conditions.

The liberating evolution made possible the full deployment of the reservoir of manpower and ability in the mellah; it also made possible the normalization of the Jewish economic structure so that Jews were no longer forced into an unequal status. Jewish merchants were able to compete with the largest European firms; Jewish bankers set up alongside the larger and better endowed financial houses; Jewish intellectuals collaborated with those who had followed the French administrators from metropolitan France. The Jews thus formed a social entity complete at all levels while, very much slower, similar classes of Moslem workers, traders, financiers and intellectuals were being formed. Wherever French influence had been established, the widening of the social scale enabled Jews to become the equal of Christians and Moslems in economic status. Poverty, however, was still rampant, especially where emancipation and advancement had not been fully promoted.

ALGERIA

The economic emancipation of the Jews of Algeria was both the earliest and the most profound in the Maghreb.[8] Their economic role in Algeria showed the deepest penetration of Western influence and the normalization of their socio-economic structure was the furthest advanced, despite the existence of an urban proletariat whose misery surpassed what was considered acceptable in the West. From demographic studies made in 1931 by Rabbi Eisenbeth[9] and in 1941 by the Vichy regime,[10] certain trends in the economic life of the Jews in Algeria can be discerned. Just over one-quarter of the population was gainfully employed. Registered unemployment among the potential Jewish labor force reached an average of 15 per cent, this group representing the proletariat which lived from hand to mouth. The proportion of unemployment grew as French influence decreased, soaring to 45.4 per cent in the backward south.

About one-third of those who were employed gave their occupation as "commerce and banking," a blanket term which included not only bankers but all manner of small traders from hosiers to grocers and barrow-men. This high percentage of traders shows that the Jews still continued to fulfill their traditional role of intermediary. The proportion of Jewish merchants was far higher (48 per cent) in the south than it was in the north (28 per cent) where Christians and Moslems had moved into what were once almost exclusively Jewish preserves. Jews predominated in the clothing, textile, leather, metal and precious stones industries, in which spheres they made up from 40 to 80 per cent of the total Algerian labor force and 10 per cent of the total Jewish working population. As was the case in commerce, the proportion of Jews in these industries was higher in the south where the opportunities for diversification were less and lower in the north where the employment mobility of the ethnic groups was greater. Other spheres in which Jews were employed in small but growing numbers indicate the degree to which they took advantage of the new opportunities: food processing, transport, building, public utilities, graphic art, rubber, paper, chemical and precision industries, mining and metallurgy.

The sense of security that was created by the French presence, and the annulment of all discriminatory laws, gradually induced Jews to turn to agriculture. There were nearly 500 Jews engaged in forestry, agriculture or stock breeding, 1.5 per cent of all those in this category. They farmed 306,000 acres in the three departments, (1.0 per cent of agricultural land).[11] The Alliance Israélite Universelle had earlier established a farm school for Jewish youths, but this was closed just after the First World War and young Jewish students who sought an agricultural training attended government establishments, many of them preferring to study in France itself.

The fact that 10 per cent of the Jewish working population were engaged in the liberal professions and in public administration which their French citizenship had made accessible to them, indicates the degree of emancipation of Algeria's Jews. In 1941, 1,336 Jews were listed as doctors, law officials, dentists and teachers. They made up an average of 15 per cent of all those exercising these professions, a proportion far beyond the ratio of the Jews to the total population. In the administration, 2,650 Jews were employed, many of them in the postal and legal services.

Jewish women too had come a long way from their seclusion of the previous century. By 1941 more than a quarter of Algerian Jewish women were working, many of them in transport, commerce, banking, the textile and garment industries and as domestic servants. Others were engaged in the teaching profession where on the whole there were more women than men, and there were even 275 women in the liberal professions. Even those women who were registered as unemployed did seasonal or odd jobs such as laundering and sewing. That women thus took so rapidly to employment outside the home reflects their desire to better their families', and their own, economic status and is a measure of the degree to which Jewish society had evolved from its traditional form to one more typical of a modern Western country.

Despite the existence of a Jewish proletariat living under extremely poor conditions, principally in the large cities, in the oases of the south and in the department of Constantine, the economic emancipation of Algeria's Jews was obviously well advanced. The rapid growth of the Jews in commerce and their increasing importance in the economic life of the country coupled with their entry into political life, fired the rise of the powerful and violent anti-Semitic movement which was described in Chapter Nine. It is a tribute to the hard work of the Jews that they could play a leading role in the development of Algeria despite this hostility which was rendered the more acute by their own maladjustment to French society. The census of 1941, designed by the Vichy regime to limit the rights of the Jews, served in fact to refute the widespread calumnies of an all-powerful Jewish conspiracy that held the Algerian economy in its grasp. On the contrary, it revealed that the Jews of Algeria, by dint of their efforts, their frugality and their commercial and intellectual ability, were playing a major role in the economic development of the country. Their function—not unlike the one they had fulfilled before the advent of the French—was essentially a leavening one. Aided by their knowledge of both French and Arabic, they acted as a bridge between the Moslem and European world until similar intermediate classes could be developed from among the Moslems on the one hand and the French colons on the other.

TUNISIA

In 1946, 28 per cent of the total of Tunisian and French Jews were listed as employed. However, this figure is highly illusory, for in the miserable conditions of the hara, "employment" frequently meant only a futile attempt to escape from complete destitution and bore no relation to any income. The term often included a poor illiterate or an unqualified laborer who, unable to find work, had set himself up in a corner of his hovel as a plumber or scrap dealer. Tunis, which held around two-thirds of the country's Jews, accounted for well over half of those gainfully employed, the remainder being in Sousse, Sfax, Gabès and the southern region, Djerba and in various smaller towns.

The rapid devolution of the Jews from their traditional occupations is illustrated by the fact that over half of those employed were engaged in industry, while only about a third were classified under commerce and banking. The industrial employees were generally to be found more in those spheres in which they had been active in the old Moslem society—the garment and leather trades, jewelry, watchmaking, joinery and cabinet making. But they also managed to adapt themselves quickly to the new industries and were employed in significant numbers in the chemical and textile industries, graphic arts, photography, paper and rubber manufacture, various branches of the building industry, transport and warehousing. The newer skills and industries had a special attraction for Jews, particularly in the larger urban centers where Jews were in closer contact with the French settlers and where they had a better chance of receiving the necessary technical training. The trade schools set up jointly by the O.R.T. organization and the Alliance Israélite Universelle furthered this tendency, furnishing Tunisia with its skilled technical workers and assuring Jewish youth of the technical specialization necessary for the attainment of remunerative positions.

Of those Jews who gave their occupation as commerce, half were cheap-jack traders living from hand to mouth on the brink of destitution. With the salaried employees, these petty traders formed the broad base of a pyramid, above whom were the

shopkeepers, wholesalers and dealers. At the top were the large
brokers and merchants, importers and exporters who held an
important position in the country's economy and whose function was recognized by the posts that were given to them in the
Chambers of Commerce of the Regency.

Unlike the Jews of other Moslem lands, those of Tunisia had
been traditionally engaged in agriculture; they had worked on
the land among the Moslem tribes in the Gabès region, near Le
Kef on the Algerian border and in the mountain massif between
Beja and La Calle.[12] These ancient Jewish shepherds had their
successors among the 115 Jews who in 1946 listed their occupation under "agriculture, forests and fisheries."

The young Tunisian Jews had a special taste for intellectual
pursuits. Even among the poorest families great sacrifices were
made to enable at least one child to study and attain one of
the professions whose prestige had an almost magical attraction
—a facet of the old respect with which the rabbi had been held
in the old days and which now was given to doctors, lawyers
and professors. The new professionals were much sought after
as sons-in-law and could be certain of a large dowry, much as
rabbis in earlier days.[13] By 1946, the Jewish intellectuals
made up 9 per cent of the working Jewish population. Nearly
15 per cent of them were rabbis, judges in the rabbinical courts,
Hebrew or religious teachers and other religious dignitaries.
They were spread throughout Tunisia in accordance with the
size of the Jewish communities but were specially numerous on
the island of Djerba which had an ancient tradition of Jewish
learning and piety. Medicine made up the next largest single
group (10 per cent) followed by lawyers, experts, technicians,
artists, writers, clerks and bookkeepers. Due to the special character of the French administration in Tunisia, there were few
Jews employed in government administration.[14]

The success that Tunisia's Jews achieved in the various trades and professions should not, however, obscure the fact that there also existed in the country a large group of Jews of the lowest social status—the Jews of the hara. This urban proletariat was only slightly less unfortunate than that of the Moroccan mellah and there were many thousands of people who did not even entertain the illusion that they were somehow gainfully employed. They were the permanently unemployed, the unemployable misfits, the professional beggars who depended on the community and public charity for their survival. Furthermore, only a decade ago, an estimated twenty thousand young people between the ages of six and twenty still needed help to be put on the road to acquiring the skills that would enable them to make a decent living. It was a problem that faced Moslem and Jewish youth alike; its seriousness served to precipitate the events that spelled the end of French rule.

MOROCCO

In 1947, 30 per cent of the Jewish population of Morocco was registered as employed, a higher proportion than in either Algeria or Tunisia. This is significant in view of the fact that one-third of the population was under fifteen years old, and that the number of adult males was slightly less than the total of those employed. If allowance is made for the sick and workless, it becomes clear that employment among women and children was common—an indication of the extreme poverty which was widespread among the Jewish masses in Morocco.[15]

Half of the working male population was registered as self-employed and the other half as laborers and employees. The classification "self-employed," like that of "commerce" in Tunisia, is misleading. It usually meant that the person was the owner of a miserable stall in the corner of a shack where he mended or sold whatever came to hand—old tin boxes, sheep's brains, stale buns, refuse from the city dump, torn rags or bent and rusty nails. For Morocco's statistics such occupations did not qualify the person as a "merchant," and since he was naturally not salaried, he was listed as a "patron." The same circumspection must be used regarding the category of "commerce," which accounted for nearly half of the total "working" population. Most of these were hawkers, riding on donkeyback with their wares to far-off Moslem villages.

Craftsmen and industrial workers accounted for more than a third of the Jewish labor force. This relatively large proportion, while still below that of Tunisia, indicates the tendency of the Jews of the Maghreb to turn increasingly to productive fields. This trend was stronger in those countries that had been most influenced by the French.[16] Forty per cent of those listed in this category in Morocco were engaged in the traditional Jewish garment and fabric trades—those in which the workers could acquire extra skills in the course of their work and escape from the mellah to work for a wider clientele, eventually reaching the European way of life. There were nearly 4,000 Jews employed in the leather trade, a very important field in Morocco, which was famous for its leatherwork. Jews were also woodworkers, employees in the food industry, goldsmiths, silversmiths, watchmakers, precious-stone workers and copper beaters. A Jewish speciality was the inlaying of engraved copper trays with silver or gold. Few Jews were employed in the newer industries in Morocco, for a further stage in their evolution was necessary to enable them to acquire the technical skills that would enable them to enter these fields. Nevertheless, there were a smattering of Jews to be found in transport, warehousing and building.

There were more Jews engaged in agriculture in Morocco

than in either Algeria or Tunisia, their number reaching over 2,000 in 1947. The majority were members of ancient Jewish agricultural communities in southern Morocco and are believed by some to be descended from Berbers converted to Judaism; they had lived in harmony with their Moslem neighbors for many centuries, cultivating the land in the same primitive manner and, like their neighbors, sharing their hovels with their animals and their produce. Though as poor as the Jews of the mellah, open-air living gave them better health and a more imposing appearance. There was also a new and growing group of young agricultural workers who had been trained in the agricultural sections of the trade schools maintained by the Alliance Israélite Universelle in Meknès and Marrakesh, and there were also 148 Jewish fishermen, two of whom were women!

By 1947, more than twice the number of women were working than had been eleven years earlier. They comprised 15 per cent of all Jewish women. This was even higher than the proportion among European women (12.5 per cent) and more than twice as high as that for Moslem women (6.4 per cent). The reason for the disparity among the communities was that the Moslem woman was the least emancipated; she worked when family conditions were extremely poor and stopped working as soon as a slightly better social status had been achieved. The Jewish woman, who did not have the same cultural inhibitions against outside employment, continued working to help her family pursue its path for social and economic advancement. Among Europeans, who were on the whole much better off, women did not have the same need to become breadwinners. (The Moslem woman was, however, catching up with the Jewish working woman, the Moslem figure for 1947 being almost identical with the Jewish figure eleven years earlier.)

Personal services such as hairdressing, manicuring and cosmetic services employed about one-third of Jewish working women. By pursuing these activities, they saw a way of escaping from the misery of the mellah and of helping to support their large families. Many young girls of twelve or even less found themselves jobs as maids, frequently giving up their chance for schooling to help support younger brothers and sisters.

As in Algeria and Tunisia, there was an intellectual—or at least an educated—class in Morocco, one-third of which was engaged in the liberal professions. The remainder were employed in the public services as clerks, bookkeepers, accountants, lawyers and religious functionaries.[17]

In Morocco, the economic élite of administrators, experts, employers, and professionals was composed largely of Europeans, while the Moslems formed the work force that kept the economy going. The Jews fell somewhere in between, some with the élite, the majority in the labor pool. The evolution of both the Jewish proletariat and the élite was rapid: between 1936 and 1947 the total of Jews of both sexes who were employed rose from 18 per cent to 30 per cent of the Jewish population. For the male population, the proportion rose sharply from 28 per cent to 46 per cent and was not far from the proportion of European males employed (56.5 per cent). The increase was most marked in commercial pursuits.

The enormous success of Jewish economic evolution in Morocco over such a relatively short period of emancipation should not hide the fact that a vast group of Jews could not adapt to the new conditions and continued to stagnate in the mellah.[18] Though the Jews of Morocco were economically retarded in comparison with those of Algeria and Tunisia, they were rapidly catching up with their coreligionists in the other countries of the Maghreb when the termination of the French Protectorate signalled the end of an era and the beginning of the rapid disappearance of the Jews from North Africa.

The Jews in the North African Economy

The growing dynamism of North Africa's economy was in itself enough to explain the extraordinary speed of the cultural and economic emancipation of the Jews of the Maghreb. Added to this general situation was the special impetus given by the French administration. The colonial structure of the economy created a pressing need for skilled and experienced cadres to run the new industries and overhaul agriculture. The colonial power tended to recruit administrators and experts either in France or among the local Jews, an ideal minority which served at all levels as a buffer between the colonizers and the colonized. This encouragement from above was one of the prime factors which induced the Jews to brave all privations in an effort to progress and to acquire an education. As the economic emancipation of the Jews gained ground, their role in the economy, while doubtlessly becoming more important, became indistinguishable from that of the French settlers and administrators.

The economic emancipation, an indication of the effective intermixing of races and cultures, caused the Jews—a community that had traditionally been turned inward onto its own resources—to burst outward in what became in fact a revolution in the group's individual psychology. It was from this that stemmed the break away from Jewish sources and traditions, the mighty movement of assimilation to the French culture, and the desire for material enrichment and technical advancement.

13

Social Conditions

Housing

As a result of their constant and growing contact with European patterns of life, the inhabitants of the mellahs and haras came to aspire to only one thing—escape from their pestilential surroundings. Once they became aware of the degradation inherent in their condition, the road before them was clear. It was only a matter of time, of relentless hard work, scrimping and saving, before little by little, they pulled themselves out of the snare of the hovels and refuse-strewn alleyways of the mellah into the fresh air, wide streets and modern apartments which were growing up around them. There was nothing in the traditions of the Jews of the Maghreb that bound them to their former way of life as was the case for the Moslems. Neither the rabbis nor the older generation had any desire to withstand this overpowering desire for emancipation, despite their misgivings regarding the break with religion which they felt would inevitably accompany it.

The children of the mellahs who brought home the lessons learned in the modern schools were a powerful element in arousing in their parents the desire for betterment. From small beginnings—the use of cutlery and earthenware plates, the permission of women to sit at the newly acquired table with the menfolk—would come the search for a better home with running water and electricity. Furniture was not always chosen with the best of taste, but the children, because of their wider contact with the new culture, would proffer their advice and prevent their parents from committing the grosser errors. It was rare that Jewish homes would show the misplaced ostentation found in the home of a newly-rich Moslem in Morocco where three pianos—a grand, a baby grand and an upright—stood side by side in one room, not necessarily in readiness for the performance of a sonata for three pianos![1]

The greatest triumph in the mellah was to be in a position to leave it. Between 1941 and 1948, Louis Villème estimated that over a thousand Jews left the mellah of Fez to live in newer quarters. He added: "This must be considered not only a necessity forced by the overpopulation of the mellah but, above all, a desire to wipe out all racial discrimination, to expunge the very principle of the mellah and to bring about an integration of the population." For this reason any attempt to enlarge the mellahs was always met by the strongest opposition on the part of the Jews. The construction of the new mellah in Meknès was in direct defiance of the general trend. Whatever the sort of housing to which the Jews of the Maghreb had been accustomed during the centuries of their oppression, whether mellah, shacks or the tents of the Jews of southern Tunisia or Morocco, their desire was the same: to acquire one day a proper apartment in the town.

ALGERIA

In northern Algeria, there was no sharp gap between the so-called Jewish quarter and the new city which surrounded it. In the 1930's, in the most densely Jewish centers in Algiers (around the Place du Gouvernement and the Square Bresson) Jews made up 70 to 80 per cent of the population, the remainder being Europeans or Moslems according to the nature of the area. Here was concentrated the less fortunate element of the community. As one got further away from this quarter the proportion dropped to reach a more or less normal level of 4 per cent in the newer areas. The situation was similar in the other towns. In Constantine, Jews constituted 90 per cent of the population of the quarter which had obviously been the ancient mellah (an area limited by the Casbah, Rue Thiers and Rue Nationale) and in Oran, the proportion was similar for the streets around Place du Maréchal Foch and Boulevard de la Revolution. The Rue des Juifs was only slightly better than the mellahs of Morocco from which much of its population came. Outside these predominantly Jewish areas, the proportion of Jews gradually fell away to a normal level.[2] The same was true in Tlemcen.

In recently built towns and villages in Algeria it was impossible to find any exceptional concentration of Jews for they were completely integrated into the general population. Even the mellah of Ghardaia in the south, despite its great vulnerability to trachoma and tuberculosis which ravaged the area, had a relatively clean appearance and many of the houses were decently built and maintained. The extreme destitution of Morocco and Tunisia were lacking here as elsewhere in the unemancipated southern territories, for the decades of French influence and the proximity of the emancipated Jews of the north had had some mitigating effect.

TUNISIA AND MOROCCO

Despite the drive for emancipation, the conditions which existed in the haras and mellahs of Tunisia and Morocco and which have been described in Chapter Eight, got worse before they got better. Infant mortality dropped and life expectancy increased with the introduction of improved hygiene and medical care; the migrants from the south and the rural areas, who flocked to the city in search of better opportunities for progress, poured into the teeming mellahs, far outnumbering those who had been able to leave them; and finally, houses crumbled and became unfit for habitation even by those accustomed to the most abject conditions. The overcrowding, filth and putrefaction of the mellahs not only endangered its inhabitants but also constituted a potential source of contagion for the cities which tolerated their existence.

Overcrowding reached unbelievable proportions. In the early 1950's, the average density of population in the area which corresponded to the old hara in Tunis (between Porte de France and the Place Sidi-Baian) was 1,000 souls per acre of built-up land. In some streets, it was two or three times greater than the average. In Morocco, the Jews of Casablanca were crowded together at the rate of 870 per acre while the average for the whole town was 24.2. (Even for the shantytown *bidonvilles* it was 374.) At Sefrou, the figure reached an incredible 1,680 Jews per acre, and living conditions were comparable with those of a concentration camp rather than of a town. In Marrakesh, Fez, Rabat, Mogador and Salé the figures were between 200 and 500 but in Meknès, where the mellah had been rebuilt it was 167. In a typical class of fifty first-grade girls in a school in Tunis in 1950, three-quarters lived with their families in one room. Most of these families had between four and nine children and some had grandparents living with them. In some cases, living space was five square feet per person[3]—not enough for a fully-grown adult to stretch his legs.

This overcrowding had a profound effect on the character of the people. The atmosphere was charged with overexcitation.

Impassioned shouting from obscure quarrels would be heard everywhere and the smallest incident would provoke screams, yells, and wild gestures accompanied by streams of colorful Oriental invective. These were the expression of the distress and confusion of a people living under conditions of emotional and physical imbalance. Families lived in small airless stone cubicles around a usually unpaved courtyard where most of their activities were carried on. There were no kitchens and no toilets and most often there was neither electricity nor running water. Water was supplied by an itinerant water seller. Furniture was rudimentary—perhaps a bed for the parents, but children would sleep on the floor on a mat, or a mattress if they were better off.[4] Exorbitant rents were charged for these hovels, landlords exploiting their destitute tenants to the maximum. They rented by the day and evicted without mercy those who could not meet their rapacious demands. The machinations of the landlords were in large measure responsible for the perpetuation of the misery of the mellah. That the Jews somehow managed to find the outrageous sums demanded of them was proof of their determination to survive.

Official indifference to and negligence of the housing situation though difficult to understand, can in some measure be explained by the aftermath of two world wars and the effect of rent control laws which were passed in France and in the French Union and which led to a curtailment of private building. The French administration was of course fully aware of the problem. Political parties and Jewish community organizations were continuously stressing the danger inherent in such inhuman housing conditions both among Jews and Moslems, but the public funds made available to remedy the situation bore absolutely no relation to the real needs.

Only by availing themselves to the maximum of the opportunities offered by the French colonial system could the Jews escape from their sub-human existence. By pulling themselves up into the newly created middle-class that lived from commerce and finance, and from there to administrative, industrial and intellectual pursuits, growing numbers of Jews were able to attain a reasonable measure of human dignity. The question of how far and how rapidly the problem of North Africa's mellahs and its inhabitants would have been resolved will remain unanswered, for the simultaneous rise of North African nationalism and the establishment of the State of Israel resulted in the sudden disappearance of these indictments of the society which allowed them.

Health

The popular beliefs and superstitions which had become deeply entrenched among the Jews during twelve centuries of close contact with the Moslems could not be eradicated by French influence in the space of a few decades. The approach of the Jews to health and hygiene which was described in detail in Chapter Eight has persisted in many parts of the Maghreb down to the present day; particularly in the southern territories where tuberculosis, trachoma and infectious diseases were rampant, little was done to remedy the situation.

ALGERIA

In Algeria, the long contact with French civilization, service in the French Army, and travel abroad had all had salutary effects on the health of the population. By the mid-twentieth century, the state of health among the Jews in the urban north approximated that of the European community. In the south, however, this was far from the case, and sickness and infirmity were widespread. In 1949 a report by the Alliance Israélite Universelle had this to say of the inhabitants of the M'zab: "The Jewish population lives with a complete indifference to the elementary rules of personal and group hygiene. Dirt reigns supreme, on the individuals as well as in their homes where they live together with animals in conditions of over-crowding which they have come to accept as normal by force of habit and indifference."[5] Added to this there were the ravages of alcoholism and inbreeding, and the absence of schools which might have served as a means of education in better habits and of welfare centers to deal at least with those ills of which the population was aware.

An estimated 85 per cent of adults and children in southern Algeria suffered from trachoma, and some 10 per cent suffered from other specific eye diseases such as leucoma and staphyloma, or were blind in one or both eyes. Conjunctivitis of all types, to which no one paid any attention, was as common as skin diseases: ring-worm, impetigo, eczema. Congenital and hereditary diseases were equally prevalent. Deaf- and dumbness, both hereditary and acquired, afflicted around 2 per cent of the population, rickets some 5 per cent; clubfeet were common and malaria was endemic. The percentage of people who suffered from tuberculosis of the lungs, the joints and the bones was never firmly established. Chronic and acute alcoholism was rife among both men and women, and the Administration's attempt to uncover the clandestine distillers of *bokha,* whose products were a grave menace to the health of the population, was without success. The women, subject to near-seclusion, were victims of obesity which often reached proportions that made them incapable of any exertion and also brought on many other diseases. The general condition of the population as a whole made it an easy prey to epidemics such as influenza, mumps and measles.

TUNISIA AND MOROCCO

Similar diseases were widespread in the two Protectorates. Their incidence was greatest in southern Tunisia, and in the mellahs of Morocco where practically nothing had been accomplished in the way of improved health and hygiene measures. In northern Tunisia 40 per cent of the Jews suffered from trachoma; in certain areas in the south 80 per cent were stricken with it. With the modest means at its disposal, O.S.E. accomplished miracles through the dispensaries it set up throughout the country. As with most diseases, it was Morocco that was in the worst situation. In 1945, 125,000 new cases of trachoma were reported; 146,000 a year later. Ophthalmological centers were set up in seven of the largest cities, but they reached only a small proportion of the victims, and none at all were treated in the smaller towns of the interior where the disease was at its worst. The Alliance Israélite Universelle set up a special school in Casablanca where children who had become infected with trachoma could receive regular attention from the best practitioners.

Malnutrition encouraged the spread of tuberculosis. At Gabès in southern Tunisia, 30 per cent of the children had this disease, half of them in a severe form, and 20 per cent of adults were affected by it. No precautions were taken to prevent contagion. In Morocco the percentage of the population suffering from tuberculosis was never established, but the effects of the disease were obviously worse than in either Algeria or Tunisia. Figures published by O.S.E. for 1945 established that the

mortality rate caused by tuberculosis among the Jewish population was 14.4 per 10,000 inhabitants. It was 5.6 for Europeans
and 26.4 for Moslems. Here once again the Jews were in an
intermediate position between the French and Moslem elements. In 1946, the state-operated tubercular centers in Morocco examined over 10,000 Jews, a similar number of Europeans and over 24,000 Moslems. Though this in itself was a
laudable achievement, it reached only a small fraction of the
total population. In 1952 the first meaningful attack on tuberculosis was launched in North Africa by the United Nations Children's Fund. A vast campaign was undertaken to innoculate
hundreds of children in Morocco, Algeria and Tunisia with the
B.C.G. anti-tubercular vaccine. The reactions of Jewish children from the mellahs revealed a great susceptibility to the
disease.

Infant mortality was high in Tunisia and Morocco. Debility
of the newborn, caused by syphilis, tuberculosis or malnutrition
in the mother, was not always the reason for this.[6] Usually the
mother had not even the most elementary notion of anti- and
post-natal care, and generally refused to submit to a gynecologi-
cal examination during her pregnancy. Spontaneous abortions
and miscarriages ended an alarming proportion of pregnancies,
though deliberate abortions were practically unknown, so great
was the respect for human life. The crude old women who
called themselves midwives no doubt were responsible for the
early death of many infants.

Only one-third of the children born in the Hara Kbira of
Djerba in Tunisia in 1946 survived their first year, many of the
deaths having been caused by gastroenteritis. In Casablanca in
Morocco the situation was no better: in 1947, nearly half the
1,100 children who died were under two years, despite the fact
that the Jewish infants weighed on an average slightly more at

birth than European children.[7] According to the official public health statistics for 1946, nearly a third of the infants who died during their first year were victims of diarrhoea or gastroenteritis, deaths which simple health precautions could so easily have prevented. Infectious diseases, as rampant here as in south Algeria and Tunisia, also took their toll.

As was pointed out in Chapter Eleven, though the birth rate among the Jews in Morocco was high, so was the mortality rate, a fact that takes on special gravity in view of the comparative youth of a population of which some 30 per cent were children under fourteen. The high death rate was in part directly attributable to the inhuman overcrowding in the mellahs of the larger cities. Whereas the national countrywide average death rate in Morocco was 135, it reached 174 per 10,000 among the Jews in the urban areas. The connection between housing and health is eloquently illustrated by the fact that the mortality rate in Meknès dropped by one-third after the new mellah had been built. In Rabat, where new roads were cut through the mellah and houses rebuilt, the death rate fell to half its former level.

The efforts of local and international Jewish organizations to fight the diseases that ravaged the Maghreb, praiseworthy as they were, were totally inadequate to cope with a situation which was characteristic of an underdeveloped country. The French administration, on whom the promotion of the health and welfare of the population should have devolved, certainly did not fulfill its obligations, not even to the Jews of Algeria who were legally French citizens. In the south of Algeria, as in the greater part of Tunisia and of Morocco, the task had hardly been started when the local Moslem population, even worse off than the Jews, finally revolted and gained its independence.

Social Ills

BEGGARY

The sudden breaking up of the old society in the Maghreb and its replacement by a more complex world threw up in the Jewish communities a mass of unfortunates who lost their precarious foothold on life. The petty tradesmen and artisans who had found a point of equilibrium in Moslem society were supplanted by the department store and the modern industry, and those who were unable to withstand the powerful competition were quickly dragged down by the new conditions of life into despair and destitution.

One could not walk through the mellahs without stumbling on an old cripple or blind man, his back against the wall, frozen in an attitude of begging, and chanting prayers with a plaint that echoed all the nostalgia of the Orient and the sorrows of a whole people. There were adult beggars, shoe-shines and errand boys, women water-sellers and ragged children—those left behind in the march toward emancipation. Schoolboys, when asked their father's profession, would often reply "a beggar at the corner of so-and-so street." The synagogues and cemeteries were favorite haunts of the disinherited. Every Friday at the cemeteries of Fez and Marrakesh, one could see hosts of miracle seekers—men and women with all the infirmities under the sun, blindness in the lead. They were an unforgettable sight, scattered among the serried rows of tombstones in the glaring sunlight.

In Algeria, the situation was better than in the protectorates for welfare departments functioned regularly in every municipality and their services were at the disposal of Christians, Moslems and Jews alike. Moreover, the Jews in Algeria had a longer period of adaptation to European ways and by the mid-twentieth century they had weathered the most difficult trials of their adaptation to the new life.

In Morocco and Tunisia, on the other hand, the new society provided no meaningful assistance for those who had not adjusted to twentieth century conditions. Apart from practically insignificant help to private welfare agencies, the governments did not concern themselves with the poor, and charity remained a private affair as it had been in former centuries. The burden of social assistance fell on the committees of the Jewish communities. Every Friday on the eve of the Sabbath, a community official would go from house to house collecting money to cover the needs of the poor for the following week. The wealthy all contributed, those who understood the meaning of sharing giving more than others. These pious customs, however, no longer corresponded to reality. In an earlier generation rich and poor had lived in the same quarter: they met in the streets, at prayer, in daily life. Now the rich man was a stranger to the poor. He lived in a far-off quarter of the town and, since he no longer had a common bond with the destitute, charity ceased to be a compelling urge close to the heart.

The Jewish communities developed a large number of welfare agencies. In Tunis, an active and vibrant community, there was financial help for widows, for the aged and for families in need. There were subsidies for day-care centers for children, for soup kitchens, for providing clothing, for protecting young girls. But in other centers, good intentions were totally inadequate to cope with the desperate situation. Thus, at Gabès, which had a Jewish population of eight hundred families, one hundred and thirty were entirely dependent on the community for their support and another hundred received occasional help at the festivals or in times of sickness. In Djerba, too, which had once been a prosperous island, the gradual change to a new way of life brought about a rapid growth in the number of destitute. The Jewish community in Casablanca, despite its innumerable charitable agencies, was unable to more than dent the general misery. Besides subsidizing agencies whose work was charitable but generally ineffective, the community directly supported a thousand completely destitute families with a weekly pittance. However insignificant was the help of the welfare agencies in relation to true needs, it nevertheless served a useful role in helping the recipients to take on a new lease in life. The smaller communities which had no welfare agencies were still served by the communal collector with his ancient chant of the mellah: "Dwellers of the upper story, dwellers of the courtyard, give alms!"

PROSTITUTION

The congestion of the mellahs and haras, where 80 per cent of families lived in one room, gave little chance for the formation of correct moral attitudes in the young; poverty did the rest. In Casablanca the position was particularly acute, and though Jewish girls made up only an insignificant 2 per cent of the officially registered prostitutes in that city, a considerable number of underpaid working girls turned to so-called "clandestine" prostitution to supplement their pay and support their families. In fact, this form of prostitution was practiced with the open connivance of the police.

By submitting to the blandishments of the great city and acquiring its new needs, the girls followed a road which quickly led to debasement and final degradation. The dangers, both to themselves and to their families were immense. The phenomenon of prostitution was one completely alien to Jewish traditions which regarded prostitution of the body as a reflection of the prostitution of the soul. The biblical injunction "There shall be no harlot among the daughters of Israel" (Deut. 23,18) inspired among the Jews a strong revulsion for this evil, the child of penury.

CRIME AND DELINQUENCY

Official statistics and the observations of judges and lawyers all concur on the disproportionately low incidence of crime and delinquency among the Jews of the Maghreb. When one considers the abnormal economic and social conditions under which the masses of the Jews lived—conditions which generally give rise to a high crime rate—this fact appears the more remarkable. The reason for it was that the Jews formed a distinct minority with a strong social structure that was deeply rooted in religious faith and practices. The Jewish community formed a closed society where everyone knew his neighbor and was ready to come to his aid. Each child received a traditional religious education which inculcated him with a whole world of spiritual values. In this cohesive society escape from misery was reflected not so much by revolt against the incomprehensible and against injustice as by an attempt to change circumstances by dint of hard work and perseverance or by prayer and submission to the will of God.

Statistics for Tunisia are typical. In 1939, out of a total of nearly 1,000 offenders sentenced to prison, only 180 or 1.8 per cent were Tunisian Jews. The figure for 1940 was similar. A rise in the general crime rate during the war reduced the Jewish offenders to a mere 0.7 per cent of the total, although during the German occupation the number of Jews sentenced also rose.

However, by 1944 the figure had fallen below the pre-war level to 136 offenders—1.0 per cent of the total. As life returned to normal, the proportion fell away sharply to reach an average of 0.6 per cent for the four years between 1944 and 1948. (Detailed figures can be found in Appendix VII.)

Of the thirty-eight Tunisian Jews sentenced to imprisonment in 1948, there was not one who had been condemned for murder[8]—no doubt a reflection of the Jewish respect for life. Drunkenness and theft made up the majority of crimes for which the Jews were sentenced.[9] Juvenile delinquency was rare, only five minors between sixteen and twenty years of age being among the thirty-eight offenders in 1948. The previous year, there were twelve adolescents among the fifty-nine Jews convicted. This picture can be regarded as typical of other years and of other countries in the Maghreb.[10] The facts thus clearly show that crime and delinquency among the Jews in North Africa were almost non-existent and that the prejudices prevalent among certain circles in Israel, according to which North African Jews are given to violence, are completely without foundation.

The Emergence of a New Man

The penetration of Western ideas into the Maghreb brought about a rapid change in the mentality and outlook of the inhabitants of the region. For the Moslems the change was less rapid and less profound, for they regarded the French as invaders and any changes introduced by them were met with disdain and suspicion. The Jews had no such hesitations. They welcomed the transformation wrought by the newcomers from Europe, taking full advantage of the educational, cultural and economic opportunities the French offered. Above all, they welcomed their liberation from the second-class status to which they had been relegated under Moslem rule.

Fortunately, the transition passed without provoking any serious crisis within the Jewish community. The Jews were encouraged by the example of the integration of their co-religionists in France who, emancipated since 1791, now hastened a similar process among North African Jewry through the work of the Alliance Israélite Universelle and other bodies. Impetus came also from the army of dedicated, wise and understanding teachers who instilled the essence of modern thought into the minds of their students. It was fortunate too that there was no clash between generations: a grandfather, clinging to the older way of life would point with pride, rather than with censure, to his grandson who had been able to enter the new world of the twentieth century whose values and standards were so different from his own. Even the rabbis, while deploring the alienation from Judaism that was the result of cultural assimilation, were careful not to antagonize the new generation in such a way as to cause an irreparable rift between the generations.

The change in outlook had indeed been great. At the turn of the century, the Jews, with their fatalistic attitude to life, accepted exile, degradation and persecution as a punishment by God for the sins of Israel, and they saw as the only ultimate hope the messianic future and the return of all Israel from exile to a miraculous Jerusalem. The first sign of change in this attitude was the migration, bordering at times on flight, of Jews from those parts of the Maghreb where conditions were worst and held no hope of immediate improvement. From the oases of the south to the small towns, from the towns to the large cities, the Jews went in search of emancipation, braving the direst privations of the urban mellahs in an attempt to attain it.

Meanwhile, the young students of North Africa had become imbued by their French teachers with the ideals of liberty and self-respect. But the deep cleft which in reality existed between the three ethnic groups of the Maghreb, the intense racialism and the spread of anti-Semitism among the European settlers struck a painfully discordant note in the lofty themes that the students had learned better than their masters. Disillusion caused many young intellectuals—Moslems and Christians as well as Jews—to flee their homeland and to seek in France and later in Israel the life of freedom and self-respect to which the French ideals had made them aspire.

It was this new man, the man of liberty, of aspirations, of self-respect, that made up the backbone of the strong contingent of Jewish soldiers from the Maghreb that fought with the French army in 1914–1918 and again, this time more personally involved, in the war of 1939–1945. It was these young Jews who worked with the underground in Algeria and made possible the successful Allied landings of November 1942. It was these young men who volunteered to fight for Israel's independence in 1947–1948 and who gave their lives in its defense in 1956 and 1967.

14

Judaism in Modern Times

The Crisis of Judaism

Under the French, temporal and spiritual rule in the Maghreb were separated for the first time and equality became the essence of the new order. The conditions of the modern world now made it possible for the Jews to leave the constraining atmosphere of the mellah without renouncing their faith or risking the bastinado.

Inevitably, there was a breakdown in the social structure as the patriarchal type of family, the *mishpacha*, crumbled under the onslaught of new concepts and in the face of new freedoms for the women and the younger generation of the family. The community that was based on religious cohesion, whose life centered on the synagogue and the liturgical calendar had to give way to the free and open secular society. Learning and religion became divorced. Though the rabbis continued to remain the guardians of the faith, of the Bible and of the prayers, and though they continued to be respected by their congregants, their teaching came to be less and less understood by those to whom Judaic learning, associated with the stagnation and imperfection of the old-fashioned Talmud Torah, seemed a threat to their progress along the road of modern culture and enlightenment.

Though Jewish learning was disappearing among the laymen (progressively fewer could even understand the meaning of the prayers that they read), faith retained its hold longer, but that too weakened slowly as individuals stepped out from their closed society into the wider world; away from the old family circle the ritual laws of food and drink tended to be ignored, on the Sabbath forbidden work was performed, the old rites and ritual were ignored and then forgotten. As emancipation progressed, old values which were no longer understood seemed doubly distasteful and the distance between the "emancipated" Jew of the Maghreb and his old culture and environment increased at an ever faster pace. Paradoxically, the secularity of the French Revolution which was ultimately one of the prime factors in the social emancipation of the Jews of North Africa, served also to sow the seeds of inner conflict between the mysticism and spirituality of the traditional world of Judaism in North Africa and the world of material intellectualism that was introduced by the French. This conflict affected each individual; each person had to find his own equilibrium between the opposing attractions of opposite worlds.

The crisis of Judaism in North Africa that eventually led to the virtual extinction of all its Jewish communities, was in part a direct outcome of the inability of the traditional institutions to adapt themselves to the new realities. Judaism in the two millennia of the exile was essentially geared to the needs of preserving the faith in exile and was a development of the ghetto-induced attitude of the Jews. Its main theme was the meaning of exile and redemption, its main concern was the preservation of the faith, the practices, the Torah and the People of Israel. Finally the mere preservation, the successive erection of "fences" to the Law to prevent the forfeiture of the least iota, became an end in itself, in itself capable of bringing about the ultimate salvation. This Judaism was effective under the conditions of the ghetto; it withstood the pressures imposed against the Jews by both Islam and Christianity; even threat of death was unable to bring about the abandonment by Jews of their ancestral faith. But this brand of Judaism, and the community structure born of the ghetto, were unable to withstand the blandishments offered by the free, democratic and secular society of the nineteenth and twentieth centuries.

The rabbis, who struggled hard to maintain the Jewish religion alive in the Maghreb and to keep it free from alien influences, were not equipped to meet the modern world. The majority had little or no secular or broadly theological learning and culture, and their horizons were sadly limited. In Morocco, for instance, only a dozen rabbis had more than a superficial knowledge of all basic Jewish subjects—the Bible, the Talmud, Hebrew and Aramaic grammar, Jewish history and theology. Even fewer had any knowledge of non-Jewish culture; only one rabbi in all of Morocco had any knowledge of Moslem culture worth mentioning. A rather one-sided opinion by José Benech considers that despite their wealth of aphorisms, "their intellectual poverty is immense, their curiosity of mind is exclusively satisfied by the interlocking of petty quibbling. Attached closely to the letter of their tomes, they never possessed the boldness to draw from them a generalized idea, a clear and practical moral (conclusion)." Indeed, many of them lacked this "curiosity of mind"; many who possessed valuable libraries, the heritage of a fine intellectual past, never took the trouble even to catalogue them; most were completely ignorant of even the elementary principles of any knowledge which was not taught at the yeshiva. Thus, they lacked in most cases the wisdom, the strength of intellect and the prudence which the new conditions demanded of them.

ALGERIA

The Algerian community, or *Kahal Hakodesh* (saintly assembly) as it was traditionally referred to, had long ceased to be an expression of the spiritual, historical and sociological reality of its so-called congregation. Until its disappearance, it was no more than the *de jure* shell of an established religion that had become almost completely emptied of all *de facto* religious content.

The Ordinance of 1845, in which the organizational structure of the consistoires in Algeria was officially defined and the appointment of rabbis was made a function of the State, was the first step in the dissolution of the old order of religious life in Algeria. The complete legal emancipation of the Jews of Algeria and the granting to them of French citizenship in 1870 was a further step in this direction. The final official act was the law of 1905 for the separation of Church and State in France as a result of which the Jews of Algeria lost their separate identity and their separate heritage by being merged into one *"Consistoire des Israélites de France et d'Algérie."* By this bureaucratic move Judaism in Algeria, such as it was, became drained of much of its specific character and traditions. An attempt to recreate some specifically Algerian structure by forming a Federation of Jewish Communities in Algeria was made in 1939 on the eve of the world war but the Federation was not established till 1947. The Federation brought together all the Jewish organizations of Algeria but it lacked creative force, it lacked breadth of vision and it lacked means.

Algeria's rabbis were concerned over the indifference to tradition, the decline of the country's Jewish institutions, and the skepticism and indifference to the faith that made many openly abandon it. Many Jews turned to communism which found fruitful ground in the lack of faith and lack of purpose of the community's youth. Others turned to Christianity; many Protestant churches had missionaries working in Algeria with the express purpose of achieving mass conversion of Jews. The situation was indeed desperate: Jewish youth had deserted the synagogues, Jewish cultural institutions were reduced to hollow shells, no Jewish organization had an assured budget and the new generation was so much at odds with its Jewish traditions that its members refused to be called by biblical or Hebrew names.

TUNISIA AND MOROCCO

In the two Protectorates, Judaism was not so severely threatened. One of the reasons for its continued strength was that, whereas the youth of Algeria attended secular government schools, those of Morocco and Tunisia were taught in schools of the Alliance Israélite Universelle. Another powerful cohesive force was the rabbinical courts. As was pointed out in Chapter Ten, the French did not interfere in Tunisia and Morocco (and in the unemancipated territories of southern Algeria) with the jurisdiction of the rabbinical courts in matters of marriage, divorce, inheritance and guardianship.[1] The courts thus remained living parts of the Jewish communal scene. Even those furthest removed from the faith had of necessity to turn to their community organizations at all important events in their lives; the only complete escape from community ties for the Jews of Morocco was by exile from the country, for those of Tunisia by requesting French nationality.

Rabbinical Justice and its Evolution. The rabbinical court in Tunisia was composed of a chief rabbi who acted as honorary president, a presiding rabbi, two rabbinical judges, two surrogate judges and one registrar. The Moroccan courts were made up of three judges (*dayanim*) and were staffed by clerks and interpreters. Although the scenes in the courts were often a sharp reminder that they were a vital part of life in the Orient, the dignity and impartiality of the judges were on a far higher plane than was common in the area. In the course of a meticulous enquiry that the author made into the conduct of the rabbinical courts, he did not find one single complaint of corruption—and this in a region of the world that is notorious for its calumnies and suspect practices.

A Moroccan Dahir of 1918 reorganized the rabbinical courts of the country into seven lower courts and one supreme court, all the rabbinical judges receiving remuneration directly from the funds of the Protectorate. A later Dahir in 1940 established an entirely new court, the *Tribunal de Serara*. This court, peculiar to the Maghreb, was set up to regulate the many differences that had arisen through the generations over *Serara,* the hereditary rights of certain families to specific public offices. In principle these rights had devolved upon all male successors capable of fulfilling the offices and, as the number of beneficiaries of *Serara* increased so did rivalry and dissention grow, until finally the French protectorate power found itself compelled to intervene to make some settlement possible. The special tribunal it established was made up of three rabbis who were not themselves beneficiaries of succession under the principles of *Serara.* This was an important provision, for the judges of the rabbinical courts were always selected (with official supervision) only from the beneficiaries of *Serara.*

The field of competence of the rabbinical courts in Morocco had been defined in two Dahirs of 1913 and 1918 and in a memorandum of 1938. The courts were empowered to deal with all matters concerning marriage, succession, adoption, pa-

ternal authority over minors, the validity of wills, the disburse-
ment of bequests, the division of inheritances, and all litigation
concerning charitable donations, religious endowments (*hekdesh*) and the administration of synagogues. The competence of
the courts was limited in every case to Jews who were also
nationals of the countries in which the courts were situated.
While this special jurisdiction safeguarded the character of the
Jewish communities, it in effect constituted a special discrimination against the Jews which they deeply resented, especially
when they were involved in litigation with a Moslem and had to
appear before the Moslem Chraa court.

The authority for all decisions in the rabbinical courts was
the Torah as complemented by the Talmud and the later codes
of jurisprudence drawn up by Alfassi, Maimonides and Joseph
Caro. To these were added previous decisions of other rabbis of
the Maghreb as published in the form of *She'elot Utshuvot*
(Responsa). Most of these had not been formally published and
in their totality they constituted a legal treasure-house for the
Jews of the Maghreb and established their legal process down to
the present.

The most important of the rabbinical courts in the entire
Maghreb was that of Casablanca which heard around two thousand cases annually. The court of Tunis, whose jurisdiction
covered Jews of Tunisian nationality throughout the country,
heard over six hundred and fifty cases in 1950. The inscription
above the judges' bench read: "Instruct with perfection, render
justice, defend the oppressed, vindicate the orphan, protect the
widow, render justice to the poor. On three things the world is
based: on justice, on truth and on peace; as it is written: 'Truth,
justice and peace shall reign within Thy gates.' Be circumspect
in your judgement. Justice is truth; it was created for its truth
and associated with the Holy One Blessed be He, in the work of

Creation." These fine maxims threw into relief the banality of much of the workings of these courts where all miseries of the mellah went on display.

The evolution of the law in the Maghreb was discernible in many fields. In matters of majority and of guardianship the biblical and talmudic traditions were naturally recognized. However, the rabbis and scholars from Spain had already modified the traditional age of majority—twelve for girls and thirteen for boys—to the age of eighteen. In 1948 the chief rabbis of Morocco, meeting at their second annual council, and acting under the influence of the French legal example, changed the age of majority to twenty while reserving for the rabbinical courts the right to emancipate youths at an earlier age when circumstances justified it.

Similar instances of progressive enactments under modern influences were discernible in other fields of law. Betrothals[2] had always had a certain legal standing, and a breaking off of an agreement to marry after betrothal had entailed legal sanctions. To prevent the many abuses over broken engagements, the rabbis of Morocco were forced to make innovations in a *Takana* (Ordinance) of 1947 which laid down stringent regulations concerning breach of promise. The same *Takana* (which was applicable to the French zone of Morocco and to Tangiers) also codified the biblical-rabbinical legislation concerning seduction consequent to a promise of marriage. By this means the new law helped to protect the young woman and safeguard her rights, purging earlier Jewish practices of the alien and regressive Arab influences. The rabbis did not, however, hasten to impute paternity unless the putative father admitted to it formally.

Women, Marriage, Polygamy and Divorce. The status of the Jewish woman in North Africa in marital affairs, the result of centuries of interaction between talmudic legislation and Moslem influence, remained an anomaly and an anachronism in the face of westernization. Although there is evidence of progressive tendencies in the *Takanot* of the higher rabbinical authorities, this evolution was of fairly recent date, and never went far enough to eradicate entirely the phenomenon.

There was, however, a notable change in the attitude of the courts in matters relating to marriage. Marriage of girls below the age of puberty had been extremely common among Jews and was in keeping with the traditions of the Moslems of the region. A few years back it was not rare to find that a girl of nine would give as her reason for not attending school the fact that she was married. The very strong reaction to this practice on the part of certain sections of the Jewish communities and of the westernized élite provoked many stern rulings by the rabbis who forbade this practice and fixed the minimum age for marriage at around puberty.

The rabbis from Spain had put restraints on the practice of polygamy which was permitted by the Bible and the Talmud. (The edict of Rabbenu Gershom [10th century], forbidding polygamy, applied to Ashkenazi Jews only.) The Spanish rabbis had encouraged the addition of a clause in the *ketuba* (marriage contract) which prevented the husband from contracting a second marriage during the lifetime of his first spouse unless he first paid her all sums due under the contract and gave her a bill of divorce so that she too would be free to enter another marriage. Unless such a provision was written into the *ketuba* polygamy was permitted under the Oriental traditions of the Jews of the Maghreb, and the only prerequisite for a husband desirous of taking an additional wife was to prove his ability to support her and all previous ones. The rabbis did all in their power to dissuade the husband from contracting a polygamous marriage unless the first marriage had been without issue for ten years at least. The result was that polygamy was virtually non-existent in recent years both in those communities that had come under the influence of Spanish-Jewish practices and in those that clung to the conservative pre-Spanish customs.

A much more serious problem, which gave rise to far more unhappiness than could ever be witnessed among the rare cases of polygamous households, was the practice of what might be called successive polygamy, made possible as the result of the ease with which divorce was granted, on the initiative and at the will of the husband. Divorce in this form was sanctioned by the Bible but in the way that it was practiced in the countries of the Orient it subjected the woman to her husband's every whim and made the children the ultimate victims. There were cases in some of the smaller mellahs where women went from divorce to marriage and from marriage to divorce practically through the hands of all the men of the town. The degradation in these practices, further enhanced by the ever-prevalent poverty, was one of the principal causes of the decline of Judaism in the countries of Islam.

In the Maghreb, at least, the rabbis, whose offices were required to make the divorce effective, tried all in their power to cut down the number of divorces, which reached frightening proportions especially among the lower classes. The disruption in the Oriental structure of the communities of North Africa provoked by the sudden confrontation with Western manners and customs, and the more rapid emancipation of the men as compared with the women, tended to aggravate the moral crisis and in certain cases brought about even more divorces at the unilateral instigation of the husband. In certain towns, especially those in the more backward south, the annual divorce rate was more than a third of the rate of marriage. Husbands who had contracted ten successive marriages in their lives were not rare and the author personally knew a woman who had been married eighteen times.

Successive polygamy naturally entailed successive polyandry. According to the workings of the divorce laws, a divorcee was usually compelled to abandon her children to her former husband, being allowed to keep only infants under six years of age who could be claimed by the former husband as soon as they attained an age when nothing could be done to thwart his request. On being divorced, therefore, the wife lost at one blow her husband, her children and her home. Abandoned, despised, incapable of learning a trade, unable to show the least initiative in solving her situation, the only recourse open to the now totally impoverished woman was to attempt to find a new husband, any husband, who could in turn divorce her with the same ease as the previous one. The process of divorce and remarriage, divorce and remarriage might thus continue for as long as the woman retained a touch of youth. After that her lot would be desperate indeed.

The more the attitudes of women became westernized, the more they suffered from their repeated marriages and divorces. Even in the more enlightened circles where frequent divorce and remarriage was not practiced, the mere fact that unilateral divorce was in theory at least possible was a severe humiliation for the young women of the modern generation. A special assembly of the chief rabbis of Morocco, perturbed by this situation, enacted a number of measures in 1947 to lessen the number of divorces and to provide better guarantees of the rights of the married woman. The provisions, which attempted to moderate the Oriental practices with innovations based on modern French examples, provided that even when a woman had agreed to renounce the sums to which she was entitled under the terms of her marriage contract, she had three days in which to change her mind. They ordered further that no *get* (bill of divorce) might be tendered till three months had elapsed since the divorce proceedings had been opened. They introduced various fundamental obstacles and delays before the rabbinical court could agree to a divorce. Most important they ruled that a woman might not be divorced against her will unless she had personally appeared before a court of three judges who had been charged with the greatest prudence, and who exercised the most explicit care for the welfare of the wife. By these means the rabbinate in Morocco tried to reduce the ravages of a law which was in theory powerless to correct these backward customs.

The rights of a widow to her husband's estate remained anomalous among the southern communities which had not adopted the procedure introduced by the Spanish rabbis in the fifteenth century and accepted in other parts of the Maghreb, according to which the wife enjoyed equal rights to her husband's property in his lifetime and substantial rights on his decease. In the traditional communities the widow had practically no share in the inheritance except in the rare instance where the husband had made a will in her favor. If the husband died intestate she could claim from his estate only the sum which had been fixed as her dowry in the *ketuba;* if she renounced this sum, the successors of the deceased had to support her with a life-long pension which ceased as soon as she remarried. The chief rabbis of Morocco attempted to unify the two systems of inheritance after 1947, preparing the draft of a regulation by which the widow would share equally with the defunct's children. The dispute engendered by this attempted

reform underlined the essential opposition of certain traditional-
ists to the total emancipation of the woman according to Western ideals.

The barbaric practices described above were the result of
the general decadence of certain particularly impoverished
groups. It would be quite incorrect to draw general conclusions
from these phenomena as to the status of the Jewish woman in
Oriental society, any more than it would be possible to draw a
general picture of the condition of women in Western societies
following a study of the evils of prostitution in the major cities.
In the many Jewish communities which did not suffer the evils
of easy and frequent divorces, the Jewish woman had the role of
guardian of the sanctity of the home and of educator of her
children which conferred upon her a natural preeminence that
complemented the rights which were hers under the true traditions of the biblical East. Arrayed in her sumptuous clothes and
her jewels, she had the beauty and the prestige worthy of a
queen.

Jewish Learning. The rabbinical court system in North Africa,
even while it was being opposed by the more emancipated of the
region's Jews who had hoped to be able to come under French
civil law in matters of personal status following the example of
Algeria, gave rise to an abundant talmudical literature. The
Talmud and its earlier glosses and commentaries naturally received most of the attention of scholars, but these were at the
same time further enriched by the writings and research of distinguished rabbis then living in the Maghreb. Many rabbis in
Tunisia and Morocco were engaged in writing exegeses on those
works in the hope of eventually publishing them. Printers in Fez
and Casablanca and particularly the firm of Bouaz Haddad in
Djerba published the more representative works, and where the

rabbi was fortunate in having a contact in Safed or Jerusalem, the book might even have the extra distinction of being printed in the Holy Land. Wealthy patrons considered it an honor to make possible the publication of these religious works whose readership was naturally limited to a coterie of the devout and the learned.

The writings of modern North African rabbis were usually in rabbinical Hebrew or, occasionally, in Judeo-Arabic, but they were always printed in Hebrew characters. Publications included prayer books with or without commentaries; talmudic argumentation and dialectic; many devotional works frequently written in Judeo-Arabic and recent translations into this dialect of earlier works of this genre; some of the major works of Jewish philosophy; manuals of Oriental folk-medicine; cabalistic writings; poetry and even historical novels.[3]

Altogether, Judaism was much more of a living reality in Morocco and Tunisia than it was in Algeria, and the vitality and intensity of life in the mellahs and haras served as the nucleus around which the social framework of the communities managed to survive.

Zionism in North Africa

The Zionist Movement had had very little success or effect in North Africa, largely because those who headed it were almost exclusively of Eastern European background and had made little effort to understand the specific traditions and attitudes of the Jews of the Maghreb. Even in their choice of emissaries to North Africa the leadership showed a singular lack of understanding, and more than once the persons who had been delegated to address the leaders of the Jewish communities or even the rank and file were unable to communicate with their hearers; few Zionist officials or speakers were able to converse freely in French, none at all in the local dialects, and none of them understood the psychology of the local masses. (The same incidentally, may be said of Zionist endeavors in the other countries of Africa and of Asia.) By not adapting its appeal and its publicity to the local requirements, the Zionist Movement was unable to reach the new group of intellectuals and the new middle classes of North Africa, most especially those of Algeria. Despite this, the three countries regularly sent delegates to every Zionist Congress, and spiritual Zionism, the hope and ideal of an eventual return of the Jewish people to their homeland, was deeply entrenched among the masses where it was nourished by the messianic spirituality of cabalistic traditions.

When the State of Israel was created, the Jews of the Maghreb were seized by a fervid excitement which equalled in many respects the popular reaction, three centuries earlier, to the messianic arousal of Shabbetai Zvi; everywhere in the Maghreb, and especially in Morocco, entire Jewish communities prepared themselves for an early departure for Israel: they sold their property and most of their belongings and waited with their bundled possessions for their return to their ancient homeland.

Christian, Moslem and Jew

In North Africa as in Europe, political and economic emancipation involuntarily brought about an alienation from the values and traditions of Judaism. But whereas in Europe emancipation was won gradually and through progressive change in the local political and sociological climate, in North Africa it was wrought suddenly—almost by force—by an outside colonizing power, entailing a much more sudden rupture with the past. In Europe, Judaism was able to retain its identity and cohesion partly because defection from Judaism implied, if only indirectly, a joining of forces with the Christian majority, and Christianity for the Jews of Europe symbolized centuries of abuse and persecution. But in the Maghreb, the emancipating power was secular, democratic, republican France. The oppressors had been Moslems, and the more the Jew advanced toward the liberating French, the greater the distance he put between himself and the degrading past he had known under Islam. Christianity, to the extent that it was identified with the French, did not arouse the same abhorrence in the Jews of the Maghreb as it did for those of Europe, for in North Africa the Church itself was a minority and the Jews had no memory of Christian persecution.

Nevertheless, the Moslem environment—its culture, its religion, its attitudes, its language and its economy—was still basically close to Jewish society. The French, for reasons to which the Jews certainly took no exception, encouraged the Jews to abandon the milieu of the colonized masses and to become an integral part of the colonizing élite. Thus the Jews lost touch simultaneously with both the North African society and the Jewish community without, however, being able to strike firm roots among the French. They never really acquired a sense of belonging to the new world they had entered.

The position of the Jews in North Africa was one of ambiguity; ambiguity in the attitude toward Orient and Occident, toward Moslem and Christian, toward colonized and colonizers, toward North Africa and France, toward past and future. This ambiguity was the ultimate cause of the disappearance of North African Jewry in the course of one decade after twenty centuries of proud and tragic history.

Part 4 Dissolution

 *Independence and Exodus*

The French presence in North Africa completely disrupted the pattern of coexistence between the Jewish and Moslem communities that had existed for over a thousand years. Instead of trying to bridge the gap between these two societies, the French had become a third force and the colonial regime brought about so rigid a separation between the three groups that each developed in almost complete isolation from the others, unaware that all were bound by a common destiny. The French in the Maghreb never succeeded in creating truly national states that transcended narrower ethnic and social groupings, or in instilling a sense of unified national allegiance; this was as true of Morocco and Tunisia, where the sovereignty of the French Protectorate administration was juxtaposed with the partially autonomous national state, as it was of Algeria, where French policy thwarted the full implementation of the oft-proclaimed principle of the unitary state.

The extent to which the three communities preserved their isolation despite the proximity of their existence is difficult to comprehend. Contacts between individuals of the separate societies were limited to the necessary minimum; neither schools nor military service nor any other factor brought about a closer understanding between them.[1] It was extremely rare for a person of one community to marry one of another, and even social

entertainment seldom managed to break through the race bar-
rier. It was not at all rare to find Europeans (or Europeanized
Jews) who had never so much as conducted a conversation with
a Moslem, who had not the least conception of Moslem thought
and culture or of the aspirations of the impoverished Moslem
masses, who had never even heard the voice of the muezzin call
out for prayer; the barriers were so impermeable that victims
and victimizers were unaware that they had become captives of
their own narrow "ghetto."

While, as we have seen, the chasm that separated the Jewish
community from the French tended to narrow, that between
these two communities and the Moslem society tended to widen
and deepen till in the end it provoked the violent overthrow of
the established order. The disintegration process was speeded
by the fact that the wealth and the means of production were
concentrated in the hands of the European communities—a situation which made the poverty of the Moslems more acute, and
brought about a growth of racial discrimination against them.
These prejudices aggravated the plight of the penniless masses
and virtually precluded any possibility that they might one day
aspire to a position of equality. Although the Jews, too, were
subjected to intense anti-Semitic prejudices on the part of the
European colons, they were fortunate inasmuch as they, like the
Europeans, benefited from their countries' economic systems.

Social and economic status in North Africa was largely governed by the community to which the individual belonged; class
barriers were reinforced by ethnic barriers; being Christian,
Jewish or Moslem was not solely an indication of religion but
also a determinant of a person's place in the economy and in
society. Though the French colonizers had such a marked success in bringing to North Africa a fine network of roads, in
establishing modern agriculture and prosperous industries and

in building splendid cities, they failed to level the enormous economic disparities between the various ethnic groups or to promote mutual understanding and harmonious coexistence among the separate communities. This was the ultimate tragedy that brought about the dissolution of France's North African empire.

The Rise of Nationalism

North African nationalism had its early beginnings in the 1930's, and it emerged from the chaos of the Second World War with both the will and the means of achieving its avowed aim: independence. The nationalists were assured of the sympathy of the newly independent Arab countries and of the emerging African and Asian nations. In addition, they could count on the support of the entire Communist bloc and on a great deal of sympathy from traditionally anti-colonialist America. To these external factors were added two important internal developments. One was the existence of a comparatively numerous Moslem élite who had been educated to a very advanced level in French universities and were thereby fitted to lead the movements for national liberation. The other was the severe famines which struck most of the Maghreb in 1944-1945. (They were in part caused by the massive purchases of foodstuffs by the armies on both sides.) Starvation was widespread, further aggravating the poverty of the Moslem masses and rendering them even more susceptible to nationalist agitation. The juxtaposition of a large majority of impoverished Moslems (80 per cent of whom had a personal income of less than fifty dollars per annum) with a ruling minority of Europeans whose standard of living was continually rising, turned the Maghreb into another of the many battlefields in which the poor of Africa and Asia fought against their domination by the rich of Europe and America. Paradoxically, it was the very wealth, both material and intellectual, that the French had brought to North Africa, that had made it possible for the leaders of the colonized masses to acquire the new patterns of thought and the new attitudes that finally enabled them to oust the privileged colonizers. The struggle for independence in North Africa was long and hard; it brought with it the unforeseen destruction of the former social and ethnic equilibrium, provoking the almost complete disappearance of the French from the Maghreb and the massive exodus of the Jewish communities who had lived there for well over two millennia.

The secret meeting during the Casablanca Conference in 1943 between President F.D. Roosevelt, champion of the right of self-determination, and Sultan Mohammed V of Morocco, who had raised the standard of his people's revolt, may quite probably have had an important influence on the turn of events in the struggle for independence in North Africa. Be that as it may, by the end of the war news had leaked out from Cairo of a comprehensive plan for the ouster of the French from their North African possessions. In 1946, Abdel Krim, Moroccan rebel leader, managed to elude his French jailers and flee to Cairo where he became the central figure around whom all those who were fighting for independence in North Africa eventually rallied. Remarkably, neither the French government nor the French residents and officials in North Africa took seriously the preparations for revolt that the Moslems in North Africa were making almost openly; the French were simply too confident of the unquestioned perpetuity of their presence in the Maghreb. An attempted revolt in the Kabyle region of Algeria in 1945 was put down with great ferocity within a week; it was blindly assumed that violence was the only sensible response to the efforts of the nationalists, that "Arabs can understand nothing but force."

Independence

TUNISIA

The real revolution in North Africa first got under way in Tunisia under the leadership of Habib Bourguiba, head of the Néo-Destour party. France, exhausted by the Second World War, crippled and humiliated by its defeat in Indochina, was internally divided. Finally, on July 31, 1954, Pierre Mendès-France, the French premier and a Jew, officially announced the recognition by the French government of Tunisia's right to independence. This courageous act brought about the fall of his government; but his successor, Edgar Faure, had no choice but to continue the policy and to enter into negotiations that led to the grant of internal autonomy for Tunisia under an agreement signed in Paris on June 3, 1955, and to the final grant of complete independence by the agreement of March 20, 1956.

In the elections for the Tunisian Constituent Assembly that followed immediately on March 25, Jews were admitted to the polls for the first time on an equal footing with their Moslem fellow-citizens. When Habib Bourguiba, now uncontested ruler of his country, presented his first cabinet to the Constituent Assembly (April 11), he included a Jew, André Barouch, as minister for planning and reconstruction. Barouch, a wealthy fifty-year-old textile merchant, had distinguished himself as a militant member of the Néo-Destour and, as such, had been exiled from Tunisia by the French. The appointment of a Jewish minister to the cabinet was intended to demonstrate the liberal attitude of the new government and also to reassure the Jewish community, whose members had been apprehensive about the revolutionary changes in the country. Barouch did not however survive the first reshuffle of the Tunisian government, and in 1957 the gesture of having a Jew in the cabinet was abandoned. Although, thanks to the political sagacity of Habib Bourguiba, the change in government was accompanied by the minimum of violence and administrative disruption (as was not the case in Algeria and Morocco), over 70 per cent of the Jewish population chose to emigrate in the years following independence.

MOROCCO

Morocco's struggle for independence was sparked by an address by Sultan Mohammed V on April 10, 1947, in which he solemnly proclaimed Morocco's desire to abrogate the Treaty of Protection that tied it to France, and to resume thereby Morocco's full independence. A fierce rebellion broke out against France. The Sultan and his entourage were exiled to Madagascar in 1953, but this only strengthened the resolve of the Istiqlal rebels to achieve victory. It also rallied all supporters of Morocco's independence, both within and without the country's borders, and brought the matter to the active attention of the United Nations. France was finally forced to capitulate in the face of the public outcry; Mohammed was recalled from exile and on November 16, 1955, Morocco gained its full independence. Mohammed V, now king, lost no opportunity to reaffirm his desire to set up a liberal, democratic regime for his country, inspired by Islam and based on the best of modern constitutions. Si Embarek Bekkai, who was called on to form the first government, reserved the cabinet appointment of minister for posts for a member of the Jewish community. After much unseemly bickering among the potential candidates, the position was finally granted to Dr. M. Benzaquen, a physician known for his philanthropic activities in Casablanca.

However, an unexpected hardening of the government's attitude to the Jews that stemmed in part from the inter-party maneuvering encouraged by Mohammed V, took place within a few months of the country's independence. The leaders of the Jewish community till then had been hopeful that the integration of their communities would proceed without special difficulties and that the Jews who were proudly accepting their new citizenship would be able to lead free and normal lives. These hopes foundered quickly under the twin influences of Arab League pressure and the economic crisis that overtook Morocco after 1956. The government of the moderate Si Bekkai fell; the right wing of the Istiqlal under Balafredj suffered defeat. When the left wing faction of the party under Mehdi ben Barka came to power in 1959 with Abdallah Ibrahim as premier and Abderahim Bouabid as deputy premier, the policy of the new government sowed panic among the Jews. In order to pacify the opposition among various political groups to its left-oriented economic policy, the government apparently used its policy toward the Jews as a bargaining counter, and the short idyll of the Jewish minority came to an end.

As part of the overall policy, the links with the Arab League were strengthened. King Mohammed toured Egypt and the Middle East; kings Saud, Faisal and Hussein visited Morocco and Morocco turned increasingly to Soviet Russia from which it obtained arms and military aircraft. The acceptance by the Moroccan government of the anti-Israel, anti-Zionist views of the Arab League led inevitably to the adoption of more or less anti-Jewish policies. Dr. Benzaquen was dismissed from the cabinet and, at the same time, postal relations with Israel were cut off. A number of highly placed Jewish civil servants were disgraced and restrictions were put on the number of Jews who could be admitted to the civil service. Finally in 1957 Jews were no longer granted passports and those hoping to emigrate were forced to do so clandestinely.

In the autumn of 1959 the Arab League held a much-publicized session in Casablanca that was attended by President Gamal Abdel Nasser of Egypt. Following this, the noose was tightened even further and the police started to hunt down Jews who were trying to leave the country illegally. Meantime, anti-Jewish measures were multiplied and all escape routes were tightly guarded. Those Jews who had braved untold hardship, days and weeks of wandering through mountains and deserts, were caught, arrested, beaten and thrown into jail on charges of "harming state security." In Meknès a Jewish leader was arrested and prosecuted because an old forgotten Hebrew almanac, published by the Jewish National Fund, had been found in his possession; another was arrested and beaten because he had prayed in synagogue with his head covered with a blue-and-white skullcap—the colors of Israel's flag. All Jewish organizations, including welfare bodies, cultural societies and even burial societies, were suspected of Zionism. The director-general of O.R.T. in Morocco was deported by the police without warning, without notice and without even the fiction of legal proceedings, despite the fact that he represented an international organization. A series of articles depicting "the many-headed Zionist hydra," which was published in a leading daily newspaper, caused further tension.

The Jews of Morocco, alarmed at the worsening of their situation, continued to try to flee the country by clandestine means, most hoping to find refuge in Israel. The saddest and most dramatic episode in this period took place in January 1961 during the visit of President Nasser to Morocco, when a fishing boat, the "Pisces," filled with Jewish refugees, foundered between Tangiers and Gibraltar and forty lives were lost.

King Mohammed V, under whom the brutal and repressive policy against the Jews had been carried out, died suddenly on February 26, 1961. (It was widely rumored that he had appeared to his intimates after his death, expressing his regret at having allowed himself to persecute the Jews whose welfare he had always wished to protect, especially during the Nazi epoch.) His son and successor, King Hassan II, who had studied in French schools and acquired Western concepts and ideals, was more efficient and more objective in outlook than his father and less inclined to political maneuvering. He took the direction of his country's affairs into his own hands and put an end to the harassment of the Jewish community by the police and the administration. The basic right of the Jews to emigrate —which had not been denied them in any other Arab country, not even in Egypt after the Suez campaign of 1956—was restored in the early days of King Hassan's reign.

ALGERIA

In Algeria the movement for independence may be dated to 1933 when Messali Hadj created the Algerian Popular Party; in 1936 Messali could proclaim the charter of his movement to a crowd of Moslems that numbered twenty thousand. The party was officially dissolved by the French authorities in 1937, together with the Tunisian Destour and the Moroccan Action parties, and Messali Hadj was sentenced to forced labor, deprived of his civic rights and his property was confiscated.

Ferhat Abbas, a pharmacist who had studied in France, thereupon rose to the leadership of a more moderate nationalist
movement but he too was hounded by the French administration so that, in final despair at the inflexible attitude of the
French, he teamed up with the more extreme elements, a step
that led to the formation of the F.L.N. (National Liberation
Front) and the start of a war that lasted seven and a half years.
The formal war began on November 2, 1954, as the National
Liberation Army, the militant arm of the F.L.N., staged attacks
in every part of the country and seized effective control of a
large area. The French army, which had been embittered and
humiliated by a seemingly unending series of defeats and disas-
ters, replied by putting a force of half a million soldiers into the
conflict in a futile attempt to crush the rebels. The rebels, however, were supported by almost the entire Moslem population
and had the backing not only of world public opinion but also
of many leading figures in France itself.

The F.L.N. saw its objective clearly as the liberation of Algeria from reactionary, cruel and unjust colonialist exploitation,
as a struggle that must continue till French domination was
terminated. It was successful in establishing diplomatic contact
abroad, in winning the support of African and Asian governments, in mobilizing world public opinion in its favor, and in
effectively neutralizing the influence of the few friends that
France managed to retain in this conflict.

The French community in Algeria, on the other hand, whose
opinion on the subject was practically unanimous, was able
virtually to dictate the Algerian policies of the successive governments in Paris and thereby nullified any attempts to grant the
Moslems a measure of emancipation. The French colons considered Algeria as their native land and as an integral part of
France, a fiction that, through long repetition, they had come to

believe. It was inconceivable for them that France might ever surrender its position in Algeria. This view was so deeply anchored in their soul that it spread, as if by contagion, to capture the minds of otherwise entirely objective leaders such as the onetime premier Guy Mollet, the majority of France's socialist leaders and men such as Jacques Soustelle. (The latter had been appointed by Mendès-France in 1954 as French delegate-general in Algeria and charged with the task of pacifying the country. He later returned to Algeria as the leader of the O.A.S., the French colonists' anti-Algerian, anti-government Secret Army Organization.) Not one single French political leader in the years 1954-1960 was able to avoid the error of proclaiming the undying perpetuity of *"Algérie Française."* Even Charles de Gaulle, when returned to power in 1958, perpetuated this myth which had become the very breath of life to the French in Algeria, and it was not till he had fully consolidated his political position that he was able, during 1961 and 1962, to impose on his people the only possible solution—the end of French rule in Algeria.

The idea that France might ever abandon Algeria was one that the French in that country had never been able to consider even vaguely. They had been born in Algeria and knew no other home. They were, at the same time, completely ignorant of the other universe, that of the ten million Moslems in their country. They lived in isolated pockets, cut off from any links with the Arab mileu. This blindness to their surroundings served only to strengthen their belief in the myth of Algérie Française, a belief which justified the fury with which they attempted to defend their way of life with the support of an army that sufferd defeat after despairing defeat. The disclosure of General de Gaulle's Algerian strategy startled the French in Algeria into open revolt against the central government; when even that failed the

O.A.S. unleashed a futile campaign of terror, anarchy and brutality in an attempt to stave off the inevitable.

Seven and a half years of warfare had sown death and devastation on the Algerian countryside, bringing ruin to a once flourishing region. The bitter warfare that had dehumanized the participants on both sides and made brutal torture and mass slaughter into commonplaces, culminated in the senseless acts of horror of the O.A.S. in which women and infants and bedridden patients were murdered with equal ferocity and the last glimmer of hope for a possible peaceful cohabitation of communities in an independent Algeria was finally shattered.

As the certainty of the eventual independent Algeria dawned on them, the non-Moslem communities in Algeria were seized with panic. Victims of the hate and disdain in which they had always held the Moslems, and fearful of being left behind among them in direct confrontation with no assistance from the outside world, the French in Algeria took headlong flight from the country of their birth to France, the country of their loyalty. The emigration, which had its early beginnings during the outbreak of hostilities in 1955, grew to gigantic proportions; between December 1961 and the final granting of independence to Algeria in July 1962 more than half a million French citizens— over three-quarters of the total—fled Algeria, abandoning everything. Among them was almost the entire Jewish community.

The precarious position of the Jews between the French minority and the mass of their Moslem subjects which, as we have seen, had brought about a noticeable loss of Jewish identity in times of peace, caused such confusion under the stress of war that it culminated in the unforeseen and sudden disappearance of the majority of the Jewish communities. But one thing, above all, was certain; the unanimity with which the Jews regretted the conflict between the French and the Moslems. In many respects, the Jews found themselves closely linked with the French; they had been the main beneficiaries of the colonial system in Algeria; their acculturation had pushed them into the orbit of French civilization; they had been almost completely integrated into French culture everywhere but for the few communities in the Saharan south. The Jews proudly considered themselves to be French in every respect. Even those who had not benefited directly from the political, social and cultural emancipation knew that the opportunities that would link them to the French culture were open to them too. But the bonds that linked the Jews to the large mass of Moslems were no less powerful. The life of the Jews in the Maghreb had, on the whole, been happier than that of those of Europe. Their coexistence had almost always been peaceful; they had lived in a symbiosis from which the Jews were generally the ones to benefit. They shared linguistic ties, and had similar attitudes, viewpoints, values and characteristics; the Jews, too, were ardently attached to the country itself, a land both rich and beautiful.

This dual loyalty, that was felt by even the poorest Jew and in the most far-flung community, posed an inescapable dilemma. It was impossible to oppose the French without betraying a deeply felt loyalty and a sense of gratitude that the Jews owed to their emancipators; it was impossible to support the French cause without becoming a traitor in the eyes of the Moslems, compromising all ties that bound the Jews to the country and its citizens and destroying all hopes for future peaceful coexistence. Heavy pressure was applied from both sides in the hope of gaining from the Jews both material and moral support; neutrality was thus also ruled out. The vast majority of the Jews in Algeria (as in Tunisia and Morocco) remained passive in the struggle, as if petrified by the imminent events which they knew would mean the end of their existence in the Maghreb. There was a small minority in Algeria as in the other two countries that wholeheartedly supported the French cause and paid for its loyalty in lives, in liberty and in property. There was similarly a small minority of varying size that supported the nationalists and paid in like manner for its loyalty.

The combatants on both sides nevertheless took great care to keep the Jewish communities clear of their military objectives. Where Jews fell victim to the struggle it was usually in retribution for a position that they had taken in support of one side or the other. Thus in the Levy family in Algiers, the father was assassinated by the O.A.S. as a sympathizer with the cause of the F.L.N., the son was killed by the F.L.N. on suspicion of belonging to the O.A.S. And in the long, bitter struggle in which human life had lost its value, there were many Jews who were killed, not necessarily deliberately but because they were within reach of the assassin's knife or bullet.

The Jewish community in Algeria, because of its historical situation and by reason of the bitterness and length of the struggle, was in an even more precarious position than that of Tunisia or Morocco. The final blow was struck on December 12, 1960, when the F.L.N., enlarging the scope of its military operations, overran the Great Synagogue of Algiers in the heart of the Casbah. The building was gutted, the Torah scrolls ripped, soiled and otherwise desecrated, the walls inscribed with swastikas and "Death to the Jews," and the furnishings ripped out and destroyed; over the ruins of the synagogue the rioters planted the green-and-white flag of the Algerian nationalists. This beautiful synagogue, built during the rein of Napoleon III, had been one of the most important houses of Jewish worship in Algeria. At Oran the nationalists similarly ravaged the Jewish cemetery and pillaged its chapel. Leading Jewish personalities including three officials of the Jewish Agency were kidnapped and assassinated. These acts of violence fell on the Jews like a thunderbolt; they were seen as a warning for the future and marked the final disintegration of the Jewish community. The despair of the Jews at these events was naturally exploited by the O.A.S. which was determined to sow chaos and confusion; in Oran the brawls between Jews and Arabs were exaggerated by the press in articles that conveyed the impression that nothing would have pleased the O.A.S. more than to see the conflict in Algeria turn into a war between Jews and Arabs, the O.A.S. (many of whose members were notorious for their virulent anti-Semitism) stepping in as arbitrators.

Peace talks between the French and the F.L.N. were started in May 1961. Two referendums later, a sovereign and independent Republic of Algeria was proclaimed on July 1, 1962. By that date no more than a few thousand Jews were left in all of Algeria.

Exodus

The exodus of the Moroccan and Tunisian Jews to Israel was spread over a comparatively long period of time. It had first gathered momentum in 1947 and 1948 under the emotional stimulus of the approaching independence of the State of Israel and had continued throughout the following years. There was a sharp decline in 1953 at the height of a grave economic crisis in Israel, but in 1955 and 1956, the years in which Tunisia and Morocco gained their independence and Arab governments came to power, emigration soared to record figures. A new low followed between 1958 and 1960, caused by the Moroccan government's refusal to allow the Jews to leave. Nevertheless, thousands of Moroccan Jews braved the hazards of clandestine immigration, an operation which displayed great courage and heroism as well as remarkable efficiency. In 1961 and 1962 the rate of emigration swelled anew and brought about the final liquidation of many Jewish communities in the Maghreb. Seventy per cent of the Jews in Morocco and Tunisia had emigrated in the previous fifteen years; in the summer of 1962 just over 30,000 Jews were estimated as remaining in Tunisia and just over 80,000 in Morocco. It has been estimated that by 1972 the Jewish population in Morocco will be less than 5 per cent of what it was in 1948 and in Tunisia less than 10 per cent.

Jewish emigration from Algeria was more precipitate; in its force and in its suddenness it resembled a flash flood in a Saharan wadi. The confidence of Algerian Jewry in their future as citizens of an Algeria that would always be French had never been shaken. Neither the Second World War with its attendant miseries nor the creation of the State of Israel nor even the outbreak of the war of liberation in Algeria itself in 1954 caused any marked change in this respect. Even in July 1961, perhaps 90 per cent of the Jews of Algeria still firmly believed that nothing would change for them in the future.

Disenchantment was sudden and brutal. It came on December 12, 1961 with the unleashing of powerful attacks by the F.L.N. on the larger cities, where most of the Jews were concentrated. The attacks spread panic among Jews and Christians alike. Within a few months both communities had vanished from the country as if by magic. In their hundreds of thousands the non-Moslems had abandoned everything, stormed airfields and ports, and sought the safety of the European coast of the Mediterranean. The unbelievable, unforeseeable, incredible, was happening. Algeria was to gain its independence. Rich and poor, pious and agnostic, leaders spiritual and temporal—all fled from the madness and pandemonium into which Algeria was suddenly plunged. The flight reached its climax just before Algeria gained its full independence on July 1, 1962. Within a matter of weeks no more than ten thousand Jews were left in all of Algeria. Of those who had fled, the vast majority were resolved never to return, not even after calm and order had been restored. Terror, murder, rape, robbery and abduction had done their part. Not all the efforts and declarations of the authorities on both sides who attempted to smooth the transition to an independent Algeria in the last few weeks, or of those who took over the leadership of the independent Algeria, were able to restore confidence. The country was in a state of utter chaos and the Jews saw headlong flight as the only escape from the prevailing anarchy.

The sudden arrival of some three quarters of a million refugees from Algeria brought vast economic disorder to France. Though the country benefited from the addition to its working force, no housing was available for the newcomers who, disheartened by their misfortune, continued to pose heavy problems to metropolitan France, shaking the Fifth Republic to its foundations.

As for the Jews, nothing and no one had been prepared for their arrival. The 115,000 Algerian Jews who poured into France within a few months caught the Jewish communities in France completely unawares. In many cities, such as in Marseilles, the newcomers soon outnumbered the resident Jewish population. Difficulties frequently arose when vast numbers of Jews from the depths of the Sahara arrived to join the old, established communities. It came as a profound shock to French Jews to realize that there existed these other Jews, disfigured by diseases and malnutrition, suffering from trachoma, tuberculosis and alcoholism, who rejected the beds they were offered and preferred to sleep on the ground. Though the sudden influx of impoverished refugees provoked certain misgivings that a new wave of anti-Semitism might be aroused in France, all necessary steps were nevertheless taken on the part of the Jewish community in France to facilitate the immigrants' integration into their new economic and social life.[2] Unlike the great majority of Tunisian and Moroccan Jews who had emigrated to Israel without any hesitation, the Jews of Algeria, with only few exceptions, had decided to settle permanently in France, for they, far more than the others, had felt themselves to be French in every respect. Their close identification with the French was further reinforced by the compensation and help that by virtue of their French citizenship they received from the French authorities to ease their economic and social integration. Despite their official welcome and acceptance by France, the Jews of Algeria tended to remain a separate entity[3] and did not entirely give up the idea that one day, when circumstances were more propitious, they too might settle in Israel.

The triumph of Moslem nationalism in the countries of Africa and Asia had everywhere been accompanied by the total or partial liquidation of the respective Jewish communities. All the Jews of Yemen, Aden and Jordan, 98 per cent of those of Iraq, and 90 per cent of those of Syria, Egypt and Libya had left their native countries between the end of the Second World War and the 1960's, as had the majority of the Jews of Afghanistan, Kurdestan and India and a large part of those of Iran, Turkey and the Lebanon. The creation of the State of Israel in 1948, because of the unrest that it caused in the majority of the Moslem countries and the attraction it exerted on the Jews who were potential candidates for emigration, doubtlessly speeded the historical process that ended in the almost total liquidation of the Diaspora in the Moslem countries. The war between Jews and Arabs in Israel in 1947–1948 and again in 1956 and 1967 cer-

16 Israel

The close links between the Maghreb and the Holy Land that had existed throughout the centuries were loosened somewhat when, following the arrival of the French in North Africa, the traditional association of the area with the vast Moslem world was supplanted by the influence and culture of France and Europe. However, the fact that the Jewish community remained a separate entity and possessed its own schools that disseminated Jewish learning to all, made it impossible for an individual, child or adult, to be unaware of his Jewish identity, even where the superimposed French culture was at its most intense. Their Jewish spiritual heritage always remained close to the Jews of the Maghreb and their yearning for Zion was never extinguished.

North African Jewry had been deeply shaken by the spread of the Nazi terror across Europe and by the sufferings of their fellow Jews there. The period of Nazi domination and the restrictive policies applied to the Jews in the Maghreb itself had opened the eyes of many to their inescapable destiny as Jews. To the rabbis of the distant Sahara the war appeared as the great cataclysmic event that foreshadowed the messianic age and the return of the Jews to Zion. That the end of the war was, in fact, followed by the creation of the State of Israel and, a few years later, by the independence of all three countries in the

Maghreb, could not but heighten the dramatic impact of the return of the Jews of North Africa to the Holy Land.

The creation of the State of Israel was accepted by the masses of North African Jewry as an act of messianic fulfillment rather than as the outcome of a political event. In the mystically charged atmosphere engendered by the war and by the interpretations given to these portents by the local rabbis, the night of November 29, 1947, when the United Nations voted in favor of the creation of an independent Jewish state in what was then Palestine, took on the character of a *Lail Shimurim*— Night of Vigil—that according to tradition preceded the Exodus from Egypt. After the centuries of suffering and privation, of fasting and of prayer, the vote at Lake Success was seen throughout North Africa as nothing less than a Divine Judgment, a palpable and visible sign of the final Redemption. If any more impetus was required, it was provided by the massacres perpetrated by the Moslems of Tripolitania on their Jewish neighbors and the similar events at Oujda and Djerada in Morocco, which have been described in Chapter Ten. These outbreaks were a further reminder to the Jews of the precariousness of their situation as a minority in the Moslem world.

Immigration

And so the mass emigration to Israel got under way. By the end of 1949 close to twenty-five thousand North African Jews had arrived in Israel to take part in the War of Independence and to participate in the resurrection of their ancient homeland. They constituted some 5 per cent of the Jews of the Maghreb, their proportion varying with the size of the respective Jewish communities and reflecting strongly the relative closeness of their ties with Israel. From Algeria, where the Jews had been most fully integrated, and where they felt most secure, only about 750 Jews came to Israel; 6,000 arrived from Tunisia and 18,000 from Morocco during the same period. From other parts of North Africa came over 22,000 Jews, 15,000 of them from Libya and the remainder from Egypt. Within the first fifteen years of the creation of the State of Israel, over a half of the Jews of North Africa had migrated to Israel. One-third had migrated to France, the Americas and elsewhere, and the rest—chiefly in Morocco and Tunisia—seemed doomed to disappear within a few years; their communities, disorganized and demoralized, dissolved one by one; the individuals who have stayed behind out of loyalty or love for their native countries or out of attachment to their property and their customary way of life remain at the mercy of every unforeseen event that might create a new atmosphere of panic. Their number, however, is dwindling constantly.

The rate of immigration of Jews from the Maghreb to Israel slowed somewhat after 1949. In 1950 and 1951 the annual total reached about 18,000; in 1952 it fell markedly to just over 8,000, while in 1953 it fell to less than half that number, totalling only 3,900. The falling off in the rate of immigration was due to the severe economic crisis prevailing in Israel at the time and to the difficulties that the new immigrants encountered in their attempts to integrate into the Israel economy. Reports of their hardships had filtered back to the Maghreb and had discouraged potential candidates for emigration. The difficult period of transition that the immigrants had to face on their arrival led to a certain proportion of return migrants, whose number reached a peak of 1,130 in 1952. However, the figure of return migration of Jews to the Maghreb was in sum negligible and never exceeded 2.65 per cent of the total immigration.

In 1954 the immigration of North African Jews to Israel started a new upward swing under the impetus of local events. Tunisia, engaged in revolutionary war, was about to negotiate its independence, warfare had broken out in Morocco, and Algeria was going through the period of tension that preceded its own war against the French. The uncertainty of the future made many Jews prefer to brave the rigors that would face them on their arrival in Israel. That year there were 11,000 immigrants from the Maghreb. In 1955, as the nationalist movements in the Maghreb achieved new successes, the figure nearly trebled, reaching just on 31,700. In 1956, as the new administrations took over in Tunisia and Morocco, there were 43,850 immigrants from the Maghreb—80 per cent of all immigration to Israel that year—and this despite the tension on Israel's borders and the frequent incursions of Egyptian terrorists that provoked the Suez campaign toward the end of that year.

The year 1956 was the last that free emigration was permitted from Morocco. As the gates clamped shut, only 12,300 North African Jews were able to reach Israel during the next year. In 1958 the number was a quarter of that (3,275) and even less than that in 1953. But, despite the refusal of the Moroccan authorities to issue passports to Jews and the hunting down and persecution of those attempting to flee, the illegal emigration was not without success. There was a slight rise to 3,838 immigrants from North Africa in 1959 and to 4,800 in 1960, the most difficult year at the turn of which the tragedy of the "Pisces" took place.

A new period of massive migration started in 1961. One of the factors was the lifting of the restrictions on Jewish emigration by the new ruler of Morocco, King Hassan II. Another was the beginning of massive emigration from Algeria. Hitherto, few Algerian Jews had reached Israel. The highest annual total had been 1,000 in 1956, and in 1953 there were only 81 immi-grants. In 1961 the figure suddenly rose to over 4,400. Yet, impressive as this may seem, it was still small compared with the number of Algerian Jews who emigrated that year to France. Of the total Jewish population in Algeria, over 90 per cent in fact had chosen to settle in France by the time Algeria achieved its independence on July 1, 1962.

As was pointed out in the preceding chapter, the Algerian Jews, French citizens, regarded France, not Israel, as their al-ternative home and, unlike the Moroccan and Tunisian Jews, they were not regarded by the French as foreigners. Economi-cally, too, conditions in France were vastly superior to anything Israel could offer: the country was going through a boom of economic expansion and could provide employment under ex-cellent conditions to all its citizens from Algeria—and this in addition to the compensation that all the new arrivals received from the authorities to ease their period of adaptation. Fur-thermore, the realities of life in Israel discouraged the Algerian refugees from settling there. The difficulties that faced the im-migrants from Morocco and Tunisia were even more pro-nounced for those arriving from Algeria. The Algerian had been used to a fairly easy life in a colonial country under full eco-nomic expansion, where he had earned a high salary and where the road to wealth was open to him. To leave such a world, artificial though its structure may have been, and settle for a hard pioneering life in the Negev desert of Israel, could not be achieved without suffering and unhappiness. One-tenth of Al-geria's Jews have nevertheless chosen to settle in Israel. This figure is bound to grow, for many of the Algerian Jews consider France to be only a way-station where they complete their ed-ucation, recover from the shock of their uprooting, acquire new skills, new savings, and new possessions, all of which will facilitate their eventual settlement and integration in Israel. Despite the attractions offered by France, few Algerians have actually re-emigrated there from Israel.

Characteristics of the North African Immigration

When Israel gained its independence in 1948, the Jews of North Africa formed only a small proportion of its population. Fifteen years later they formed the largest and the most cohesive community in the country. If the *Moghrabim* (the Jews of Maghrebian origin who had been living in the Holy Land for many generations before the State achieved its independence) are included with the more recent immigrants, and the immigrants from Egypt and Libya are added, and if account is taken of the high rate of natural increase among this group which is one of the highest in the world and the highest of all communities in Israel, the Jews of North African origin may now be estimated as making up a quarter of Israel's Jewish population.

Besides being the largest community, the North African is also in aggregate, the youngest, with a median age of 25—as against 31 for immigrants from Asia and 45 for immigrants from Europe. Half of the immigrants from the Maghreb are under 25; the average size of a household is five persons and many families number eight, ten, even fifteen children. A family with only three children is the exception among Jews from North Africa.

Another characteristic that distinguished this mass immigration from that from other countries was the fact that it arrived in Israel lacking its social and economic élite. The well-educated, the affluent, the trained technicians, the intellectuals and the businessmen among them, like their counterparts in other countries, had chosen to make their homes in the West—in France or the Americas—rather than face the difficulties of Israel. Israel had drawn those who lacked possessions or resources, those who, more deeply imbued with Judaism and messianic fervor, chose to return to their ancient homeland as if by instinct. This inverse selection naturally aggravated the absorption into Israel of those who did come. The imbalance, however, is slowly being corrected as the better educated and more substantial type of North African immigrant has been arriving in Israel in increasing numbers, in part attracted by the better economic climate and in part because those factors that had tended up till now to keep him in North Africa have gradually changed and made his situation there untenable.

The masses who came to Israel were poor; their poverty was that of North Africa alongside which European-type poverty would seem to be the lap of luxury. They included the blind, the paralyzed, the tubercular and the syphilitic. For them, living in a world that twenty centuries seemed to have bypassed, the promise of a new future dawned as they saw the coasts of the Maghreb disappear beyond the horizon.

Encounter

The sudden and unexpected arrival of nearly 57,000 immigrants from North Africa (including those from Libya and Egypt) between 1947 and 1949 had caught the Israel authorities unprepared. Like Western Jews in general, they had been almost unaware of the existence of what have been referred to as "the forgotten million" Jews of the Orient. In fact one might go so far as to say that except for the work of the Alliance Israélite Universelle and the activities of the Hilfsverein, the Anglo-

Jewish Committee and the Joint Distribution Committee, there had been almost no contact between the Jews of Europe and those living in the Arab world since about the sixteenth century.

The Jews of Europe and America, for their part, found it difficult to accept the idea that these people of darker hue, imbued with Arabic culture and customs, were in fact Jews and their brothers. The Israelis of European origin, like the pioneers who half a century earlier had been dumbfounded at the sight of fellow Jews in Jaffa who looked for all the world like Arabs, tended, consciously or not, to look down on the new arrivals from the Moslem countries in much the same way. They found that they had little in common with these newcomers from the Atlas Mountains or the Saharan deserts; they understood neither their language nor their customs nor their reactions. Among certain sections of the population, there existed a hostility that assumed racial overtones. Regrettable and unexpected as it was, it heightened even more the difficulties that the immigrants from the Orient and from the Occident experienced in their mutual encounters.

During the 1950's, Israel was following a courageous policy of permitting and encouraging free immigration for all Jews from any part of the world. But it lacked the resources to cope with the many problems posed by the arrival of the mass immigration from North Africa, not the least of which was the absence of an economic or intellectual élite among them. Israel at that time was seeking formulae for integration. It was a period of experimentation, of trial and error. The unexpectedly long period in which the immigrants were obliged to stay in the transit camps (*ma'abarot*)—immense shantytowns which were hurriedly set up to house them pending their final settlement into proper homes and permanent employment—produced untold social and economic hardship, leaving a canker of bitterness that was not to be eradicated for a long time.

While the Jews of Israel had not been prepared for the arrival of the first Jews from North Africa, the truth of the matter is that the Jews of North Africa had not been prepared for Israel. The World Zionist Organization, set up at the turn of the century, had never made the effort to draw them into the orbit of active Zionism in which later, as builders of Israel, they were to play such an important part; the contribution to practical Zionism on the part of North Africa's Jews was as a result negligible. That which had attracted them to Israel was neither Zionism nor even Jewish nationalism but an uncompromising spiritual tradition based on the Bible, the Talmud, the Cabala, Jewish liturgy and the teachings of the great Jewish philosophers and teachers. These elements played a relatively small part in the Zionist vision and even religious Zionism had never been able to penetrate deeply into the lives of the Jews of the East; the spirit of Orthodox Judaism, such as had developed in Europe after the eighteenth century, was far removed from that of the Sephardi and Oriental Jews.

For the majority of the North African immigrants, then, the adventure of their arrival in Israel was, and for many still is, an event of an essentially religious, messianic, spiritual, almost mystic nature. For many the reality was a sad delusion. Thus it was for a certain rabbi whom the author had met in a distant Saharan village in the dark days of 1942; even then the rabbi had predicted with propehetic accuracy the resurrection of the State of Israel, which in an apocalyptic vision, he saw as the outcome of the world turmoil. The next meeting took place fourteen years later at Kfar Ono, a small village near Tel Aviv. The rabbi's encounter with the secular character of the State of

Israel was beyond his comprehension; it had left him disillusioned, quietly resigned, helpless and far from happy.

The vision of redemption that had been nourished in the darkness of the mellah, and that had seemed on the point of fulfillment as the immigrants' ship came within sight of Haifa, was dispelled almost on the first contact with the reality of Israel. A typical case was that of a boatload of new immigrants from North Africa who in 1954 had been selected by the immigration department of the Jewish Agency before their departure from the transit camps in France to spearhead a new venture. The immigrants had no doubt dreamed of Israel as a blissful home where they would dwell in eternal tranquillity within the turreted walls of Jerusalem; they were taken by truck straight from the ship to the site that had been chosen as their new home: an isolated spot in the Negev—wilderness, sand and rocks as far as the eye could see and jackals howling in the distance. The immigrants flatly refused to leave their trucks; they demanded to be taken away at once; anywhere at all, just so long as they would not have to remain in this God-forsaken desert. Explanations were of no avail; they bounced off a solid wall of refusal. At last, one of the accompanying officials staged an "incident." Rifles were shot off at random in the dark, the immigrants were told that this was an attack by Arab raiders, and in a second the reluctant immigrants had left their trucks to seek shelter in the huts that had been prepared for them. Today that forsaken site in the desert is Dimona, a modern industrial town of 17,000 inhabitants, most of them immigrants from North Africa. It is a tribute to their courage, hard work and capabilities.

The lack of communication between immigrants of vastly different geographical, social and historical backgrounds did nothing to relieve the disillusionment of the new arrivals. They lacked a common language, or common ties with the recent past, and the Arabic and French-speaking immigrants were frequently unable to make their needs and fears comprehensible to their neighbors and to the officials with whom they were dealing. And then, there was the distress that resulted from the break-up of the customary social order into which the Jews of North Africa had been born and under which they had lived. The close, cohesive life of the Maghreb had collapsed with one blow and there was nothing, at first, to replace it. To the complications caused by the sudden uprooting from their established social framework, the disillusionment and the painful process of adaptation to the new life, was added another problem, that of discrimination, of which virtually all new immigrants from Moslem countries believed themselves to be the victims, especially at the hands of the Jewish Agency. In fact, arrangements for the reception of new immigrants had been made with the needs of European Jews in mind. Housing, for instance, was perfectly adequate for a family that had no more than three children, but for the large families customary among immigrants from North Africa and other Moslem countries the resultant overcrowding caused great unhappiness. Neither were salaries and wages scaled to the needs of large families.

The tension that arose from this social and economic maladjustment reached breaking point in the summer of 1959, when a series of incidents forcibly brought the gravity of the problem to the public's attention. The spark was fired in Wadi Salib, a crowded quarter in downtown Haifa near the port that had been abandoned by its Arab population in 1948 and was later settled largely by immigrants from North Africa. The police tried to arrest a drunkard who was sleeping in a cafe. In the ensuing altercation a policeman fired a bullet that injured the drunk, who as it turned out was a Jew from North Africa. A crowd of two hundred soon gathered in the streets of the quarter, stoned a police car and roughed up some policemen. Their cries of "assassins" and "exploiters" reflected their conviction that they were the victims of deliberate discrimination and exploitation. At dawn a newly formed organization, "The Union of North Africans," headed by a young, unemployed immigrant from Morocco, David ben Harrosh, incited new demonstrations. Inflammatory leaflets were distributed and a crowd marched out of the lower town headed for the residential and business quarters on the slopes of Mount Carmel, causing a certain amount of damage—and a considerable degree of fear—on its way. The disturbances spread from Wadi Salib and Haifa to other towns where there were large concentrations of dissatisfied immigrants —Tiberias, Beersheba and Migdal Haemek in particular. The North African immigrants there poured into the streets, smashed an occasional shop or office, and roughed up some of their antagonists. There was a feeling of impending revolt in the air that gave rise to fears of a widespread flare-up whose results would have been disastrous for the whole country.

Around the world even the most serious newspapers featured sensational stories of the inter-communal unrest. This new picture of Israel spread consternation wherever concern for the interests of the new State were felt. Understandably it was more pronounced among the Jews still living in North Africa who were receiving letters that spoke of the tension and despair gripping the North African community in Israel. The Israel government immediately set up a commission of enquiry to investigate the matter and to seek the underlying causes of the tension. Its conclusions, commented on at length by the press, were published a month later and brought to light the unsolved problems of the integration into Israel life of the immigrants from Oriental countries.

Settlement and Absorption

The North African immigration placed an enormous strain on the absorption capacity of Israel and of the Jewish Agency. Altogether the immigrants from the Maghreb made up some 25 per cent of total immigration during Israel's first fifteen years. (Another 10 per cent came from Egypt and Libya.) The inconceivable poverty of the new arrivals from North Africa meant that all, almost without exception, were dependent on the Israel authorities for every step of their integration into the country. The number who became social welfare cases surpassed even the most pessimistic estimates. The task was further complicated by the fact that most of the North African Jews who came to Israel were those who had remained part of the under-developed Oriental society that had not yet evolved under French influence. They had to adapt themselves at one and the same time to the economy, the culture, the techniques and the patterns of living of a pioneering country developing along Western lines. For Israel, itself grappling with problems of national development, its security under constant threat, the attempt to integrate these people so totally unprepared for what was before them, was indeed a courageous undertaking.

HEALTH

Immediately upon arrival the North African Jews placed before the Israel health authorities an unprecedented emergency: not only were there hundreds of cases of tuberculosis, trachoma, syphilis, ringworm and other highly infectious diseases that required urgent treatment, but there was also an imminent danger that epidemics would break out in the immigrants' camps and spread throughout the country. The fact that, despite the make-shift medical facilities, no such situation arose is eloquent proof of the efficiency and devotion with which the health services met the crisis. Today, many of the T.B. sanitoriums in Israel have been closed and the eye clinics are relatively deserted in comparison with what they were fifteen years ago. Furthermore, thanks to the nationwide network of mother and child welfare clinics, the infant mortality rate among the North African community is now identical with that of the country as a whole —28 infant deaths per 1,000 live births. (The figure in the United States is 25.) In general, the state of health of this community today is similar to that of Israel's total population.

PIONEER SETTLEMENT

The first priority of the State of Israel after its boundaries had been secured was to settle the sparsely populated areas of the country. Those regions most suited for immediate settlement were in the Galilee, certain areas in the center of the country and in the narrow "corridor" of the Judean hills which links Jerusalem with the coastal plain, and then, the northern and western Negev. The departments of Immigration and Settlement of the Jewish Agency were concentrating their efforts on the development of these areas and to them the majority of the new settlers from North Africa were directed. In the eighteen months from October 1956 to April 1958, 66.5 per cent of the North African immigrants who arrived were directed to "development towns"—either those that had been expanded around the nucleus of a small town abandoned by its hitherto predominantly Arab population such as Beersheba and Migdal Ashkelon, or entirely new cities like Dimona and Hatzor: 8.5 per cent

settled in the relatively fertile, well-developed and densely populated coastal region; 3 per cent settled in *kibbutzim* (collective
villages) some of which, like Regavim and others in the Negev,
had been founded originally by immigrants from North Africa;
5 per cent joined *moshavim* (cooperative villages); 14.5 per
cent settled in the larger, old-established cities or joined relatives. Over six hundred youngsters (2.5 per cent of the total)
were accepted by the agricultural and industrial training centers
of Youth Aliyah. Thus, 77 per cent of the immigrants from
North Africa in this typical period took to a pioneering life in
agricultural settlements and development towns under the
harshest conditions that the country could offer. That they
tended to resent the hardships is axiomatic. That over three-
quarters of a people, so thoroughly unprepared for these new
conditions and so recently and brutally uprooted, could succeed
in striking new roots despite such difficulties speaks for their
stamina and fortitude.

The statistics on agricultural settlement in Israel project a
similar picture. Of the 251 new agricultural villages and settlements founded in Israel from 1948 to 1959, 82 were entirely or
in large part settled by immigrants from North Africa. Of these
13 were in the north of the country, 15 in the Galilee, 16 in the
coastal plain, 11 in the Jerusalem "corridor," 13 in the Lachish
region (between the Judean foothills and the northern Negev),
and 14 in the Negev itself. The number of villages settled by
North Africans has since risen to well over a hundred. The part
played by the North Africans in the settlement of new agricultural villages since the independence of Israel is greater than
that of any other single group in the country, and it is in this
sphere that their success has been most marked. These Jews,
whose contact with the soil had been almost non-existent for
two thousand years, returned to a soil that had been abandoned

for almost as long and, by revitalizing it, were themselves revitalized. "This soil recognizes us and now it is beginning to talk to us," one of them explained graphically. The proportion of North African immigrants who gave up the challenge of agricultural life is remarkably similar to the national average for all immigrants—31 per cent.

The conditions to which the settlers from North Africa were subjected were disproportionately difficult: less than one-third were directed to settlements whose soil was classified as "best" quality, a similar number went to settlements of "medium" quality and 37 per cent to settlements whose soil was described as the "worst." The fortitude shown by the new pioneers from North Africa was thus certainly no less than that of the others. A survey conducted by the Jewish Agency in 1960 revealed that, despite all obstacles and despite the youth of both the settlements and the settlers, the general condition of the villages colonized by North Africans was close to the national norm. Fifty-four per cent had "good conditions" (the nation-wide average was 55.1 per cent), 21 per cent of the villages were in "medium condition" (against 22.3 per cent) and 25 per cent had poor conditions (against 22.7 per cent). It is more difficult to evaluate the real stability of these new settlements. The survey considered a number of elements such as communal stability of the village council, stability of other communal bodies, level of investment and of the economy, degree of exploitation of individual holdings, organization of marketing procedures, and relations with outside groups and with the various authorities. Taking all these factors into consideration, the villages were classified variously as "flourishing," "average" and "poor." The villages settled by North Africans tended to fall below the general standard in certain areas of the country. Overall, 15.4 per cent were considered poorly developed (as against the nationwide average of 8.6 per cent), 54 per cent were classified as "average" (42 per cent national average) and 30.8 per cent as "flourishing" (as against the national 49.3 per cent). Taking account of the ages of the settlements and of their settlers, of the regions and the quality of the soil and also of the large number of children in their households, this points to a remarkable achievement. As the report of the Jewish Agency stated: "The immigration from North Africa has played a considerable role in the new colonization. . . . The level of development of these settlements inhabited by North Africans is equivalent to the general mean of the other communities." These lines highlight the revolutionary process by which the North Africans, within a few years of their arrival in Israel, have been transformed into a highly productive group, especially as tillers of the soil.

The celebration of the first harvest in a new village in the Jerusalem "corridor" was a significant event. The village was occupied by North Africans; this was the first harvest for them and for the land that had lain fallow for centuries. The men were carrying their sheaves and their fruits; they radiated pride and satisfaction. "Are you happy on this land?" the author asked an old woman who had once lived in the Atlas Mountains. Bending down to encompass the earth with a sweep of her hand, she asked in reply: "How could you expect this land to be happy with me if I were not happy with it?"

Many young immigrants from the Maghreb joined *kibbutzim,* either as a transitory stage prior to their settlement elsewhere in Israel, or as a permanent way of life. The first group, who migrated from Tunisia with the express purpose of setting up a *kibbutz* in Israel, have been successfully established at Regavim in the Negev for a dozen years and many more *kibbutzim,* especially in the Negev, have since been established primarily with young settlers of North African origin.

A story from Yanuv, a *moshav* set up by Tunisian immigrants in the narrow coastal plain not far from the Jordanian frontier, throws humorous light on the agonies through which these new farmers passed in their metamorphosis on Israel's soil. The welcome accorded to this group upon arrival in their new home had been especially warm. Together with other supplies given them to make their start, were fifteen huge Mexican mules for use in hauling farm carts and implements, but the only effect that the huge animals had was to terrorize the new farmers, who were unanimous in their desire to rid themselves of these dangerous, unfamiliar monsters. One night, mysteriously, the beasts strayed across the Jordanian frontier; but the Jordanians, probably no happier with the monsters, drove them straight back, to the disappointment of the men of Yanuv. Finally, somehow, the mules disappeared, but today the villagers of Yanuv, proud of their well-tended fields, and capable of handling any agricultural challenge, still regret the disappearance of their first Mexican mules!

ECONOMIC INTEGRATION

A fundamental obstacle which hindered the integration of many North African immigrants into Israel's economic life was the fact that 40 per cent of them were illiterate. Among women the rate of illiteracy reached 58 per cent. This was due to the fact that a large proportion of the immigrants came from those regions of Morocco where the scholastic network of the Alliance Israélite Universelle had not penetrated and where, in consequence, schools were virtually nonexistent.

In 1960, the percentage of North Africa immigrants of working age who were actually employed was the lowest of any group of immigrants at 51.7 per cent—76.2 per cent of men and 26.2 per cent of women. (The low proportion of working women was due both to their lack of education and to the necessity for them to look after their large families.) In the same year, 54.8 per cent of all Israelis over fourteen were employed. However, many of the North Africans registered as employed worked only sporadically. Whereas 80 per cent of Israelis, and 87 per cent of workers of European origin worked throughout the year, only 68 per cent of North Africans were fully employed. Because most marginal benefits such as paid holidays, sick leave and pensions are linked to the number of days worked, these immigrants found themselves at a distinct disadvantage vis-à-vis other Israelis. In addition to the overall low level of employment, the North African immigrants were further disadvantaged by the fact that they were usually employed in the more menial and therefore lower paid jobs in the various spheres. This, coupled with the fact that they had large families to support, further aggravated their economic situation. Among the 24 per cent engaged in the "public services," only about 2,000 were civil servants, half of whom were classified as laborers. The rest held positions in the lowest rungs of the service. Only two were to be found in the highest grades.

Twenty-four per cent of the active North African labor force was employed in public services, 23.4 per cent in agriculture, 18.6 per cent in industry, 14.7 per cent in building and construction, 11.5 per cent in trade and the rest in transport, public utilities and other minor spheres. Thus, well over half were engaged in the three productive fields of agriculture, industry and construction, while only a meager 11.5 per cent were to be found in commerce. This represented a marked transformation in their role in the economy in comparison with that which they had played in their former homes. Some 74 North African immigrants were employed as engineers, technicians, doctors and journalists in 1960—not a large number perhaps but an indication of positions to which others could aspire, given training and opportunity.

The increased facilities for adult education and vocational training which have been set up throughout the country are helping to eradicate illiteracy and to raise the professional and technical capacity of the immigrants of Oriental and North African origin with a view to easing their employment situation. Another powerful factor is the Army which each year equips large numbers of young men with a basic education and a useful trade. However, the absolute improvement in the economic situation of the immigrants, due both to the fact that they have benefited from the general amelioration in Israel's economy and to the improvement in their own skills, has tended to be neutralized by the even greater strides that have been made by the already more advanced sections of Israel's population over the past few years. The fact that the means of production have tended to be concentrated in the hands of those who have been in the country the longest and who have the best skills has further widened the disparity.

There is a difference between being poor and being the most poor. In North Africa the Jews, as a group, had been poor but they had not been the most poor. The poorest, the most famished, the worst off, the sickest, were the Arabs. Even the most miserable Jew might feel himself king in comparison with the penury he could see all around him. And, even for the most wretched among them, there was always hope that he might profit on some little deal with an Arab, hope for the unexpected, hope that his children would one day escape the poverty and despair of their parents and benefit from the best available education. In Israel, however, the North African Jews are, as a group, the poorest. The Arabs of Israel are much better off. The North Africans, perhaps because they were the last to arrive,

are the poorest, and the least accepted. As such, they feel themselves entrapped with no apparent escape. Israel is not like the
Maghreb; the little business deals are out of the question; the
pay, as laborer or petty clerk, scarcely suffices to provide food
for a large family. Moreover, unless the children are fortunate
enough to obtain some kind of scholarship for their post-primary education, the chances that they will enjoy a brighter
future than their parents are small.

The immigrant from North Africa below a certain poverty
level regards himself as a member of the most unfortunate
grouping of any in Israel. He is not a philosopher; the socio-
economic reasons for his poverty mean nothing to him. He
knows only that he is badly off, that no one seems to take his
problem seriously. He believes himself to be the victim of deliberate discrimination. Though this feeling is entirely unjustified,
it is widely enough held to constitute a potential danger, the
more so because there are irrefutable statistics that can be interpreted in support of this view, even though the real explanations lie elsewhere. When passions run high, there is neither
the time nor the inclination to engage in socio-economic
analyses. This is a problem which must be eradicated at its
source through a thorough modification in Israel's economic,
educational and social structure.

SOCIAL WELFARE

While waiting for the integration process to take its course, a
large proportion of the new immigration became a charge on
the State. One quarter of the 93,300 families who were receiving some form of support from the Ministry of Social Welfare in
1961 were of North African origin. There were many other
families who could have qualified for assistance but did not

claim it, perhaps out of repugnance for the idea of charity; many accepted their misery and adapted themselves to the difficulties of their new existence. The majority of families receiving assistance had more than six children. The social welfare workers were devoted but hopelessly overburdened. Family benefits as paid under the national welfare scheme for large families were practically meaningless, and a family that might have played a happy and productive role often became transformed into another "welfare case." The 23,100 families receiving various kinds of support, who posed such a severe burden on the State's economy, situated at the lowest point of the social pyramid of the State, clearly demonstrated the condition of the immigration from North Africa; they constituted fully one-third of North African families.

In 1965 the government increased family allowances, and families became eligible for them as from the first child and not from the fourth as hitherto. New legislation regarding assistance for large families is at present under review. Though separate statistics on the number of families of Oriental or North African origin still receiving some form of state aid are no longer available, there is no doubt that the vast drop in the overall figure for the total population during the past five years has been reflected in the situation of Israel's citizens from North Africa.

HOUSING

The housing situation in 1960 was not better than that in other fields. Although conditions had improved from the 1957 level, Israelis of Oriental origin, among whom were included the North Africans, were shown to be living under conditions of far more severe overcrowding than the general population. As Appendix VIII shows, immigrants from Europe were vastly better housed than those from Africa and Asia whose condition was on the whole similar to that of Jews of Oriental origin who had been established in Israel for some time.

The housing that was provided by the Jewish Agency for immigrants on arrival was generally one of three standard types: 260–300 square feet; 365–410 square feet or 490 square feet. An average room measured 130 square feet. While adequate for a European family, this bore no relation to the needs of families with anything from five to ten children. In 1961, over a quarter of the immigrants from Oriental countries were living at a density that allowed 32 square feet or less per person. Since then, much larger apartments have been provided—between 500 and 850 square feet in area—but the problem still remains a serious one.

CRIME AND DELINQUENCY

The crime rate among North African Jews, which, as has been shown in Chapter Thirteen, was extremely low in North Africa, has unfortunately grown considerably within this community since its arrival in Israel. The North African community has the largest crime rate of any in the country. During the period 1951 to 1960, there were 20.7 convictions per thousand adults (over 15) among the North African immigrants, 12.7 per thousand among immigrants from Asia and 4.9 per thousand among those from Europe. The results for juvenile delinquency were similar: 13.7 per thousand among North Africans, 9.5 per thousand among immigrants from Asia and 4.1 per thousand for immigrants from Europe.

Social and economic factors are at the heart of these statistics. Where a family is crowded with more than four persons per room and where the monthly income per head is less than the equivalent of twenty dollars, it is only too easy for the weakest to succumb to bad influences and to give way to temptations. As living conditions improve, the rate of delinquency decreases; three-quarters of the offenders proved to have come from the most recent immigrants, those who had not yet managed to find their place in the society or in the economy; for immigrants long established in Israel, who have been integrated into the country's life and have acquired a certain patience to deal with frustrations and aggravations, the tendency is for the crime statistics to taper off and reach a "normal" level.

There is also an important psychological factor in the astonishing crime statistics. The immigrants had lived in their home countries in strict, clearly defined, closely associated, traditional societies where religious and spiritual values reigned supreme. They were uprooted, cast into a harsh adventure for which they were totally unprepared, into a world that rejected their way of life and culture as antiquated and made its youth question not only parental authority and tradition but also the validity of its moral and spiritual values. They found themselves in a bewildering environment they could not understand and, to try and understand it in the light of that which was familiar to them or of that for which they had hoped, only increased their sense of bewilderment to the point of revolt. The sense of frustration was further aggravated by a feeling of isolation that can drive even the strongest to the limits of despair. The isolation was very real; at one blow the immigrant had lost contact with his friends, his relatives, his customs—in brief the whole world to which he had been accustomed. The new world that replaced it was a foreign world. The language spoken was one that he knew, at best, only slightly. When his grasp of it improved he became even more disappointed, for he realized then that he lived in a different society and a special mental universe that went beyond the mere problem of language.

A further complication, one that is a negative by-product of what is in itself a positive phenomenon, is that of the young men who, after being discharged from Army service where they have learned a useful occupation and adjusted to the Israeli way of life, find themselves without employment and with no suitable place in society. Their homes are their homes no longer for they have acquired a totally different outlook and set of values and they no longer have anything in common with the older generation. Unless they are absorbed into the economy immediately upon their release, they create another potential source of maladjustment and crime.

EDUCATION

The social and economic position of the Jews of North Africa would be more encouraging if the picture as regards education —which will determine the future of the country—were brighter. Unfortunately, while Israel has made remarkable progress in the fields of agriculture, industry and defense, education still leaves much to be desired. There is a crisis in education at present in even the most developed countries of the West; in Israel, where the population has more than trebled in the past eighteen years, the difficulty of finding teachers and adequate finance has further complicated the issue.

Though primary education from the age of six to fourteen is nominally free, except for various fees and dues, parents must under normal circumstances pay for nursery schools, high schools and university education. Fees are so high for post-primary education that unless scholarships are available, it is entirely beyond the reach of the North African and other Oriental immigrants' children. In 1961, only 12 per cent of secondary school pupils were of Oriental or North African origin. At the university level the Oriental element made up 5 per cent.

(It is significant that at that time the total university population was less than one half of one per cent of the population, less than a quarter of what is considered adequate in the West and certainly insufficient for the special requirements of a small developing country like Israel that must maintain the high standards set by its founders.) There were only 29 students from the Maghreb at the Hebrew University in Jerusalem in 1961; 15 were in the faculty of arts and the others were dispersed in the social studies, the natural sciences, the faculty of law, the medical school, the school of agriculture, and the school for social workers. In Algiers, it will be remembered, over a third of the student body was Jewish, and every French university, especially the Sorbonne, was enriched by groups of Jewish students from North Africa who achieved remarkable successes there.

Great efforts have since been deployed to help solve the education problem among the Oriental communities. The budget of the Ministry of Education and Culture has been more than trebled and has risen from 5 per cent to 8.3 per cent of the national budget. Nursery schools have been provided to help close the gap between the elementary knowledge of children from different backgrounds, so reinforcing the efficacy of the primary schools. The proportion of Oriental secondary school pupils has risen from 12 to 30 per cent thanks to a system of state education grants. At the university level, the proportion has risen from 5 to 13 per cent, also due to an increase in the number of university scholarships. However, the proportion of secondary school and university students who do not complete their studies remains considerable. A special campaign has been launched by the government in cooperation with the ODED (Hebrew for "encourage") organization to promote free university education among students of North African origin and to encourage young Jewish students at present in France to immigrate to Israel. In this way, it is hoped to create the requisite intellectual cadres so lacking among this community.

But there is still an inherent imbalance in educational opportunities and successes and these have tended to create and confirm the notion of the intellectual inferiority of immigrant youth from the Orient. The well-intentioned experiments of fixing a lower passing grade for the admission of these youths to secondary schools, and the provision of two-year vocational high schools for them, have, by creating a double standard, resulted in bitterness and failure at the expense of the children. It would seem to perpetuate the conditions of disparity and make of these children the potentially depressed class of Israel's population. The true reason for the seeming failure of the North Africans in the educational system is to be found not in any intellectual inferiority but in the economic condition in their homes, in the overcrowding that denies them quiet for study or thinking, in the inability of their parents, by reason of their own poor education, to help their children in their studies. Though Israel lacks the facilities to compensate for this initial disadvantage, the Ministry of Education and Culture is nevertheless trying to strengthen the influence of the school in the lives of the pupils. Attempts are being made in certain areas to extend the hours of teaching to cover a full day, not as at present only half a day. There is a move to extend preschool education further and to provide one hot meal at school for the pupils. But further assistance must be given to make secondary schooling entirely free, to provide stipends for the specially gifted and to set up a network of residential schools for those who, for one reason or another, cannot make use of the educational facilities available locally. Finally, at the university level, where the number of students must grow, it will be necessary to increase the number and value of scholarships so as to free more students not only from fees but also from material need while studying.

Only a bold and generous policy will enable Israel to correct the defects in its educational system and, as a result, in its social and economic structure. This will impose a serious financial burden on the country but it must be done. The North Africans are a dynamic group, their birthrate will double their size and importance within twenty years. Such a large group cannot be allowed to stagnate. Unless drastic steps are taken to improve their education, Israel will become a very poor nation, lacking a cultural élite and cut off from its roots with world Jewry.

Citizens of Israel

Jews from the Oriental countries, among whom are counted the North Africans, today make up just one half of Israel's total population and, given their high birth rate, they are likely to constitute 75 per cent of the country's Jewish population by 1978 unless some unexpected factor should provoke mass immigration from Russia or the Western countries. The confrontation of Jews from East and West created in Israel a microcosm of the problem, albeit in a less extreme form, that lies at the base of the world's present conflicts—that of the disparity between the wealth of the developed nations and the poverty of the underdeveloped. The situation was unprecedented: no other advanced society had ever been called upon to absorb within fifteen years a group of backward immigrants that outnumbered its own population by two to one; no other society has demonstrated that, with a maximum of willpower and a minimum of resources, such a rapid evolution in the general level of the underdeveloped element can be obtained. Indeed, certain aspects of this social experiment have come to be recognized as workable prototypes for other developing nations.

Though the problems inherent in the integration of the Jews of North Africa remain vital issues demanding immediate solution, the generation that has been born and brought up in Israel is palpable proof of the extent to which the community has advanced in less than two decades. The youth of North African origin have become practically indistinguishable from those of European background in their outlook, their way of life and their sense of national and personal responsibility. Over the past few years there has been a sharp drop in intercommunal tension and the number of marriages between youth of different origins is growing slowly but constantly. As time passes there are increasing indications that the process which will eventually make an anachronism of the term "Jews of North Africa" is beginning to work itself out.

Israel's citizens from North Africa have become a feature of the Israel scene. They are dispersed in the north and the south, in towns, villages, *moshavim* and *kibbutzim*. Recent years have seen the arrival of an intellectual and technical élite that has enriched the community with doctors, businessmen, engineers and educators. This movement is likely to grow as the élite, whose members were the last to leave North Africa and have tended to tarry in France, arrive in Israel. But even without its élite, the North African community has contributed handsomely to the present and the future of Israel. At least a third of what has been accomplished in the revival of the Galilee can be attributed to the North Africans, over half of what has been accomplished in reclaiming the desert of the Negev is due to their endeavor. A new élite has emerged; a youth that is devoted to communal betterment, that is active in the pioneering youth movements and in political parties. They have made a name for themselves by their dynamism, by their willingness to work hard, by their imagination and by their readiness to take a calculated risk. An outstanding example of their courage was the supreme sacrifice made by Nathan Elbaz, a young soldier from Morocco, who saved the lives of his comrades by absorbing with his own body the explosion of a hand grenade which was accidentally released in the midst of an army camp. Israelis of North African origin are also playing an increasingly important role in public affairs. Four were elected to the Sixth Knesseth in 1965, one of whom was appointed Deputy Minister of Agriculture; and over three hundred hold elected office as members of municipal councils, labor councils and representatives of communal and collective agricultural villages.

In Israel's War of Independence, recent arrivals from North Africa played a noticeable part. In the Suez campaign of 1956 they were even more prominent, fighting in the front ranks of battle and giving their lives in defense of their homeland. However, it was the Six-Day War which indisputedly revealed their complete integration within Israel society which, during the months of May and June, 1967, proved its real vigor and deep unity both to itself and to the world. At that moment, as every citizen confronted the Arab menace, each felt that Israel was one people and that barriers no longer existed in its midst; no longer were there differences between Easterners and Westerners, rich and poor, old-established citizens and new immigrants. Every individual faced the same danger and fulfilled his duty with the same determination, often with the same heroism. A large number of those who lived in the border areas were Jews who had come from North Africa and Oriental countries. As civilians they carried out their duty to the full. As for the Army, a vast majority of its ranks were filled by youths of African or Asian parentage. Their courage in the hour of trial was eloquently demonstrated. Indeed, in that time of danger, Israel society strikingly proved that it had overcome its inner contradictions. One of the most extraordinary phenomena resulting from the Six-Day War was the incontrovertible fact that in only 20 years communities brought together in the crucible of Israel from 102 countries of the world, communities of disparate economic and cultural levels, diverse origins and different patterns of settlement in the country, had become welded into a perfect whole, capable of presenting an indomitable front to the enemy.

But the achievements of the North African immigration and its contribution to Israel's life and development are heroic by other standards too. This young generation, that would have been reduced to a life of futile sterility in North Africa, has been transformed into conquerors of the desert, builders of cities, redeemers devoted to the resurrection of a people and of a land. They are the heirs and the continuers of the great tradition of Sephardic Judaism, of the poets, philosophers and judges of North Africa who kept the lamp of Judaism alight in the Maghreb in the face of all vicissitudes. This new generation has fulfilled the dreams and aspirations of its ancestors. With its return to Israel, twenty centuries of history have come a full circle.

Abbreviations used in the Notes

A.I.U. Alliance Israélite Universelle

I.F.A.N. Institut Français d'Afrique du Nord

I.H.E.M. Institut des Hautes Études Marocaines

P.L. Patrologia Latina

R.E.J. Revue des Études Juives

R.P.J. Revue de la Pensée Juive

Notes

PART I

From Antiquity to the Byzantine Period

1 The Carthaginian Era: 813-146 B.C.E.

1. Procopius, *The Vandal War* (*De Bello Vandalico*) 2, 10. Cf. Moïse de Korène, *Histoire d'Arménie,* French translation V. Langlois, Paris, 1869, p. 70, and Gauthier, *Le Passé de l'Afrique du Nord,* Payot, 1942, p. 141. Henri Cambon refers to the legend in his *Histoire de la Tunisie* (Paris, 1948, p. 5) and, drawing on the work of Maspéro and Mesnage (*Romanisation de l'Afrique,* p. 29), regards as authentic the inscription brought to light by Procopius and the theory he advances on the basis of it.

   Tigisis has been identified with Aïn el Bordj, fifty kilometers southeast of Constantine.

2. Ibn Khaldun, *Histoire des Berbères,* Slane translation, (Algiers, 1852-1856), Vol. I, p. 177.

3. Marcel Simon, in his masterly work, *Judaïsme berbère en Afrique ancienne,* points to an inconsistency in Ibn Khaldun's view. A few pages later (p. 183) Ibn Khaldun comes out "against the idea of a migration" and regards the Berbers as the indigenous population of Africa. Nevertheless he mentions the quarrels between their Canaanite ancestors and the Israelites.

4. Cf. Charles, *Book of Jubilees,* London, 1902.

5. Josephus, *The Antiquities of the Jews,* I, 15. Josephus is followed

by Eusebius of Caesarea, *Praep. Evang.*, I, 20. Cf. Genesis XXV, 1.

6. According to Slousch, who wished to give scientific cohesion to the theory of the Berbers' Asian origin, ancient Egyptian documents show that under the 19th dynasty of the Pharaohs, and therefore before the establishment of the Jews in Palestine, the Hyxos, defeated by the Pharaohs, emigrated to the Maghreb. Slousch ascribes the idea of the Canaanite origin of the Berbers to the Jews of Cyrene.

7. *Midrash Leviticus Rabba,* XVII. Cf. *Jerusalem Talmud, Sukkah* 5a; 23a. It is interesting to note the use of the proper name Girgash in Tripolitania. Cf. Simon, *op. cit.,* p. 14; Slousch, *Étude sur l'Histoire des Juifs au Maroc,* Paris, 1906, p. 17; *Hébréo-Phéniciens et Judéo-Hellènes,* Paris, 1909; *Hébréo-Phéniciens,* Paris, 1909; *Judéo-Hellènes et Judéo-Berbères,* Paris, 1909; Paul Monceaux, "Païens Judaïsants," an essay explaining an African inscription, published in *Revue Archéologique,* 1902, pp. 208-226. In *Tosefta Shabbat,* VII, 25, there is a slightly different version of the same story, in which the Amorites take the place of the Girgashites. Cf. Slousch, *Judéo-Hellènes,* p. 59. The variation between Girgashites and Amorites confirms the general idea of the Canaanite origin of the African peoples. An anonymous Christian chronicle of the third century (Migne, *P.L.,* 3, 665) extends the legend to include the inhabitants of the Balearic islands as being also of Canaanite origin. Cf. *Jerusalem Talmud, Shabbat,* VI, 36. See Paul Monceaux, "Les Colonies Juives dans l'Afrique Romaine," in *R.E.J.,* Vol. 44, Paris, 1902, and *The Jewish Encyclopaedia,* Vol. I, p. 225.

8. Ibn Khaldun evidently holds to the Josephus tradition and regards the Berbers as the descendants of Abraham. Other Arab writers, fond of etymology, trace the descendance from Abraham through Afrik-Opher, the son of Abraham. Cf. *Encyclopaedia of Islam,* Art. "Ifrikya II," p. 483 *et seq.*

9. Saint Augustine, "Epistolae ad Romanos Inchoata Expositio," 13 (*P.L.,* 34, 2096). Cf. Simon, *op. cit.,* p. 8; Gauthier, *op. cit.,* p. 139. Cf. William M. Green, "Augustine's Use of Punic," in *Semitic and Oriental Studies* presented to W. Poppes, Berkeley, 1951—the most recent and most complete work on St. Augustine's knowledge of Punic. Cf. C. Courtois, "Saint Augustin et

la survivance du Punique" in *Revue Africaine,* 94 (1950), pp. 259-283. Courtois follows Trend in confirming that no conclusions can be drawn from the texts of St. Augustine with regard to the survival of Punic, for they refer to the ancient spoken language of Numidia. Unfortunately, Courtois does not make use of Green's latest work.

10. Marcel Simon, Christian scholar and Dean of the Faculty of Letters at the University of Strasbourg.

11. Tacitus, *Annals,* V, 2.

12. *P.L.,* 3, 665.

13. P. 109 *et seq.*

14. Jews, Moslems and even Christians flock to the *Marabout* of Nedromah, famous for his miraculous cures.

15. Gsell, *Histoire Ancienne de l'Afrique du Nord,* Hachette, 1913, Vol. IV, p. 494. The masterly history of Carthage in Gsell's monumental work throws new light on E.-F. Gauthier's *Le Passé de l'Afrique du Nord,* Payot, 1942.

16. Dhorme, *Langues et Écritures Sémitiques,* Paris, 1930.

17. On the Jews during the Punic period see also the well-documented article by Mièses, "Les Juifs et les établissements puniques en Afrique du Nord," *R.E.J.,* Vol. XCIII, Paris, 1932.

18. On Punic literature, see *ibid.,* p. 70.

19. The passages in which Augustine speaks of the Punic language have been collected by Bochart in *Phaleg et Canaan* (ed. 1707). Cf. William M. Green, *op. cit.,* pp. 179-190.

20. It is remarkable that Latin never penetrated deeply among the peoples of the Maghreb. All that survived the Arab invasions were a few borrowed terms of Roman civilization. Judah ibn Kuraïsh of Fez, writing in the tenth century, mentions some Latin words in his Epistle (Risala) on the comparison of the Hebrew, Aramaic and Arabic languages. See Mièses' article quoted above, in *R.E.J.,* No. 184, Paris, 1932, p. 134.

21. Saint Augustine, "Epist. ad Rom. Inch. Expos." (3, *P.L.,* 34, 2096).

22. Marcel Simon, *op. cit.,* pp. 21, 22, 23. Cf. Dr. Carton, *L'Afrique du Nord devant les civilisations anciennes.* Georges Vajda considers Simon's conclusion somewhat daring since a simple reading of the biblical text quoted could, in any translation, just as

well as in Hebrew, suggest the etymological connection adopted.

23. Quaest. in Gen., 36, 24: "Nonnulli putant aquas calidas juxta punicae linguae viciniam quae hebraeae contermina est, hoc vocabulo signari. . . ."

 Comm. in Is. Proph., III, 7, 14: Lingua quoque punica, quae Hebraeorum fontibus manare dicitur . . . (*P.L.*, 24, 108 B.).

 Comm. in Jer. Proph., V, 25, 21: "Unde et Poeni sermone corrupto quasi Phoeni appellantur: quorum lingua hebraeae linguae magna ex parte confine est." (*P.L.*, 24, 837 D).

24. Priscian, *Institutione Grammaticae*, 1, V, C. II.

25. E. Renan, *Histoire Générale des Langues Sémitiques,* Paris, 1878, p. 148. Nahum Slousch, *Civilisation Hébraïque et Phénicienne à Carthage,* Tunis, 1911, p. 16. Slousch states that the only differences between Hebrew and Punic are in the spelling and pronunciation.

26. On the relationship between Punic and Hebrew, cf. Gsell, *op. cit.,* Vol. IV, p. 179. Gsell's conclusions regarding the spread of Punic in North Africa are clear and are worth quoting: "Saint Augustine reveals that in his time Punic was widespread throughout the countryside. Procopius shows that it was still spoken in the sixth century. From then until the Moslem conquest the interval is short. However, Arabic, a language related to Punic, could easily supplant it just as Aramaic, another Semitic tongue, supplanted the Phoenician dialect in Phoenicia several centuries earlier. One can therefore assume that the Berbers adopted the language of Islam because, knowing Punic, they could learn it easily." Gsell, *op. cit.,* Vol. IV, p. 498. M. Simon, *op. cit.,* pp. 30 and 31 and note 101, echoes Gsell's opinion.

27. Slousch, *Hébréo-Phéniciens,* 1909; *Judéo-Hellènes et Judéo-Berbères,* Paris, 1909. It is not impossible that, at the beginning of the Phoenician colonization, Jews settled in the first trading posts established on the coast.

28. M. Simon, *op. cit.,* pp. 23-25.

29. M. Simon, *op. cit.,* advances the theory of the continued existence of Hebrew-speaking communities in the hinterland after the use of Latin had spread in the coastal towns.

30. *Babylonian Talmud, Rosh Hashana,* 26a.

31. R. Isaac, R. Hanan, R. Abba. Cf. *Jerusalem Talmud* XVI, 1;

Kil., 1b; *Babylonian Talmud, Bera,* 29a; *Ketubot,* 27b; *Baba Kamma,* 114b.

32. Augustine, Ep. 71, 5 and 75, 22 (*P.L.,* 33, 242-243 and 263). Cf. note 15.

33. Tertullian, *Apol.,* 8 and *De Jejuniis,* 16 (*P.L.,* 1, 311-313 and 2, 975-977).

2 Pax Romana: 146 B.C.E.-430 C.E.

1. G.-G. Lapeyre and A. Pellegrin, *Carthage Punique,* ed. Payot; by the same authors, *Carthage latine et chrétienne,* Paris, 1949.

2. Neubauer, *Mediaeval Jewish Chronicle,* I, p. 190.

3. North Africa later became an important province of the Church. According to Gsell ("Chron. Archéol. Afric.," in *Mélanges d'Arch. et d'Histoire,* XX, 100), it was the North Africans who insisted on Latin being adopted as the official language of the Western churches.

4. *Babylonian Talmud, Rosh Hashana,* 26a.

5. Josephus, *Bell. Jud.,* 7, 11.

6. Simon, *Judaïsme berbère,* p. 123. Slousch, *op. cit.,* p. 14 *et seq.* See also Cahen's analysis, *Les Juifs dans l'Afrique Septentrionale,* Paris, 1867, p. 14 *et seq.*

7. Gauthier, *Le Passé de l'Afrique du Nord,* p. 226.

8. A talmudic text, *Gittin,* 57b, describes savage excesses and merciless massacres, Cf. Dion Cassius, I, 11. Eusebius, *The Ecclesiastical History,* Bk. IV, I-II. Cf. *Babylonian Talmud, Succah* 5a. *Gittin,* 57b, gives the number of victims as 1,200,000. This Oriental exaggeration or copyist's error provides an indication of the impression made by the events. See also Renan, *Les Évangiles,* pp. 502-505 on the Cyrenaica revolts.

9. Albertini, *L'Empire Romain,* Paris, 1939. Delafosse, *Les Noirs de l'Afrique,* Paris, 1922. J. J. Williams, *Hebrewisms of West Africa,* New York, 1930. Slousch, *op. cit.,* p. 23 *et seq.*: the fugitives would have fled across the south along the routes between Djebel Demmer in Tripolitania and the Aurès mountains in Numidia. On Mediterranean influences in Black Africa cf. E.-F. Gauthier, *L'Afrique Noire Occidentale,* Larose, 1935. Mordecai

Aby Serour, who guided Charles de Foucauld in his *Reconnaissance au Maroc,* mentions the Daggatun, Jewish but superficially Moslem tribes, who lived in the Western Sahara from the Tafilalt to Tombouctou. (*Bulletin de l'Alliance Israélite Universelle,* 1880). Cf. *Hespéris,* 1928, 3rd and 4th quarters. Y.T. Semach, *Un Rabbin Marocain Voyageur.*

10. A complete list of these has been prepared by Juster on the basis of P. Monceaux's work, "Les Colonies Juives dans l'Afrique Romaine," *R.E.J.,* Vol. 44, Paris, 1902.

11. Cf. Monceaux, p. 5. In *The City of God* (XXII, 8, 21), Augustine mentions the presence of a Jewish sorcerer from Uzali or Carthage.

12. Cf. Tissot, *Géographie comparée de la Province Romaine d'Afrique,* Vol. II, p. 630.

13. Collection du Musée Alaoui, Paris, 1880, p. 57 *et seq.* Gsell, *Mélanges de l'École de Rome,* 1901, p. 205.

14. St. Augustine, *Sermo.,* 196, 4.

15. *Corpus inscript. lat.,* VIII, 7150, 7155, 7530, 7710.

16. *Ibid.,* suppl. 16701.

17. According to the *Passio Sanctae Salsae.* Monceaux, p. 23, writes that the synagogue replaced the sanctuary of a demon, and it was later turned into a church.

18. Ph. Berger, *Bull. Arch. du Comité des Travaux Historiques,* 1892, pp. 64-66. Rabbi Eisenbeth gives a different rendering from that of Berger: "Yehuda Noah, daughter of Rabbi Matrona." Cf. Eisenbeth, *Les Juifs au Maroc,* p. 9.

19. Ibn Khaldun, *Histoire des Berbères,* Slane translation (Algiers, 1852-1856), Vol. I, p. 208.

20. Slousch, *Étude sur l'Histoire des Juifs et du Judaïsme au Maroc,* Paris, 1906, p. 40, note 1, suggests that the name Djerawa was derived from the Hebrew word "ger" meaning proselyte. It is uncertain if this explanation takes all the philological facts into account.

21. Saint Augustine, Epist. 71, 35 (*P.L.,* 33, 242-245). Cf. p. 9 *supra.* I wish to take this opportunity of thanking Father J. Leroy for his guidance in the texts quoted from *Patrologia Latina.*

22. The Locus Judaeorum Augusti of Peutinger's Table. Tissot, *op.*

cit., Vol. II, p. 237. On the importance of the Jewish community at Cyrenaica, cf. J. Mesnage, "Le Christianisme en Afrique," in *Revue Africaine,* Algiers, 1913; cf. Slousch, *Archive Morocaine,* XIV, p. 249. Philon, *Leg. ad Caïum,* 30. Schürer, *Geschichte des Jüdischen Volkes im Zeitalter Jesu Christi,* III, p. 72. On other Jewish settlements see N. Slousch, *Un Voyage d'Études Juives,* pp. 48 and 82. By the same author, *The Jews of North Africa,* Philadelphia, Part I, pp. 3-104.

23. Tissot, Vol. II, p. 238.

24. Mesnage considers that the Falashas (the name means exiles) in Ethiopia had their origins in a Jewish community which existed between Assuan and Elephantine at the time of Xerxes in 471 B.C.E. See Slousch, *Arch. Maroc,* XIV, p. 332 *et seq.,* 459 *et seq.; Jewish Encyclopaedia,* Art. "Falasha" and "Africa." On the Jewish communities scattered all over Libya from Egypt to Lake Tritonus, cf. Herodotus, *Hist.* IV, 186, notably at Borium, Praesidium, Iscina, Mesrata, Zlitin, Msellata, etc. On the Jewish communities which formed an uninterrupted chain from Mauritania to India, cf. St. Jerome, *Epist. ad Dardanum,* 129, 4: "A Mauritania per Africam et Aegyptum, Palaestinamque et Phoenicem Coelensyriam et Osrohenem Mesopotamiam atque Persidem tendunt ad Indiam. Haec est, Judaee, tuarum longitudo et latitudo terrarum: in his gloriaris, super his te per diversas provincias ignorantibus jacititas."

25. Such as the Jewish writers Nahum Slousch and Mathias Mièses, the Christian writers Paul Monceaux and Father T. Mesnage and others without religious affiliations.

26. Cf. Héron de Villefosse, *Bull. des Antiquités de France,* 1895, p. 150. The inscriptions which were found at the Naro synagogue are preserved at the Museum of Bardo. The mosaics are at the Museum of Toulouse. Besides the seven-branched candelabra, the mosaics are decorated with a wealth of images, despite the fact that this is expressly forbidden by biblical commandments. As in contemporary synagogues discovered in Palestine, they depict lions, hyenas, partridges, guinea-fowl, ducks, fish, trees, fruit and human figures.

27. P. Monceaux, "Les Colonies Juives dans l'Afrique Romaine,"

R.E.J., 1902, Vol. 44, p. 16. For a detailed description of the necropolis, see P. Delattre, *La Nécropole Juive de Carthage,* Lyon, 1895. Cf. A.L. Delattre, *L'Épigraphie funéraire chrétienne à Carthage,* Tunis, 1926. By the same author, *La Nécropole des Rabs, Prêtres et Prêtresses de Carthage,* Paris, 1905, and *Une Visite à la Nécropole des Rabs,* Palerme, 1906.

28. *Corp. Inscript. Graec.,* Vol. III, No. 5364. Cf. Slousch, *op. cit.,* p. 9.

29. On Hadrian's legislation cf. Bernard d'Orgeval, *l'Empereur Hadrien,* Thèse, Paris, 1950.

30. In principle, the Romans granted the right of religious practice only to those who were Jews by birth, and not to proselytes, but the distinction disappeared as the wars between Israel and Rome were forgotten.

31. Under Marcus Aurelius (161-180) and Verus (161-163) certain Jews risked compromising the peace by trying to take advantage of Rome's difficulties in the war against the Parthian king Vologaeses III. Once the Parthians had been overcome, Verus severely punished the Jews by depriving them of their judicial autonomy. The restriction was repealed after his death.

32. One of Claudius's rescripts states: "We regard it as just that nowhere, not even in the Greek villages, should the Jews be deprived of the privileges granted them by the divine Augustus. We regard it as equitable that the Jews be permitted to observe their national customs throughout our Empire. We desire that our edict be engraved on tablets by the magistrates in the towns, colonies and municipalities both within and outside Italy." Josephus, *Antiquities,* XIX, 5. Cf. J. Juster, *Les Juifs dans l'Empire Romain,* Paris, 1914, 2 vols. The study of Juster is necessary for a more detailed understanding of this question. Cf. Marcel Simon's exposition, *Verus Israël,* Paris, 1948, pp. 52-53.

33. The Caracalla edict of the year 212, which granted citizens' rights to the Jews as well as to the other free inhabitants of the Empire, imposed a supplementary tax which was levied only on the wealthy classes.

34. The non-Jewish partner had to be converted to Judaism according

to the Mosaic law before the conclusion of the religious marriage.

35. Cf. p. 19.

36. E.-F. Gauthier, *Le Passé de l'Afrique du Nord,* "Les siècles obscurs," p. 214 *et seq.* Cf. Gsell, "La Tripolitaine et le Sahara au IIIe siècle de notre ère," in *Mémoires de l'Académie des Inscriptions,* 1926. On the introduction of the camel to North Africa, cf. Gsell, *Histoire Ancienne de l'Afrique du Nord,* Vol. I, p. 60.

37. The classification of the Botr as nomads and the Beranese as sedentary tribes was brought out by Gauthier, *op. cit.,* pp. 229-243. M. Simon qualifies Gauthier's clear-cut distinctions and adds some sound propositions.

38. Ibn Khaldun, *Histoire des Berbères,* Slane transl., Vol. I, p. 208. See p. 22.

39. E.-F. Gauthier, *Sahara Algérien,* Colin, 1908, p. 251. Cf. E.-F. Gauthier, *Le Passé de l'Afrique du Nord,* p. 225. Cf. A. Koller, *Essai sur l'Esprit du Berbère marocain,* Fribourg, 1949. Cf. Quedenfeld, *Division et Repartition de la population berbère au Maroc,* trans. H. Simon, Alger, p. 63 *et seq.*

40. M. Simon, *le Judaïsme berbère en Afrique ancienne,* p. 131.

41. See M. Delafosse, *op. cit.* Cf. A. Bernard, "Afrique Occidentale," *Géographie Universelle,* XI, 2, Paris, 1934, p. 424. Raymond Mauny, "Le Judaïsme, les Juifs et l'Afrique Occidentale," in *Bulletin de l'Institut Français d'Afrique Noire,* Vol. XI, July-October, 1949, Dakar, pp. 354-378.

42. M. Simon, *Judaïsme berbère,* p. 105 *et seq.*

43. Historians of North African Jewry dwell at length on these sects about which, on the whole, we know little. See M. Simon's excellent analysis in *Le Judaïsme berbère en Afrique ancienne.*

44. M. Simon, *ibid.,* p. 109. On the connection between the Coelicolians and the worshippers of Regina Coelistis, cf. M. Simon, pp. 111-114. On the Abelonians and the Coelicolians, cf. Mesnage, *op. cit.,* p. 537. Mièses, *op. cit.,* p. 146.

45. Theodosian Code, 16.8.19.

46. M. Simon, *Judaïsme berbère,* p. 116.

47. Cf. Monceaux, "Païens Judaisants. Essai d'Explication d'une Inscription Africaine," *Revue Africaine,* 1902, pp. 208-226. Cf. F. Cumont, "Un fragment de Sarcopharge Judéo-Païen," in *Revue*

Archéologique, 1916, II, p. 9, No. 4 which analyzes an authentic Jewish inscription.

48. According to J. Juster, *op. cit.*, Vol. I, pp. 180-209, the 80 million inhabitants of the Roman Empire included 6 to 7 million Jews, a proportion of 7 per cent. This figure does not include proselytes, whose number cannot be determined, or sympathizers.

49. Tertullian, *Ad Nationes*, 1,3.

50. Commodianus was probably of North African origin. Cf. Pierre Albers, *Manuel d'Histoire Ecclésiastique*, Paris, 1925, 1,3.

51. Cf. Mièses, *op. cit.*, p. 145.

52. The origins of Christianity in North Africa are somewhat obscure. Ibn Khaldun suggests that Simon the Cananaian was the first apostle from Ifrikya. Cf. Mesnage, *op. cit.*, p. 389, *Contra Duchesne, Origines chrétiennes*, p. 407.

53. Cf. Margolis and Marx, *History of the Jewish People*, p. 210.

54. On the Jewish status under the Roman Empire after Constantine, cf. Theodosian Code, 16.8. Also Juster, *op. cit.*, Vol. I, p. 160 *et seq*. M. Simon explains the conflict between Jews and Christians from the second to the fifth centuries in his work *Verus Israël, Étude sur les Relations entre Chrétiens et Juifs dans l'Empire Romain*, Paris, 1948, pp. 135-425. Cf. especially *Le Statut des Juifs dans l'Empire Chrétien*, pp. 155-166, and Chap. VIII: the practical repercussions of the anti-Semitism; the destruction of synagogues; the gradual modification of the Jewish status; the limits of Christian anti-Semitism. Its real cause: the religious vitality of Judaism, pp. 264-277.

55. On this subject, see M. Simon, *Verus Israël*, Chap. V: La Polémique anti-Juive. Caractères et Methodes, pp. 166-208, and Chap. VIII: l'Antisémitisme Chrétien, pp. 239-264.

56. Monceaux, *La Vraie Légende dorée*, Paris, 1929, pp. 239-326. Simon, *Verus Israël*, p. 265.

57. Cf. M. Simon, *Judaïsme berbère*, p. 137; *Verus Israël*, p. 264 *et seq*. Cf. Rachmuth, "Die Juden in Nord-Afrika bis zur Invasion der Araber," in *Monatschr. für Gesch. und Wissensch. des Judent.*, 1906. Cf. Dubnov, *Weltgeschichte des jüdischen Volkes*, III, 265.

3   Vandals and Byzantines: 430-642

1. Gaiseric used Carthage as a base from which to launch his wars and raids. Amongst the valuable objects he brought back as booty from his Italian campaign in 455 were the trophies of the Temple of Jerusalem which Titus had brought to Rome after the year 70. A century later, Belisarius, conqueror of the Vandals, took them to Byzantium. Ed. G.-G. Lapeyre and A. Pellegrin, *Carthage latine et chrétienne,* Paris, 1949.

2. The ruins were restored fifteen centuries later by the French archeological services which uncovered the remains of the Roman cities. Among them were those of Timgad which are comparable with the ruins of Pompei. Timgad was laid waste by the Vandals around 508.

3. According to Procopius.

4. Others bearing debased names were Abdias, King of the Aurès who fought fiercely against Byzantine Carthage in the sixth century; and Isfidaias who fought around the Matmata mountains.

5. Cf. *Histoire de l'Église* published under the direction of A. Fliche and V. Martin, Paris, 1939, Vol. 3.

6. Two hundred and seventeen bishops from all over the region attended the council—proof of the vitality of Catholicism in Africa and the force with which it must have opposed the Vandals.

7. As from 303, the Donatist schism, which came into being in Carthage, endangered the unity of the Church, especially by its progress in Africa. After several efforts at conciliation, the schism was condemned by Constantine, the secular arm of the Church. The Donatists were exiled and their property confiscated. Constantine's decision set off a conflict which reached its most brutal stage in Africa. The Council of Carthage which met after the Vandals had been conquered, continued to persecute the Donatists, in spite of the edict of toleration of 521. Cf. *Histoire de l'Église,* pp. 50-52.

8. Theodosian Code, 3.7.2 (the year 388) and 16.8.6 (the year 339) on the Jews, the Coelicolians and the Samaritans.
9. Theodosian Code, 3.12.2 (the year 355); Justinian Code, 1.9.7 (393).
10. See El Kairouani, Pélissier and Rémusat translation, p. 42. Also R. Thouvenat's study, "Chrétiens et Juifs à Grenade au IVe siècle après Jésus-Christ," in *Hespéris*, Vol. XXX, 1943, pp. 201-213.
11. The University of Carthage maintained the Latin tradition. The poet Corripus and Victor de Tonnona were educated there.
12. Cf. G.-G. Lapeyre and A. Pellegrin, *op. cit.*, p. 179 *et seq.*

PART II

The Rule of Islam

4   The Moslem Conquest of the Maghreb: 642-ca. 900

1. "No, it is not Ifrikya, but the treacherous country which deceives and leads one astray and which no one will attack so long as I am alive." This saying, attributed by Arab historians to Omar, indicates the importance attached to the Berber warriors. Cf. Gauthier, *Le Passé de l'Afrique du Nord*, p. 125 pas.
2. On Kahena see Ibn Khaldun, or Kitab el Adouani published by Féraud in *Recueil des Notices et Mémoires de la Société Archéologique de Constantine*, 1868. Cf. Masqueray's research on the remains of this period in popular tradition in "Traditions de l'Ouras Oriental" in the *Bulletin de Correspondance Africaine*, 1885, p. 72 *et seq*. On the origin of the name "Kahena" see J.W. Hirschberg, *A History of the Jews in North Africa*, Bialik Institute Publications, Jerusalem, 1965, pp. 65-66.
3. Gauthier considers they were nomads who had recently arrived in Ifrikya. Simon, on the other hand, regards them as a sedentary tribe converted to Judaism during the Roman period and established for a long period in the Aurès. Ibn Khaldun classified the tribe as nomads recently established in the Aurès which, hav-

ing become rich, practiced a form of semi-nomadism. Cf. François Plessier, *État Juif et Monde Arabe*, p. 26.

4. El Bayan, *Histoire de l'Afrique et de l'Espagne*, Fagan trans., Alger, 1901, p. 25.
5. Ibn Khaldun, *Histoires des Berbères*, p. 214.
6. El Bayan wrote that this took place on the day of the combat. Kahena, in full battle and her hair flying, cried "Take care of the future for I am as good as dead."
7. Khaled was the young Arab warrior who had attracted Kahena's attention at the battle on the Meskyana river and whom she adopted. Bayan reported: "You are the bravest and most handsome man I have ever seen," Kahena said to him (Khaled). "Therefore, I wish to give you of my milk so that you may become a brother to my two sons. Among us Berbers, a foster child who is suckled by the mother receives the rights of heredity." Thereupon, she took some barley flour, mixed it with oil and placed it on her breasts; then, she called her two sons and made them eat it together with Khaled, saying: "You have become brothers."
8. Ibn Khaldun, *op. cit.*, Vol. I, p. 29.
9. El Bayan, *op. cit.*, p. 29.
10. *Ibid.*, p. 29, note 1.
11. Cazès who collected this ballad considers that it recalls the memory of Kahena. It appears in his *Essai sur l'Histoire des Israélites de Tunisie*, Paris, 1888, p. 46.
12. *Chronique d'Abu Zalearya*, p. 124 *et seq.* 191-197. This chronicle, translated and interpreted by Émile Masqueray, was published in Algeria in 1870.
13. *Ibid.*
14. *Encyclopaedia of Islam*, Art. "Algeria."
15. Roud el Kartas, *Histoire des Souverains du Maghreb et Annales de la Ville de Fès*, Beaumier trans., Paris, 1860, p. 16 *et seq.*
16. *Ibid.*, p. 16.
17. Roger le Tourneau, "Fès avant le Protectorat," *Publications de l'Institut des Hautes Études Marocaines*, Casablanca, 1950, p. 41 *et seq.*
18. See Julien, *Histoire de l'Afrique du Nord*, Paris, Payot, 1932, and

Henri Terrasse, *Histoire du Maroc,* 2 vols., Paris, 1950.

19. H.-P.-J. Renaud, "Divination et Histoire Nord-Africaine au Temps d'Ibn Khaldun," in *Hespéris,* Vol. XXX, 1943, p. 213.

20. The first work of any value which was done was the publication and analysis of Y.T. Semach of Yahas Fès by Rabbi Avner Sarfaty. It appeared under the title "Une Chronique juive de Fès" in *Hespéris,* XIX, 1934, fasc. I and II.

Georges Vajda, in his "Recueil de Textes Historiques Judéo-Marocains," published in *Hespéris,* XII, Paris, 1951, demonstrated the interest of similar work. The Institute for Research on the Jewish Communities of the Middle East at the Hebrew University in Jerusalem has undertaken to assemble and analyze a large number of manuscripts.

On the basis of Jewish sources, Robert Brunschvig was able to reconstruct Jewish life in eastern Barbary under the Hafsids. He used the collections of *Consultations* of the chief rabbis of Algiers, Isaac ben Sheshet Barfat, Simon and Solomon Duran. His work is entitled *La Berbérie Orientale sous les Hafsides, des Origines à la fin du XVe siècle* and was published in Paris in 1940-1947. Vol. I, Chap. VII, pp. 396-430 deal with Jewish life and p. 92 *et seq.* with the chief rabbis of Algiers.

21. Cf. the basic *Sources Inédites de l'histoire du Maroc* published by H. de Castries and P. de Cénival between 1906 and 1936 which continued to appear after the Second World War.

22. In this connection, mention should be made of the work of the late Rabbi Jacob Moses Toledano of Tiberias which was published in Hebrew in Jerusalem in 1911. It was entitled *"Ner Ha'Ma'arav* (Light of the Maghreb)—a History of the Jews of Morocco from their settlement in that country till our times." It claimed to be based on authentic documents. The book was widely read among Hebrew scholars and was regarded as an authority by the Jewish communities of Morocco. Pierre de Cénival deplored the damage done to the oral traditions by this, and other, insufficiently prepared works. See "La Légende du Juif Ibn Meshal" by de Cénival in *Hespéris,* 1925, 2nd quarter, p. 182.

5 *The Status of the Jews under Islam*

1. See Louis Gardet's work on the rights of the dhimmis, in particular "Islam et Démocratie," in *Revue Thomiste,* Sept.-Dec. 1946.
   See Al Mawardi, *Les Statuts Gouvernementaux,* Fagnan commentary and trans., Alger, 1915, p. 52 *et seq.;* 299 *et seq.;* 362-492.
2. Cf. A. S. Tritton, *The Caliphs and their non-Moslem Subjects,* London, 1930.
3. When the French arrived in Algiers, the *djezya* amounted to 336,000 *budjus* which was paid at the rate of 7,000 *budjus* per week. The tax was delivered to the Pasha by the "head" of the Jewish nation every Thursday evening before sunset. Goldsheider and Pharaon, "Lettre sur l'État des Juifs en Algérie et sur les moyens de les tirer de l'abjection," *Archives Israélites,* Vol. I, 1840, p. 578.
4. For a commentary on this verse which served as the basis for all legislation relative to the dhimmis, see Al Mawardi, *op. cit.,* p. 299 *et seq.*
5. Care should be taken not to be carried to extremes when regarding the Moslems as excessively tolerant on the one hand, or cruel and barbaric on the other. For further information on this point see Chukri Cardahi, *La Conception et la Pratique du Droit International Privé dans l'Islam,* in Académie de Droit International. See also Ahmed Reshid, *L'Islam et le Droit des Gens,* Académie de Droit International, 1937, II, p. 371 *et seq.*
6. Louis Gardet, *op. cit.;* Cf. Chukri Cardahi, *op. cit.,* pp. 511-642.
7. Cf. Terrasse, *Histoire du Maroc,* p. 333 and A. Chouraqui, *La Condition Juridique de l'Israelite Marocain,* A.I.U., Paris, 1950, Chap. II.
8. Al Mawardi, *op. cit.,* p. 53-54.
9. Terrasse, *op. cit.,* Vol. II, p. 39.
10. Pierre de Cénival, "La Légende du Juif Ibn Meshal et la Fête du Sultan des Tolbas à Fès," in *Hespéris,* 1925, II, pp. 137-218.
11. The Turks never controlled more than a sixth of the Tunisian and Algerian territories.

12. Albert Cousin and Daniel Saurin, *Annuaire du Maroc,* 1905, p. 50.

13. Quoted by Eisenbeth, *Le Passé du Maroc,* p. 30. Abraham ibn Ezra (1092-1167) is famous for his religious poems, and for his work as a grammarian and a biblical commentator. He had a profound influence during his lifetime.

14. Léon l'Africain brings evidence of this. He is quoted by N. Slousch, *Judéo-Hellènes et Judéo-Berbères,* Paris, 1909, p. 236.

15. Cf. Terrasse, *op. cit.,* p. 305, and Vajda, "Recueil de Textes historiques judéo-marocains," p. 79 *et seq.*

16. Cf. Cazès, *Essai sur l'Histoire des Israélites de Tunisie,* p. 92 *et seq.*

17. In Tunisia, the tax was higher for the indigenous Jews that it was for Spanish immigrants. Cf. Rabbi Abraham M. Hershman, *Rabbi Isaac ben Sheshet Perfet and His Time,* New York, The Jewish Theological Seminary, 5704, 1943, p. 36.

18. Cf. José Benech, *Essai d'Explication d'un Mellah,* p. 59

19. In 1530, when Charles V previously attempted to attack Tunisia, the Jews of Mahdia were obliged to seek refuge in Moknine where they remained permanently.

6 Judaism in the Maghreb: The Oriental Components

1. On Hebrew pronunciation in Morocco see Slousch, *Jews in North Africa,* p. 431, Philadelphia, 1944; in Tunisia, *ibid.,* p. 277. See also Cazès, *Essai sur l'Histoire des Israélites de Tunisie,* p. 180 *et seq.*

2. Rabbi Raphael Alnaqua of Rabat was among those consulted.

3. Cf. Brunot and Malka, *Textes judéo-arabes de Fès,* p. 222.

4. Marcel Cohen, *Le parler arabe des Juifs d'Alger.* Collection Linguistique, published by the Société Linguistique de Paris, Paris, 1912. Louis Brunot, "Notes sur le parler arabes des Juifs de Fès," in *Hespéris,* 1936, fasc. 1, pp. 1-33. Brunot and Malka, *Textes judéo-arabes de Fès; Glossaire judéo-arabe de Fès,* Rabat, 1940.

5. *Les Juifs de l'Afrique du Nord,* Alger, 1936, p. 69.

6. Brunot and Malka, *Textes* . . . pp. 199, 205, 239, 240, notes 3 and 4; 270, 274, notes 14 and 15; 283, 285, notes 9 and 10; 316, 333, 334, 336, 370, 378. Jeanne Jouin, "Le Costume de la femme israélite au Maroc" in *Journal de la Société des Africanistes,* Vol. VI, 1936, pp. 167-186.

7. Tajouri, "Le Mariage Juif à Salé," in *Hespéris,* 1923, 3rd quarter, p. 400. Mr. and Mrs. V. Danon have also provided some useful details about Jewish costumes in Tunisia. Louis Brunot, "Noms de vêtements masculins à Rabat," in *Mélanges,* René Basset, Paris, 1923.

8. In certain mellahs untouched by French influence, the author had occasion to see men and women who had been married and divorced more than eighteen times, each time with a different partner. This legal and widespread prostitution was to the detriment of all concerned and the rabbi was unable to stop it.

9. Ryvel and Vehel, *Le Bestiaire du ghetto,* Tunis, 1934.

10. Mathieu, "Notes sur l'enfance juive de Casablanca," in *Bulletin de l'Institut d'Hygiène du Maroc,* nouvelle série, Vol. VII, 1947, pp. 29-30.

11. I am indebted to J. Shebabo for this description.

12. There was a similar case in Egypt where the tomb of Rabbi Abu-Hatzirah was venerated by Moslems, Jews and Copts.

13. Cf. *L'Univers israélite,* 7 October, 1932.

14. Voinot, *Pèlerinages Judéo-Musulmans du Maroc,* Éditions Larose, Paris, 1948, Institut des Hautes-Études Marocaines, notes et documents.

15. *Ibid.,* p. 51. Cf. Godard, *Histoire du Maroc;* Doutté, *Les Marabouts;* Aubin, *Le Maroc d'aujourd'hui;* Montet, *Le Culte des Saints Musulmans.* De La Martinière, *Souvenirs du Maroc.* See also Brunot and Malka, *op. cit.,* p. 215.

16. Voinot mentions the case of the escorts of the Klot tribe who, when accompanying pilgrims, saw a paralytic walk. They then burnt their cloaks on the tomb of the saint. Cf. p. 50. Machaux-Bellaire, *Quelques tribus de montagne de la région du Habt;* Aubin, *Le Maroc d'aujourd'hui: Villes et tribus du Maroc; Rabat et sa région; Moulieras Fez.*

17. *Bulletin de la Société géographique et d'Archéologie de la Province d'Oran,* Vol. 64, fasc. 219, 1943.
18. Cf. André Zaoui, "Djerba, ou l'une des plus ancienne communautés juives de la Diaspora," *R.P.J.,* October 1950, pp. 129-136.
19. A useful study could be made of the division of pilgrims according to age, social standing, etc. It would reveal the general direction of the evolution of Maghrebian Judaism.
20. Raoul Darmon, *La Déformation des cultes en Tunisie,* Paris, 1945, p. 215 *et seq.*
21. Abraham I. Larédo. Cf. Noar, 17 October 1951.
22. Nissim's daughter was to marry the son of Samuel Ha-Nagid and, to mark the event, many Jews of Kairouan visited Granada where they met Solomon ibn Gabirol, still a young poet at that time.
23. Dr. Simon regarded him as a resident of Cairo. Cf. *Revue de la Pensée Juive,* April 1951, p. 21. In fact, he was born in Cairo but lived and taught in Kairouan.
24. Cf. the documented study published by Isaac Rouche, "Un Grand Rabbin à Tlemcen au XVe siècle," in *Bulletin de la Société géographique et d'Archéologie de la Province d'Oran,* Vol. 57, September-December, 1936.
25. This text is quoted in Hebrew by D. Cazès, *op. cit.,* p. 81.

7 *Judaism in the Maghreb: The Spanish Component*

1. Cf. Hasdai Crescas' letter to the Community of Avignon, in *Shevet Yehuda,* Wiener edition, pp. 260-263.
2. Cf. Margolis and Marx, *History of the Jewish People,* p. 413. Cf. Lorenzo Nino Azcona, *Felipe II y la Villa de El Exorial a travès de la Historia,* Madrid, 1934, in which mention is made of the conversion of Maghrebian Jews at the end of the sixteenth century in Spain. Cf. Robert Picard, "Baptême d'un Juif de Fès à l'Escorial (1589)" in *Hespéris,* Vol. XXXIV, 1937, p. 136.
3. Cf. Margolis and Marx, p. 437.
4. Abraham ben Solomon mentions the violence at Arzila and Salé. Cf. Eisenbeth, *Les Juifs de l'Afrique du Nord,* p. 36. Cf. also

Terrasse, *Histoire du Maroc,* Vol. II, p. 219; "The Jews were very badly received in North Africa." This should be understood as localized events. Hebrew writings of the period show that on the whole their settlement was made possible.

5. Cf. Cl. Martin, *Les Israélites Algériens de 1830 à 1902,* Paris, 1936.

6. Michal Molho, *Usos, y costumbres de los sefardies de Salonica,* Madrid, Barcelona, 1950; p. 227 mentions the survival of Maghrebian customs in the synagogues founded in Salonika in the seventeenth century by Jewish refugees.

7. Acoca, Albo, Allerzouz, Aloro, Alzira, Amigo, Arama, Arbon, Arenos, Azuelos, Belmes-Benara, Benaroyo, Benbico, Bendjo, Benicha, Benoudiz, Bensenior, Benta, Bentito, Berdugo, Berros, Bibas, Blanca, Boros, Bouja, Buenos, Cabalo, Cabessa, Cacon, Calvo, Cardozo, Canizo, Carotche, Carralho, Castiel, Castro, Caxtalan, Checlair, Cheriqui, Chikitou, Corcos, Coriat, Costa, Dadoun, Delouya, Djian, Eminente, Escudero, Fayon, Feelias, Franco, Henriquez, Hombres, Karmès, Karo, Karsenty, Larat, Larédo, Loubaton, Louski, Luisada, Mansano, Marchina, Mastora, Matcho, Médina, Mendez, Mendozo, Méniane, Miara, Minhos, Molina, Molson, Morali, Moreno, Nino, Noguerra, Nouchi, Nourry, Nunez, Ossona, Pacifico, Palas, Parerou, Pariente, Paz, Pene, Picho, Pimienta, Pinto, Pisson, Prissiado, Raudaza, Ribas, Roch, Rosilio, Sarragossi, Serero, Serezo, Sierra, Silverra, Soria, Sotto, Soudri, Spinoza, Strologuo, Tapiéro, Tolédano, Trigan, Valensi, etc. Cf. Eisenbeth, *Les Juifs de l'Afrique du Nord,* Algiers, 1936.

8. A. Chouraqui, *La Condition Juridique de l'Israelite Marocain,* Chapter VI, Section 3a.

9. Cf. Eisenbeth, *Les Juifs au Maroc,* p. 37.

10. Cf. J. Vehel, Lecture delivered at the Popular Jewish University of Tunis, and Cazès, *Essai sur l'Histoire des Israélites de Tunisie,* p. 114.

11. A. M. Larédo, *Los Taḳanot de Castilla,* Sépharad, Madrid, 1949. A. Chouraqui, *op. cit.,* Chapter VI, Section 3b.

12. Rabbi Abraham M. Hershman, *Rabbi Isaac ben Sheshet Perfet and His Time,* (N.Y., 1943), has given an account of Jewish life at this time based on the Consultations of the Ribash.

13. Cf. Is. Epstein, *The Responsa of Rabbi Simon ben Zemach Duran*, London, 1930.

14. Cf. Hershman, *op. cit.*, p. 61, note 11.

15. Saadia Chouraqui was dubbed by his contemporaries "The Ocean of Knowledge." His commentary on Psalm 119 entitled "The New Song" is particularly worthy of attention.

16. Translated into French by Ventura in the collection *Judaïsme*, Rieder.

17. Maurice Eisenbeth, *Le Judaïsme nord-africain, études démographiques sur les Israélites du département de Constantine*, Paris, 1931, pp. 40-43.

18. G. G. Scholem, *Major Trends in Jewish Mysticism*, Schocken, 1941.

19. The first edition of this work appeared in 1567 and spread rapidly throughout the Diaspora.

20. On the doctrine of the Ari, see Scholem, Chap. 7.

21. Rabbi Tubiana Abraham, a Dayan of Algiers who died in 1792, introduced into the liturgy certain modifications which were inspired by the Cabala of the Ari. On customs in Algiers, see the works of Rabbi Ayashe Juda who died in 1756, notably *Beth Yehuda*.

22. On other functions of the *Chevra* which were common to Judaism everywhere, cf. Brunot and Malka, *op. cit.*, p. 231 *et seq.*

23. A. Bel, *La Réligion musulmane en Berbérie*, Paris, 1938, p. 71 *et seq.*

24. In certain civilizations, the hand is that of a goddess who is shown weeping at the sufferings of the world. Her tears fall onto her breasts where they become milk and whence they flow to the earth, making it fertile. Cf. H. de Keyserling, *Méditations Sud-Américains*, p. 185.

8 The Condition of the Jews in the Nineteenth Century

1. Cf. Terrasse, *Histoire du Maroc*, Vol. II, p. 111 *et seq.*, "Les Entreprises chrétiennes au Maroc," and F. Braudel, *Les Espagnols et l'Afrique du Nord de 1492 à 1577*, Alger, 1928.

2. William Shaler, *Sketches of Algiers,* Boston, 1826.

3. Dubois-Thainville in Esquer Gabriel, *Le Prise d'Alger,* Paris, 1923, III, 134.

4. See also Edmond Norès, *L'Oeuvre de la France en Algérie,* "La Justice," Paris, 1931, Chap. III, p. 81. Cf. Genty de Bussy, *De l'Establissement Français dans la Régence d'Alger,* Paris, 1835, I, 117. Cf. Pananti, *Relation d'un séjour à Alger,* Paris, 1820, p. 229-230. D.J. Montagne, *Physiologie morale et physique d'Alger,* Paris, 1834.

5. Almanac of the Bey's secretary Titteri, *Revue Africaine,* 1874, p. 316, Féraud trans.

6. On the struggle with Bacri and Duran and its outcome, cf. Eisenbeth, *Les Juifs d'Afrique du Nord,* p. 17-18. Claude Martin, *Les Juifs d'Algerie,* p. 20 *et seq.*

7. Cf. Isaac Bloch, *Les Israélites d'Oran de 1792 à 1815,* Alger, 1886, p. 12.

8. Cf. Bloch, *Inscriptions tumulaires des anciens cimetières israélites d'Alger.*

9. Ernest Mercier, *Histoire de l'Afrique Septentrionale,* Paris, 1891, Vol. III, p. 501.

10. Cf. Terrasse, *op. cit.,* Vol. II, p. 264.

11. Georges Vajda, "Un recueil de textes historiques judéo-marocains," Paris, 1951.

12. Y.T. Sémach, "Un Rabbin voyageur marocain," in *Hespéris,* 1928, 3rd-4th quarter, a portrait of Mordecai aby Serour and his journeys with de Foucauld.

13. *Ibid.,* p. 397.

14. Cf. Eisenbeth, *Les Juifs du Maroc,* for further documentation on Moroccan Jewry.

15. On the Jews of Fez, cf. Le Tourneau, *op. cit.,* pp. 73-75; Chap. IV: "La Communauté Juive," pp. 183-186; Chap. V: "Le Mellah," pp. 268-271, 350-353; Chap. VII: "Les Moeurs du Mellah," pp. 569-583. Cf. L. Massignon, *Le Maroc dans les premières années du XVIe siècle,* Alger, 1906, p. 157. Leon L'Africain in his *Description de l'Afrique,* Schefar ed., Paris, 1897, Vol. II, p. 177, confirms that the Jews were confined to the mellahs to protect them from massacres. Cf. Brunot and Malka, *Textes*

Judéo-Arabes de Fès, Rabat, 1939, pp. 197-205. Bel, *La Réligion Musulmane en Berbérie*, Paris, 1938, p. 299. On the mellah of Marrakesh in the 16th century, see P.-Henry Kochler, "La Kasba Saadienne de Marrakech," from the manuscript of a man from the year 1585, in *Hespéris*, Vol. XXVII, 1940, pp. 1-21.

16. Cf. Terrasse, *op. cit.*, p. 30, and Le Tourneau, *op. cit.*, pp. 66-67.

17. According to M. Terrasse.

18. According to Yahas Fès, *op. cit.*, p. 91.

19. Dr. H.-P.-J. Renaud, "Recherches Historiques sur les épidémies du Maroc," in *Hespéris*, 2nd quarter, 1921, p. 160-182; first quarter, 1925, pp. 83-90, and 1939, Vol. XXVI, pp. 293-321.

20. Cohba Lévy, "Enquête dans la région sud de Marrakech," in *Les Cahiers de l'Alliance Universelle*, June, 1949. Cf. the well-documented monograph by J. Mathieu, R. Baron and J. Lumman, "Études de l'alimentation au mellah de Rabat et contrôle de l'état de nutrition de ses habitants," extract from the *Bulletin de l'Institut d'Hygiene du Maroc*, III, IV, 1938.

21. M. L. Dubouloz-Laffin, *Le Bou-Mergoud*, Folklore Tunisien, Paris, 1946.

22. José Benech, *Essai d'explication d'un mellah*.

23. Paul Lapie, *Les Civilisations tunisiennes*, Alcan, Paris, 1898.

24. Research carried out by A. Ribbi and published in the A.I.U. *Bulletin*, No. 26, 1901, p. 83.

25. Georges-S. Colin, "Un Juif marocain du XIVe siècle constructeur d'astrolabes," in *Hespéris*, Vol. XXII, 1936, p. 183.

26. A. Ribbi's report published in A.I.U. *Bulletin* of 1st April, 1900.

27. José Benech, *op. cit.*; Paul Valence, "La Yéchiba talmudique," in *Bulletin de l'enseignment public au Maroc*, January and February, 1939.

28. On elementary talmudic scrolls, see Goulven, *Les Mellahs de Rabat Salé*, Paris, 1927. Also Brunot and Malka, *op. cit.*, p. 237.

PART III

The French Period

9 *The Emancipation of Algerian Jewry: 1830-1962*

1. Cf. Cl. Martin, *Les Juifs d'Algérie*, pp. 20-21.
2. The affair of the "Slap with the Fan" (Le Coup d'Éventail) is discussed in all the works dealing with the French conquest of Algeria. Cf. Norès, *op. cit.*, p. 38, and the bibliography. On the Bacri-Busnach affair, cf. Maurice Eisenbeth, "Les Juifs en Algérie, Esquisse Historique depuis les origines jusqu'à nos jours," extract from the *Encyclopédie Coloniale et Maritime*, Paris, 1937, pp. 17 and 18.
3. A French officer, who was held prisoner in Algeria from 1811 to 1814, foresaw that France would have the support of the "slaves" of the feudal Moslem state. Countremoulins, *Souvenirs d'un officier français prisonnier en Berbérie pendant les années 1811, 1812, 1813, 1814*, pp. 29-30. Cf. Martin, *op. cit.*, p. 40. Martin's opinion of the indifference of the Jews to the arrival of the French (pp. 40-41) is contradicted by the facts in subsequent paragraphs (pp. 41 and 42).
4. Martin, *op. cit.*, p. 42.
5. Cf. Rousset, *L'Algérie de 1830 à 1840;* Rozet, *Voyage dans la Régence d'Alger*, p. 238; Frégier, *Les Israélites Algériens*, Paris, 1865, p. 465; Martin, *op. cit.*, p. 50 *et seq.*
6. Cf. Martin, *op. cit.*, p. 44.
7. Ménerville, *Dictionnaire de Législation Algérienne*, p. 380.
8. Pellissier de Reynaud, *Annales Algériennes*, Paris, 1854, Vol. I, p. 132 *et seq.*
9. Procès-verbaux et rapports de la Commission d'enquête nommée par le Roi le 7 juillet, 1833, pp. 177-178. Cf. Instructions pour la Commission d'Afrique du Maréchal, duc de Dalmatie, président du Conseil, ministre de la Guerre, *ibid.*, p. 23.

10. Martin explains the Jews' acceptance of this measure as a consequence of their "lack of political acumen" (p. 47), and not as an expression of their wishes. On page 41, however, he accuses them, on the contrary, of extreme Machiavellism in their zeal to serve the French forces.

11. Ménerville, *op. cit.,* p. 206 *et seq.* Cf. Martin, p. 47 *et seq.*

12. On the complaints of the Jews against the administration of the rabbinical courts, cf. *Archives nationales,* F.80, 1631, F.80, 1671, *et seq.* On the ordinances quoted, see Ménerville, *op. cit.,* p. 409 b.

13. On the support given by the French Consistory to Algerian Jewry, cf. Martin, *op. cit.,* p. 65 *et seq.*

14. The ordinance was drawn up by a Commission headed by the deputy Janvier. It included Max Cerfberr and Crémieux, both deputies; Anspach, acting Attorney; Artaud, General Inspector of the University; Cuvier, head of the Department for non-Catholic Religions; Fellman, Director of the Algerian Department of the Ministry of War. Maurice Meyer, *Archives Israélites,* 1843, p. 288.

15. The Chief Rabbi received 4,000 francs plus an allowance of 1,500 francs, the provincial rabbis 3,000 plus 1,000 francs, and the secretary of the Consistory, 8,000 francs. The cost of material and installation were budgeted at 1,500 francs. *Archives nationales,* F.80, 1631; Martin, p. 72.

16. Martin remarks that by leaving responsibility for the care of the poor in the hands of the consistories, the basic significance of the ordinance was compromised since one of the characteristics of the former structure of the Jewish community was thereby maintained.

17. For details of this campaign, see Martin, *op. cit.,* Chap. VI: "L'évolution"; Chap. VII: "La campagne pour la naturalisation"; Chap. VIII: "Les Israélites et la réorganisation algérienne," pp. 94-136.

18. *Arch. Nat.,* F. 80, 1748.

19. Cf. Pellissier de Reynaud, *op. cit.,* Vol. III, p. 337. The decree of February 2, 1852 withdrew this right from the Algerians.

20. Frégier, *op. cit.,* p. 103; *Echo d'Oran,* January 18, 1859; *Univers Israélite,* December 1859. The Moslems were represented by two councillors in each of the provinces of Algiers, Oran and Con-

stantine. The decree of July 7, 1864 altered this proportion by granting one quarter of the Council seats to Moslems.

21. *Archives Israélites,* 1844, p. 735.

22. The first article of the decree of March 15, 1860 confuses Jews and Europeans. Cf. J. Cohen, *Les Israélites de l'Algérie et le Decrét Crémieux,* Paris, 1900, p. 90 *et seq.*

23. Martin, *op. cit.,* p. 114.

24. Frégier, President of the Court of Sétif, was their most ardent spokesman. He wrote a 478-page volume in support of a decree, the first article of which was to read thus: "All the Jews of Algeria are French and French citizens." Article II made provision for those Jews who had reached their majority to preserve their right to their former status by means of a declaration made within two months of the publication of the decree. (Frégier, *Les Israélites Algériens, leur passé, leur avenir juridique, leur naturalisation collective,* Paris, 1865, p. 383.) Frégier's arguments were based not only on Christian principles but also on his experience as a magistrate in Algeria.

25. The Algerian press of the time—*Echo d'Oran, Indépendant de Constantine, Africain, Akhbar d'Alger,* etc.—reflected their vigorous campaign. See Saint-Hilaire Delsieux, *Essai sur la naturalisation collective des Israélites Algériens,* Alger, 1860, pp. 22-23.

26. Adolphe Crémieux was their eloquent spokesman. On his campaign, cf. S. Posener, *Adolphe Crémieux (1796-1880),* Paris, 1933.

27. *Echo d'Oran,* May 28, 1865. Frégier, *op. cit.,* p. 446 *et seq.* Martin, *op. cit.,* p. 119. For the full text of the petition, see Frégier, p. 446.

28. A decree relative to public administration which was in accordance with the provision of Article V of the Senate decree was issued on April 21, 1866 (Estoublon et Lefébure, *Code d'Algérie,* p. 313). Article IV dealt with the process of naturalization and put the Jews and the Moslems on the same footing. In the following four years, only 1,039 people were naturalized, of whom 289 were Jews, 116 Moslems and 634 Europeans. For a criticism of the resolution, see Cohen, *op. cit.,* p. 124 *et seq.*

29. Crémieux's note to General Allard, President of the War Depart-

ment of the Conseil d'Etat, *Bulletin de l'Alliance Israélite Universelle,* 1872, p. 32; Compte rendu des notes, p. 69.

30. In Algerian courts, daughters of the deceased had the right to only one-tenth of the inheritance, in accordance with the personal statute. In the French court, in which questions of inheritance were settled according to the French civil statute, they had equal rights with the sons.

31. This draft was similar to Frégier's proposition. See Frégier, *op. cit.,* p. 383. The Legal and War Departments of the Conseil d'Etat appointed Manceau chairman, and Émile Ollivier was requested to consult the Governor General of Algeria, Marshall MacMahon. MacMahon was in favor of the reform although he suggested that Article II should be deleted and that such an important reform should be made by law and not by decree.

32. According to a speech delivered at the Alliance Israélite Universelle in May 1877.

33. *Journal Officiel* of July 20, 1870, p. 1290.

34. At the general assembly of the Alliance Israélite Universelle, Crémieux declared: "What would you think of me today if a complaint were made that the Minister of Justice in 1870, member of the Government of the Fourth of September, had not wished to grant French citizenship to the Jews whose naturalization he had been demanding since he became a deputy." He further stated: "Besides our patriotic duties, we, the Jews of the Alliance Israélite Universelle, have a great mission in common which together we wish to accomplish on the widest possible scale. No separation between us is possible; in the sacred cause we serve— Jews of Germany, Austria, England, Belgium, Spain, Holland, Russia, the Jews of East and West, of North and South—we constitute a unifying entity which maintains an inviolable link." *Bulletin de l'Alliance Israélite Universelle,* 1st quarter 1872, pp. 32 and 57. It was Crémieux who proclaimed his devotion to France before the National Assembly: "I do not believe that there is anyone in this Assembly who loves France as I do." L. Durrieu, *Les Juifs Algériens,* Paris, 1902, p. 17.

35. This decree has been frequently analysed and discussed. For a detailed legal analysis, see J. Cohen, *Les Israélites d'Algérie et le*

Décret Crémieux, Chap. V: "Examen juridique du Décret Crémieux," pp. 292-361. The preceding chapters include material on the collective naturalization (pp. 149-222) and on the political effects of the decree from 1870 to 1900.

36. Louis Bertrand, commenting on Algerian anti-Semitic literature in 1898 remarked: "The perpetual delirious incitement to murder and pillage would seem to have been written by slaughterhouse workers who learnt French from the Negroes."

37. Martin, *op. cit.,* p. 148 *et seq.*

38. Decree of October 7, 1871, *Journal Officiel* of October 9, 1871, p. 3885.

39. The decree was signed by the Prime Minister Thiers and the Minister of the Interior, Lambrecht.

40. Cf. Michel Ansky, *Les Juifs Algériens, du Décret Crémieux à la Libération,* Paris, 1950, pp. 75-76. Cf. J. Cohen, *op. cit.,* p. 208 *et seq.* Martin, *op. cit.,* pp. 153-166.

41. See Z. Szajkowski's study, "Socialists and radicals in the development of antisemitism in Algeria (1884-1900)," Conference on Jewish Relations, New York, 1948, reprinted from *Jewish Social Studies,* Vol. X, No. 3, pp. 257-280.

42. Drumont, *La France Juive,* particularly Vol. II, Book IV, p. 4 *et seq.*

43. Cf. Gustave Touanet, *L'Antisémitisme Algérien,* Paris, 1900 (text of a speech delivered in the Legislative Chamber on May 19 and 24, 1899).

44. See Chapter V above. Cf. André Chouraqui, "Témoignage sur les relations judéo-arabes en Algérie," *Vendredi Soir,* 2nd year, No. 1250, November 14, 1947. Also S.-D. Goitein's article, "The Common Heritage of the Jews and the Arabs, *"Zionist Information Bulletin,* Jerusalem, 1949.

45. Cf. Jean Mélia, *L'Algérie et la Guerre,* Paris, 1918.

46. "So long as this attitude persists, peace in the streets will depend on the ability or lack of it of agitators to exploit to their own advantage the hatred of the Christians for the Jews." Martin, p. 368. Jules Isaac's analysis of the causes of anti-Jewish hatred which appears in his work *Jésus et Israel,* is also valid for Algeria.

47. On this period, see Michel Ansky, *op. cit.;* Cf. Maurice Eisenbeth, *Pages Vécues, 1940-1943,* Algiers, 1945.

48. For a detailed study of the Jewish Resistance in Algeria, see Michel Ansky, *op. cit.,* p. 175 *et seq.*
49. *Ibid.,* Chap. XII, p. 261.
50. *Ibid.,* p. 289 on the note drawn up by the staff of Prof. René Cassin, then National Commissioner of Justice.
51. R.P. Jean Maynard, Jacques Maritain, Prof. Viard, Francis Perrin and Emile Buré were among those who voiced their indignation at the survival of Nazism in Algeria after the liberation.
52. On his arrival from London on August 20, 1943, René Cassin assumed his new functions as President of the Legal Committee of the F.C.N.L. His first act was to express his agreement with André Philip's report on the legal position of the Algerian Jews.
53. Law No. 47-1853 of September 20, 1947 which established the Algerian Constitution. *Journal Officiel,* September 21, 1947, Art. 2.

10 The Status of the Jews in Tunisia (1881-1956) and French Morocco (1917-1956)

1. Such as the hundred families who fled from Algiers after the 1805 massacres. See Chapter VIII above.
2. It was he who built the exquisitely beautiful palace, today the Museum of Bardo, to house the 1,200 women of his harem.
3. See Chapter VII above on the Schism of the Grana and British intervention in the affair of the hats.
4. M. Fabré and MM. Foa and Carcassone.
5. Henceforth, soldiers were chosen by drawing lots.
6. R. Arditti, *Receuil des textes législatifs et juridiques concernant les Israélites de Tunisie de 1857 à 1913,* notes and commentary by Chief Rabbi R. Arditti, Tunis, 1915, p. 209. Cazès, *Essai sur l'Histoire des Israélites de Tunisie,* Paris, 1888, p. 151 *et seq.* Henri Cambon, *Histoire de la Régence de Tunis,* Nancy, 1948, p. 111 *et seq.* On the Sfez case, see Léon Roches' eyewitness account, *Trente-deux ans à travers l'Islam*—an outstanding account of the history of the Moslem countries during the July Monarchy and the Second Empire, and particularly of Tunisian affairs.

7. On the causes of the revolt, cf. Cambon, *op. cit.,* p. 115 *et seq.*

8. Cf. a curious pamphlet, in the form of a letter signed by General Henssein and his lawyers, printed in Florence by J. Civelli, 30 Panicale Street, and entitled, "Exposé des Réclamations du gouvernement Tunisien contre le feu Caid Nissim Scemama et contre ses ayants cause." (The document is undated.)

9. Four hundred and twenty-seven had Italian protection, 726 Spanish, 206 Dutch (of whom 17 were Moslem), 109 Belgians, all residents of Sfax etc. Cf. Chalom, *Les Israélites de la Tunisie, Leur Condition Civile et Politique,* Paris, 1908.

10. Cf. Cazès, *op. cit.,* p. 160.

11. *Bulletin de l'Alliance Israélite Universelle,* 1877, p. 248.

12. Barthélemy Saint-Hilaire, Minister for Foreign Affairs, refused to hold an official conversation on Tunisian affairs with the Turkish ambassador "for fear that a debate, as ill-timed as it would have been useless, might ensue." Dispatch of April 18, 1881, to the French Ambassador in Istanbul.

13. A Decree of September 13, 1876, relative to the organization of slaughterhouses and welfare funds provides useful information of the organization of the Jewish community prior to the establishment of the Protectorate. Cf. R. Arditti, *op. cit.,* pp. 2-4.

14. Cf. *ibid.,* pp. 1-123 for details of the texts of these.

15. Decree of July 16, 1884.

16. Decree of June 10, 1884.

17. Decree of June 10, 1885.

18. Decree of June 7, 1896.

19. Decree of May 17, 1902.

20. Decree of July 8, 1903.

21. Cf. M. Smaja, *De l'extension de la juridiction et de la nationalité française en Tunisie,* Tunis, 1905.

22. Chalom, *op. cit.,* p. 131.

23. In its resolution of June 9, 1905; cf. Chalom, p. 132.

24. The Radical Socialist Congress of Tunis passed a resolution to this effect on August 17, 1906.

25. Chalom, p. 182.

26. *Journal Officiel,* July 13, 1923, report of parliamentary discussions.

27. Of the 13,996 Tunisians naturalized, 7,004 were Italians and 787 Moslems. Cf. *Annuaire Statistique de la Tunisie,* 1948, p. 42.

28. A total of 9,669 Tunisians were naturalized during this period, of whom 139 were Moslems.

29. Out of a total of 3,563 of whom only 2 were Moslems.

30. Out of a total of 2,301, of whom 2 were Moslems.

31. Out of a total of 4,769, of whom 15 were Moslems.

32. Paul Ghez, *Six mois sous la botte,* Tunis, 1942.

33. Gaston Guez, *Nos martyrs sous la botte allemande, les ex-travailleurs juifs racontene leurs souffrances,* Tunis, 1943. Severe economic and financial measures were also taken against the Jews.

34. There were 238 amicable suits dealing with the management of inheritance, guardianship, the purchase and sale of property and emancipation from legal restraints; 402 cases were in litigation and dealt with alimony, divorces, disputed wills, and legal incompetence. Seven women, granted *Halitza,* were freed from the levirate laws; there were 8 suits for the recognition of paternity, 2 for its disavowal and 3 requests for legal adoption.

35. Cf. Jacques Chalom, *op. cit.;* and Salomon Tibi, *Le Statut personnel des Israélites et spécialement des Israélites tunisiens,* 4 volumes, Tunis, 1923.

36. See Chapter VII above, p. 92.

37. Cf. A. Chouraqui, *La Condition Juridique de l'Israélite Marocain,* Chap. II. For details of Sir Moses Montefiore's mission, see Refutation of an anonymous article in the *Jewish World* entitled "Secret History of Sir Moses Montefiore's Mission to Morocco in 1863-1864" by H. Guedalla Esq., London, 1880.

38. Terrasse, *Histoire du Maroc,* p. 328.

39. See Chapter VI above, "Veneration of Saints."

40. There were fourteen Jewish communities in the interior of Tripolitania: in Amrous, 1,240 Jews; Misurata, 912; Zliten, 604; Homs, 902; Syrte, 180; Cussabat, 410; Tarhuna, 191; Beni Ulid, 185; Zuara, 794; Zavia, 676; Zanzur, 150; Ifren, 407; Garian Tigrina, 464; Tagiura, 202. There is not one Jew left in any of these towns.

41. There are also perhaps a few score still in Bengazi.

11 Population Trends Among the Jewish Communities

1. Maurice Eisenbeth, *Les Juifs de l'Afrique du Nord: Démographie et Onomastique,* Algiers, 1936, p. 69 *et seq.*
2. *Statistiques de la Population Algérienne,* Vol. I, September, 1934, p. 17.
3. Ruppin, *News from Palestine,* July, 1938.
4. *American Jewish Year Book,* 1951, p. 195 *et seq.* These figures presumably estimate that there are two million Jews in the Soviet Union.
5. This figure is based on the 1941 census and the estimated rate of natural increase.
6. 70,971 Jews of Tunisian nationality were listed in the 1946 census, to which must be added those of French or foreign nationality, and an allowance made for natural increase on one hand and a high rate of emigration on the other.
7. There were 203,850 Jews of Moroccan nationality according to the 1947 census. To this must be added Jews of other nationalities, those resident in Tangiers and Spanish Morocco, 26 per cent for natural increase and then a deduction made for emigration. See André Chouraqui, *La Condition Juridique de l'Israélite Marocain,* Chap. I.
8. In Spanish Morocco, the Jews made up 2.8 per cent of the total population and 20 per cent of the European colony.
9. This is equivalent to an annual rate of increase of 4.06 per cent.
10. That is, 6.4 per cent or an annual rate of increase of 0.61 per cent.
11. There was an overall increase of 21 per cent in the total number of families.
12. The precise figures are: department of Constantine 6,285 families with 18,863 children; department of Oran 13,338 families with 37,442 children; department of Algiers 10,755 families with 26,750 children.
13. See Chapter IX.
14. Cf. Régence de Tunis, Protectorate français, Secrétariat général du Gouvernement tunisien, *Annuaire Statistique,* 1940 to 1946, 1947, 1948.

15. Cf. Secrétariat général du Protectorate du gouvernement chérifien. Service des Statistiques, Dénombrement de la population de la zone français de l'Empire chérifien carried out on March 1, 1947. Fasc. Nos. 1-4.

16. Charles de Foucauld, *Reconnaissance au Maroc, 1881-1884,* Paris, 1888, p. 395 *et seq.*

17. See Louis Massignon, *Le Maroc dans les premières années du XVI siècle.* Tableau géographique d'après Léon l'Africain, Algiers, 1906, p. 159. Massignon shows that from the sixteenth to the nineteenth century the distribution of the population hardly changed. Cf. Eisenbeth, *Les Juifs au Maroc,* Algiers, 1941, p. 12.

18. A. Chouraqui, *La Condition Juridique,* etc., Chap. I.

19. According to André Adam, "La Population Marocaine dans l'Ancienne Medina de Casablanca," in *Bulletin Economique et Social du Maroc,* Nos. 47-48, 1950.

20. Cf. P. Flamand, "Statistical information on the Jewish poulation of southern Morocco" in *Hespéris,* 1950, 3rd-4th quarter.

21. According to Louis Villème, "L'Evolution de la vie citadine au Maroc," in *Cahiers de l'Afrique et de l'Asie,* December 1, 1948, p. 92, the Jewish population of Fez counted 17,580 souls. Of these 14,180 were Moroccan citizens 1,490 of whom lived in the new city and 13,690 in the mellah. The 2,400 Jews of French nationality lived in the new city.

22. According to N. Slousch, *The Jews of North Africa,* pp. 388-430.

23. Agadir Command Region.

24. The statistical details given in this section are based on the Dénombrement de la population de la zone français de l'Empire chérifien of 1947.

25. For every six marriages where the wife was Jewish, there were seven where the husband was Jewish.

12   Facing West

1. *Archives Israélites,* 1840, p. 275. See also Claude Martin's history of French education for Algerian Jews, *Les Juifs d'Algerie,* pp. 94-99, 176-178.

2. E.-F. Gauthier, *Le Passé de l'Afrique du Nord*, pp. 2 and 439.

3. According to statistics furnished by Mr. Robert Montagne.

4. Cf. Narcisse Leven, *Cinquante ans d'histoire, l'Alliance Israélite Universelle*, Paris, Alcan, 1920, Vols. I and II.

5. See André Chouraqui, *La Condition Juridique*, etc. Chap. IV, section 1.

6. *Bulletin de l'A.I.U.*, 1901, pp. 76-77.

7. *Ibid.*, p. 78.

8. J. Monsonégo, *l'Activité économique de Mostaganem de 1830 à nos jours*, Larose, Paris, 1950, p. 77.

9. Cf. M. Eisenbeth, *Les Juifs de l'Afrique du Nord*, Alger, 1936, p. 58.

10. The results of the 1941 census were obtained from Mr. R. Montagne.

11. Cf. M. Eisenbeth, *Pages Vécues, 1940-1943*, Alger, 1945, pp. 49-51.

12. Cf. Cazès, *Essai sur l'Histoire des Israélites de Tunisie*, p. 29, note 2.

13. See Dr. Saul Chemla, *Le Judaïsme tunisien se meurt: Un Cri d'Alarme*, Tunis, 1939, Chap. III.

14. See *Annuaire Statistique de la Tunisie*, 1948, pp. 12 and 13.

15. André Chouraqui, *La Condition Juridique*, etc. Chap. I, Section III.

16. On the transformation of the traditional economy in Morocco, see L. Massignon, "Enquête sur les Corporations d'Artisans et de commercants au Maroc (1923-1924)," in *Revue de Monde Musulman*, Vol. L, VIII, 1924.

17. See André Chouraqui, *La Condition Juridique*, etc. Chap. IV, section III.

18. On living conditions in the old medina of Casablanca, see *Bulletin Economique et Social du Maroc*, 1st quarter, 1950, pp. 247-256.

13 *Social Conditions*

1. According to Louis Villème: "L'Evolution de la vie citadine au Maroc," *Cahiers de l'Afrique et de l'Asie*, Paris, 1950, p. 92.

2. According to Maurice Eisenbeth, *Pages Vécues,* pp. 28-37.

3. According to an enquiry, made at the request of Mr. Paye by Messrs. R. Lévi and V. Danon, which was laid before the Congress for Scientific Progress held in Tunis in May, 1951.

4. E. Donio, "L'habitat des Juifs de Tunisie" in *Bulletin Economique et Social de la Tunisie,* No. 34, pp. 73-79.

5. From an unpublished report by Dr. Franier.

6. Dr. R. Tibi, on infant mortality in *Bulletin de l'O.S.E.,* Tunisie, No. 3, 1948. Dr. Fajerman, *Mission en Tunisie et au Maroc,* September, 1948, O.S.E. Union, Paris.

7. Cf. Mathieu, *Notes sur l'enfance juive du Mellah de Casablanca,* p. 37 *et seq.*

8. *Annuaire Statistique de la Tunisie,* 1946-1948, p. 54.

9. Three offenders were sentenced for assault and injury, fifteen for theft, ten for public drunkenness, one for bankruptcy and eight for various crimes. Only one was sentenced to a term of over three years, and none was condemned to forced labor or death.

10. Raoul Darmon, *La Tunisie Criminelle,* Tunis, 1948.

14 Judaism in Modern Times

1. On the rabbinical courts in Tunisia see Raoul Darmon, *La Situation des cultes en Tunisie,* Paris, 1930, pp. 72-97; Jacques Chalom, *Les Israélites de la Tunisie,* Tunis, 1908; Salomon Tibi, *Le Statut personnel des Israélites et spécialement des Israélites de Tunisie,* Tunis, 1923; on the courts in Morocco, see André Chouraqui, *La Condition Juridique,* Chap. V.

2. On betrothal ceremonies, see Goulven, *Les Mellahs de Rabat Salé,* Paris, 1927, p. 36; Tajouri, "Le Mariage juif à Salé," *Hespéris,* 3rd quarter, 1923, p. 393; Brunot and Malka, "Textes judéo-arabes de Fez," *I.H.E.M.,* Rabat, 1939.

3. See Eugène Vassel, *La Littérarie popularie des Israélites tunisiens,* 4 fascicules, Leroux, Paris, 1905-1907.

15 *Independence and Exodus*

1. Cf. Jacques Berque, *Le Maghreb entre deux guerres,* Paris, Editions de Seuil, 1962, p. 446.
2. See Claude Tapia's article "Le rapatrié en 1965. Portrait d'un inconnu?" in *L'Arche,* January 1965, pp. 16-23. See also "Les Nouvelles frontières," *L'Arche,* February 1964, pp. 24-27.
3. *Ibid.*

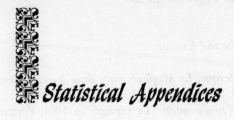 *Statistical Appendices*

Editor's Note: The following tables contain selected material only. Those wanting further statistical information should refer to Dr. Chouraqui's earlier work, *Les Juifs d'Afrique du Nord,* Presses Universitaires de France, Paris, 1952.

APPENDIX I

List of occupations in which Jews in Meknès were engaged at the end of the nineteenth century.

Occupation	Number employed
Bellows makers	4
Bookbinders	3
Carpenters	14
Clockmakers	3
Cobblers and helpers	59
Cotton goods retailers	5
Distillers	10
Dressmakers	62
Druggists and hardware mongers	102
Dyers	5
Embroiderers on velvet	11

Flour merchants	22
Furnace operators	6
Gardeners	15
Gold and silver inlayers of stirrups	4
Goldsmiths	48
Grocers	7
Hairdressers	14
Lace and button makers	150
Masons	2
Money changers and money lenders	25
Muleteers	6
Public criers	55
Rabbis and teachers	18
Scabbard makers	3
Scribes	7
Shoemakers and helpers	81
Silk thread retailers	7
Slaughterers and notaries**	24
Snuffmakers	2
Tailors and helpers	136
Tinsmiths and helpers	52
Waxmakers	15
Weavers	13
Wool carders	6
Total	996

Other trades included furnishers, kiln operators, suppliers, stokers and wagoners.

* Research done by A. Ribbi and published in the *Bulletin de l'A.I.U.* No. 26, 1901, p. 83.
** These two trades went together because those who had the necessary rabbinical training to act as slaughterers could also serve as clerks of the rabbinical court.

Growth of the Jewish Population in Algeria 1872-1921

Year	Population
1872	34,574
1881	35,663
1886	42,595
1891	47,459
1901	57,132
1906	64,645
1911	70,271
1921	73,967

*Growth of the Jewish Population in Oran, Algiers and Constantine
Compared with that of the European and Moslem Population*

	ORAN			ALGIERS			CONSTANTINE		
	1881	1931	Growth %	1881	1931	Growth %	1881	1931	Growth %
Europeans	41,714	111,031	233	38,850	156,971	403	14,679	34,493	235
Moslems	9,084	32,219	355	21,005	76,601	365	17,900	52,299	292
Jews	3,549	20,493	577	5,372	23,550	438	5,213	13,110	252
Total	54,347	163,743	301	65,227	257,122	394	37,792	99,902	263

Table I
Growth of the Jewish Population in Tunisia 1921-1946

1921	48,436
1926	54,243
1931	56,248
1936	59,485
1946	71,543*

Table II
*Births and Deaths Registered by the Jewish Community in Tunisia 1914-1945***

Year	Births	Deaths
1914	1724	995
1924	2004	1225
1934	1862	988
1945	2795	1349

* Includes 572 Jews who were neither "Tunisian" nor "European."
**Based on *Annuaire Statistique de la Tunisie* 1940-1946, p. 53.

Table I
Birth Rates per 10,000 Population among the
Various Ethnic Groups in Tunisia 1919-1938

Average for five year period	Jews	Moslems	Italians	French nationals
1919-1923	373	229	287	267
1924-1928	334	253	305	316
1929-1933	330	?	316	336
1934-1938	302	288	289	277

Table II
Mortality Rates per 10,000 Population among the
Various Ethnic Groups in Tunisia 1919-1938

Average for five year period	Jews	Moslems	Europeans	
1919-1923	219	163	155 (Italians)	172 (French Nationals)
1924-1928	198	181	169 (all Europeans)	
1929-1933	180	173	154 (all Europeans)	
1934-1938	166	170	141 (all Europeans)	

Table III
Births and Deaths Registered by the Jews
of Tunisian Nationality 1940-1945

Year	Births	Deaths
1940	1047*	515
1941	1012	669
1942	1210	695
1943	1059	1132
1944	1427**	754
1945	1344***	597

* Including 44 still-births
** Including 44 still-births
*** Including 63 still-births

Table IV
Infant Death Rates per 1,000 Live Births According to
Religious Communities in Tunisia 1940-1945

Year	Moslems	Jews	Europeans
1940	194	107	82
1941	255	164	83
1942	234	132	104
1943	259	266	158
1944	280	130	105
1945	224	130	105

Distribution of the Jews of Tunisian Nationality by Age Groups—1946 Census

Age	Percentage of Population
0-1	2.7
1-4	9.6
5-9	10.7
10-14	11.0
15-19	10.3
20-24	9.0
25-29	7.5
30-34	7.3
35-39	6.9
40-44	5.6
45-49	4.5
50-54	4.4
55-59	3.2
60+	7.3

Tunisian Jews Sentenced between 1944 and 1948
as Percentage of Total Convictions

Year	Total Convictions	Jews Convicted	Jews as % of Total
1945	8906	82	0.9 %
1946	8920	56	0.6 %
1947	8263	59	0.7 %
1948	8335	38	0.45%

Percentage of Families in Each Immigrant Group in Israel in 1960 According to the Density of Occupation Per Room

Persons per room	1 or less	1-2	2-3	3-4	4 or more
Immigrants from Europe	11.7	58.9	24.2	3.1	2.1
Immigrants from Asia and Africa	2.4	20.6	30.4	20.7	25.9
Long-time residents of Oriental origin	3.9	24.9	33.2	15.6	22.4
All Israelis	7.0	41.4	30.9	10.3	10.4

Bibliography

An exhaustive bibliography on Judaism in North Africa would consist of about two thousand titles, the majority of which refer to revues and articles. In 1961, Mr. Robert Attal published such a bibliography in *Sefunot,* an annual publication for Research on the Jewish Communities in the East published by the Ben-Zvi Institute in Jerusalem (Vol. V, 1961, p. 467). It also appeared under the title "Bibliography on North African Jewry" in the publication *Be'tfutsot Ha'golah* in 1961. The following list contains only the most important titles. Those wishing for further information should refer to Mr. Attal's thorough research.

The number of original scientific studies made on North African Jewry does not amount to more than three or four score—few indeed for two thousand years of rich and eventful history. This work should be regarded first and foremost as an appeal to historians, sociologists, musicians and students of folklore to record and preserve for posterity the vestiges of a world which is on the point of disappearing.

Abdelkader, A.R., *Le Conflit Judéo-Arabe,* Paris, 1961.

Ansky, Michel, *Les juifs du décret Crémieux à la libération,* Paris, 1950.

Benech, José, *Essai d'explication d'un mellah,* Baden-Baden, 1949.

Brunot, Louis and Elie Malka, *Glossaire judéo-arabe de Fès,* Rabat, 1940.

Brunschvig, Robert, *La Berbérie Orientale sous les Hafsides,* Paris, 1940-47.

Cazès, David, *Essai sur l'histoire des israélites de Tunisie,* Paris, 1888.

Chouraqui, André, *La condition juridique de l'israélite marocain*, Paris, 1950, and in translation, *The Social and Legal Status of the Jews in French Morocco*, American Jewish Committee Publication, New York, 1952.

Cohen, Marcel, *Le parler arabe des juifs d'Alger*, Paris, 1912.

Corcos Abulafia, David, "North African Jewry Boasts of Glorious Constructive History," *Jerusalem Post*, Dec. 1959.

——, "The Attitude of the Almohadic Rulers towards the Jews," *Zion*, XXXII year, number 3-4, Jerusalem, 1967.

Darmon, Raoul, *La situation des cultes en Tunisie*, Paris, 1930.

Dubouloz-Laffin, Marie Louise, *Le Bou Mergoud*, folklore tunisien de Sfax et de sa région, Paris, 1946.

Elmaleh, Abraham, "Les juifs d'Afrique du Nord et la terre d'Israel," *L'Orient*, 1933.

Eisenbeth, Maurice, *Les juifs d'Afrique du Nord, démographie et onomastique*, Algiers, 1936.

——, *Les juifs en Algérie, esquisse historique*, Paris, 1937.

——, *Les juifs du Maroc*, Algiers, 1948.

Flamand, Pierre, *Diaspora en Terre d'Islam*, Vols. I and II, Casablanca, no date.

de Foucauld, Charles, *Reconnaissance au Maroc*, Paris, 1888.

Gardet, Louis, "Islam et Démocratie" in *Revue Thomiste*, Sept. 1946.

Goulven, *Les Mellahs de Rabat Salé*, Paris, 1927.

Hershman, Abraham M., *Rabbi Isaac ben Sheshet Perfet and His Time*, New York, 1943.

Hirschberg, J.W., *Au pays du soleil couchant*, Jerusalem, 1956.

——, *A History of the Jews in North Africa*, Bialik Institut Publications, Jerusalem, 1965.

Israeli, Isaac, A translation of his works and a commentary by A. Altman and S.M. Stern, *Scripta Judaica* I, Oxford University Press, 1958.

Lapie, Paul, *Les civilisations tunisiennes*, Paris, 1898.

Lévi Provençal, Evariste, *Histoire de l'Espagne Musulmane*, Vols. I and II, Paris, 1950.

Laredo, *Los Taķanot de Castillo in Sepharad*, Madrid, 1949.

Malka, Elie, *Essai d'ethnographie traditionnelle des mellahs*, Rabat, 1946.

Martin, Claude, *Les israélites algériens de 1830 à 1902,* Paris, 1936.

Mauny, Raymond, "Le judaisme, les juifs et l'Afrique Occidentale," *I.F.A.N.,* Dakar, 1949.

Ortega, Manuel, *Los Hebreos in Marruecos,* Madrid, 1934.

Rouche, Isaac, *Un grand rabbin à Tlemcen au XVe,* Oran, 1936.

Sebag, Paul, *La hara de Tunis,* Paris, 1959.

Simon, Marcel, *Le Judaïsme berbère dans l'Afrique ancienne,* Paris, 1946.

Slousch, Nahum, *The Jews of North Africa,* Philadelphia, 1944.

Szajkowski, Zoza, *Socialists and radicals in the development of anti-semitism in Algeria (1884-1900),* New York, 1940.

Toledano, Jacob Moïse, *Ner Hama'arav,* Jerusalem, 1911.

Vajda, Georges, "Un recueil de textes historiques judéo-marocains," *Hespéris,* 1948.

Vassel, Eugène, *La littérature popularie des israélites tunisiens,* Paris, 1904-1907.

Voinot, Louis, *Pélerinages judéo-musulmans du Maroc,* Paris, 1948.

Williams, J.J., *Hebrewisms of West Africa,* New York, 1930.

Index